Misplaced I

GW00391718

One week loan
Benthyciad un wythnos

Please return on or before the due date to avoid overdue charges
A wnewch chi ddychwelyd ar neu cyn y dyddiad a nodir ar eich llyfr os gwelwch yn
dda, er mwyn osgoi taliadu

CRITICAL STUDIES IN LATIN AMERICAN CULTURE

SERIES EDITORS:

James Dunkerley
Jean Franco
John King

This major series – the first of its kind to appear in English – is designed to map the field of contemporary Latin American culture, which has enjoyed increasing popularity in Britain and the United States in recent years.

Six titles will offer a critical introduction to twentieth-century developments in painting, poetry, music, fiction, cinema and 'popular culture'. Further volumes will explore more specialized areas of interest within the field.

The series aims to broaden the scope of criticism of Latin American culture, which tends still to extol the virtues of a few established 'master' works and to examine cultural production within the context of twentieth-century history. These clear, accessible studies are aimed at those who wish to know more about some of the most important and influential cultural works and movements of our time.

Other Titles in the Series

DRAWING THE LINE: ART AND CULTURAL IDENTITY IN CONTEMPORARY LATIN AMERICA by Oriana Baddeley and Valerie Fraser

PLOTTING WOMEN: GENDER AND REPRESENTATION IN MEXICO by Jean Franco

JOURNEYS THROUGH THE LABYRINTH: LATIN AMERICAN FICTION IN THE TWENTIETH CENTURY by Gerald Martin

MAGICAL REELS: A HISTORY OF CINEMA IN LATIN AMERICA by John King

Misplaced Ideas

Essays on Brazilian Culture

———◆———

ROBERTO SCHWARZ

Edited with an Introduction by John Gledson

VERSO

London · New York

First published by Verso 1992
Essays © Roberto Schwarz
Selection © Verso 1992
All rights reserved

Verso
UK: 6 Meard Street, London W1V 3HR
USA: 29 West 35th Street, New York, NY 10001-2291

Verso is the imprint of New Left Books

ISBN 0-86091-382-1
ISBN 0-86091-576-X (pbk)
ISBN 978-0-86091-576-8

British Library Cataloguing in Publication Data
A catalogue record for this book is available from the British Library

Library of Congress Cataloging-in-Publication Data
A catalogue record for this book is available from the Library of Congress

Typeset by Leaper & Gard Ltd, Bristol
Printed in Great Britain by Biddles, Guildford

Contents

Introduction *by John Gledson*   ix

1   Brazilian Culture: Nationalism by Elimination   1

2   Misplaced Ideas: Literature and Society in Late-Nineteenth-
    Century Brazil   19

3   Beware of Alien Ideologies   33

4   The Importing of the Novel to Brazil and its Contradictions
    in the Work of Alencar   41

5   Machado de Assis: A Biographical Sketch   78

6   Complex, Modern, National and Negative   84

7   The Poor Old Woman and Her Portraitist   94

8   'Who can tell me that this character is not Brazil?'   100

9   The Cart, the Tram and the Modernist Poet   108

10 Culture and Politics in Brazil, 1964-1969   126

11 Cinema and *The Guns*   160

12 On *A Man Marked Out To Die*   166

13 Is There a Third World Aesthetic?   173

CONTENTS

14 Anatol Rosenfeld, a Foreign Intellectual 175

15 A Historic Landmark 187

16 Chico Buarque's New Novel 197

Index 202

Sources

The texts used have been taken from the essays' publication in book form, mostly in the following books: *Ao Vencedor as Batatas: Forma Literária e Processo Social nos Inícios do Romance Brasileiro*, Duas Cidades, São Paulo 1977 (*AV*), *O Pai de Família*, Paz e Terra, Rio de Janeiro 1978 (*PF*), and *Que Horas São?* Companhia das Letras, São Paulo 1987 (*QHS*). The relevant book is indicated in parentheses in each case. Unless otherwise indicated, the essays are published in English for the first time, and are translated by John Gledson.

'Brazilian Culture: Nationalism by Elimination': originally a lecture given in a series entitled 'Tradição/Contradição', organized by Adauto Neves for Funarte. First published as 'Nacional por subtração' in the *Folha de São Paulo*, 7 June 1986 (*QHS*). English translation by Linda Briggs, first published in *New Left Review* 167, 1988.

'Misplaced Ideas': original title: 'As idéias fora do lugar', *Estudos Cebrap*, 3, 1973 (*AV*). English translation by Edmund Leites and the author, published in *Comparative Civilization Review*, 5, 1980.

'Beware of Alien Ideologies': first published as 'Cuidado com as ideologias alienígenas (Respostas a *Movimento*)', in *Movimento* 56, 26 June 1976 (*PF*).

'The Importing of the Novel to Brazil and its Contradictions in the Work of Alencar': original title 'A importação do romance e suas contradições em Alencar' (*AV*).

'Machado de Assis: A Biographical Sketch': first published as the second part of an introduction to a Spanish translation of Machado's *Quincas Borba*,

Biblioteca Ayacucho, Caracas 1979, of which 'Who can tell me that this character is not Brazil?' ('¿Quién me dice que este personaje no sea el Brasil?') was the first part (*QHS*).

'Complex, Modern, National and Negative': first read at a Lunchtime Seminar at the Institute for Advanced Study (Princeton, New Jersey) in 1980. First published as 'Complexo, moderno, nacional e negativo' in *Novos Estudos Cebrap, 1*, São Paulo 1981 (*QHS*). English translation by Edmund Leites and Roberto Schwarz, published in *Social Science Information* 22, 1, 1983.

'The Poor Old Woman and Her Portraitist': first published as 'A velha pobre e o retratista' in *Os Pobres na Literatura Brasileira* (organized by Roberto Schwarz), Brasiliense, São Paulo, 1983, pp. 46-50.

'Who can tell me that this character is not Brazil?', as 'Machado de Assis'.

'The Cart, the Tram and the Modernist Poet': was a lecture given at the Centre d'Étude des Mouvements Sociaux, Paris, in 1983, at the invitation of Luciano Martins, Daniel Pecaut and Silvia Sigal, in a seminar on the intelligentsia in Latin America. First published as 'O carro, o bonde e o poeta modernista' in *QHS*.

'Culture and Politics in Brazil, 1964-1969': first published as 'Remarques sur Culture et Politique au Brésil, 1964-1969' in *Les Temps Modernes*, January 1970, pp. 37-73. (*PF*)

'Cinema and *The Guns*': first published as 'O cinema e *Os fuzis*', *Revista Civilização Brasil* 9, 196, (*PF*). English translation published in R. Johnson and R. Stam, eds, *Brazilian Cinema*, Associated University Press 1982.

'On "*A Man Marked Out To Die*"': first published as 'O fio da meada' in the *Folha de São Paulo*, 26 January 1985 (*QHS*).

'Is There a Third World Aesthetic?': first published as 'Existe uma estética do Terceiro Mundo?', a reply to a survey in *Leia Livros*, 15 December 1980 (*QHS*).

'Anatol Rosenfeld, a Foreign Intellectual': first published as 'Anatol Rosenfeld, um intelectual estrangeiro', in *Debate Crítico* 3, 1974 (*PF*).

'A Historic Landmark': first published as 'Marco histórico' in the *Folha de São Paulo*, 31 March 1985 (*QHS*).

'Chico Buarque's New Novel': first published as 'Sopro novo' in *Veja*, 7 August 1991.

The editor is extremely grateful for the help of Peter Anti in the translations of chapters 4 and 10, and would also like to thank the series editors, James Dunkerley and John King, for their timely advice and encouragement.

Introduction

In 1977, Roberto Schwarz, who had recently returned from Paris to São Paulo, published two books: *Ao vencedor as batatas* [*The Winner Gets the Potatoes*] and *O pai de família* [*The Father of the Family*]. Soon afterwards, a friend recommended me to read the first of these, which deals with the early fiction of Machado de Assis and its ideological context. I was immediately gripped by the daring of the argument, the tightness of the style, and the sensitivity to language and its social context, that the essays – two of which are included here – convey. Many Brazilians were similarly impressed, as much by the essays of more immediate relevance in *O pai de família* (like 'Culture and Politics in Brazil, 1964-1969', originally published in *Les Temps Modernes*) as by Schwarz's radical rereading of their nineteenth-century literature, without doubt the richest of all the national literatures in Latin America in that period.

In recent years, Roberto Schwarz's reputation has steadily grown, and the originality and sheer usefulness of his ideas has become plainer not just in Brazil but in the rest of Latin America. As a result, the pressures on him to publish have been great. But he will not be hurried. The end of the eighties saw two further quite slim volumes, another collection of essays with a bias to contemporary topics, *Que horas são?* [*What Time Is It?*] (1987) – from which many of the essays in this volume are taken – and, at last, the second volume of his study of Machado de Assis, *Um mestre na periferia do capitalismo* (1990). It would be no exaggeration to say that these two books have led to a process of consecration in Brazil – the kind of public acclaim that Brás Cubas, the cynical narrator of Machado's first great novel, thinks we all thirst after, and the extraordinary phenomenon of a book of literary criticism reaching the bestseller lists for a few weeks.

This kind of success is obviously not just due to the quality of Schwarz's writing, nor to the fact that he often writes about Machado, who remains a problematic and highly creative figure in Brazilian culture. It lies in undoing - not cutting - a Gordian knot which affects a great deal of Latin American culture: the 'problem' of national identity. Sometimes assertively (as in José Enrique Rodó's *Ariel*, 1900), but increasingly with a note of frustration and despair (as in Octavio Paz's *The Labyrinth of Solitude*, 1950) Latin Americans have reflected on what 'makes' a Mexican, an Argentine, or on what unites the area in a wider sense. Paz, for instance, goes back to a kind of primal rape, a loss of identity, in the original conquest by Spain. For Schwarz, these are misuses, mythicizations, of a history that has much more obvious material causes. Ultimately, I suspect, they are for him derogations of the intellectual's duty to remain on the level of universal truth. As far as Schwarz is concerned, this obsession with identity is a vital fact, to be seen and understood within the context which explains it. But, in the end - as a quick reading of the short essay 'Is There a Third World Aesthetic?' reveals - we are all parts of a single world, with its varied inequalities, oppressions and accompanying distortions and misunderstandings. It is because he allows us - and 'us' means anybody, wherever we come from, as that same essay makes plain in its final paragraph - to put our misplaced ideas back where they belong, without ignoring the realities which have caused them to get misplaced, that he finds his echo in his readers.

Schwarz is stimulated by the *unrealities* of culture, by the comic or tragic adoption of a set of ideas, an artistic form, or a fashion, which does not fit the actual circumstances of the writer or his audience. Whether it be the dominant liberal ideology of the nineteenth century in a country whose economy was based on slavery, or the flower-power optimism of the sixties in Brazil, a country under military rule and rapidly stumbling into extremely savage repression (see the measured attack on the Teatro Oficina in 'Culture and Politics in Brazil, 1964-69'), the revelation that circumstances are relative only encourages him to find the common ground which will explain them. Such things were embarrassingly evident a hundred years ago. If Paris, in Benjamin's often repeated phrase, was the capital of the nineteenth century, there were also plenty of aspiring, resentful provincials. As João da Ega, the sarcastic dandy and failed author in *The Maias*, Eça de Queirós' panorama of upper-class Portuguese life in the 1870s, says: 'Here, we import everything. Laws, ideas, philosophies, theories, subjects of conversation, aesthetics, sciences, style, industries, fashions, mannerisms, jokes, everything comes in boxes on the boat. Civilization is very expensive, what with the customs dues: and it's all secondhand, it wasn't made for us, it's short in the sleeves.'[1] Such attitudes are equally important today, though they find less cheerfully overt expression. 'How can I paint in a Brazilian way?' I remember one member of the audience asking Schwarz after a lecture – an early version of 'Nationalism by Elimination' – intended to question the very notion of a Brazilian essence or identity. Schwarz's reply was typically courteous and serious, somewhat in the manner of his mentor Anatol Rosenfeld, as he describes him in this volume. Obviously, Schwarz's own awareness of the dualities of Latin American culture, and his unwillingness to resolve them into a single identity, spring in part from his own background. The son of Jewish immigrants (a lawyer and aspiring novelist, and a biologist), he was born in Vienna in 1938. His parents soon had to leave Austria, and, finding no safe haven in Europe, finally obtained visas for Paraguay: they stopped on the way, and ended up staying in Brazil, though for a while illegally. There, Schwarz's father worked in a hat factory in the interior of the state of São Paulo. Schwarz, then, is bilingual in German and Portuguese, which he learnt in the street with his playmates. Life was an exercise in comparative sociology: an only child, he remembers how he was fascinated by the large families of his friends, with their quantities of distant cousins. From his German background comes his thorough familiarity and sympathy with Marx, with the tradition of Marxism, and with the Frankfurt School in particular. As he puts it quite explicitly in the introduction of *Um mestre na periferia do capitalismo*: 'My work would be unthinkable without the – contradictory – tradition of Lukács, Benjamin, Brecht and Adorno, and without the inspiration of Marx.'[2]

An important part of the origins of Schwarz's thought lies in the critique of the version of Marxism espoused by the Brazilian Communist Party in the years before the 1964 coup, when he was a student at the University of São Paulo. As he explains above all in 'Culture and Politics, 1964-1969', the Party placed most of its ideological and strategic emphasis on anti-imperialism. In order to establish a solid basis for ultimate revolution (and to go through the necessary stages of the Marxist interpretation of history) it preached an alliance between the working class and the national – and, it hoped, nationalist – bourgeoisie. Only by means of a strong, assertive middle class could the next stage of progress towards ultimate proletarian control be made, and if sacrifices – calling off strikes, for instance, or making political alliances with parties of the centre – had to be made in the here and now for this ultimate goal, so be it. Obviously such a position had less confessible conveniences for the intellectual élite of the Party, many of them middle-class themselves, and for whom (it is strongly implied) the working class became something of an abstraction.

In the years of developmentalist enthusiasm and then of social ferment that preceded the 1964 military coup, a group of intellectuals, among them some of the most distinguished philosophers, historians and sociologists of present-day-Brazil – Fernando Henrique Cardoso, José Arthur Gianotti, Octávio Ianni, Fernando Novais – began to question this interpretation of Brazilian history and politics, and to think, as Schwarz says, 'of ways of rewriting the history of Brazil so as to understand the way that our backwardness formed a part of the development of modern society ... that is, backwardness was not something separate in the modern world, but a part of it.'[3] Rather than understanding Brazilian society as a rather more backward version of European capitalism – an earlier stage or version of the same thing, whose fate was to follow the pattern of the original – they began to see that its backwardness was necessary to the system in which Brazil had a crucial though structurally subordinate role (as a provider of cheap raw materials). This was the period of the rise of dependency theory, many proponents of which, like André Gunder Frank, argued that, since capitalism had a structural interest in the reproduction of poverty, the cycle could only be broken by revolutionary means. The Communist Party's interpretation of Marxism was a crucial example of 'misplaced ideas', in effect the *a priori* imposition of an ideological system on a reality that was more recalcitrant than seemed to be the case at first sight. It shows, too, how practically important such questions can be, and why so much passion is devoted to discussing them.

Having spent two years at Yale as a postgraduate, Schwarz returned to the turbulent Brazil of 1963. In the first years of the military regime (whose artistic atmosphere is brilliantly described in 'Culture and Politics 1964–69'), he was active in the continuing process of rethinking on the left. But when, in 1969, during the brutal hardening of the regime following the 1968 'coup within a coup', his flat was broken into and searched, he took the bus to Uruguay, and then a plane to Paris, where he stayed for the next eight years, teaching for part of the time at the University of Paris. It was there that the ideas conceived in the early sixties began to bear fruit – a process culminating in the publication of *Ao vencedor as batatas*, which was subtitled 'Literary Form and the Social Process in the Beginnings of the Brazilian Novel', when he returned to Brazil in 1977.[4]

The crucial influence in attracting Schwarz to the study of literature was Antonio Candido, now Emeritus Professor of Comparative Literature at the University of São Paulo, and author of a path-breaking history of Brazilian literature between 1780 and 1870: the *Formação da Literatura Brasileira*. Candido treats the history of literature from the point of view of the intellectual formation of the nation, and the growth of its self-consciousness – though his view is anything but crudely nationalist. He is the founder of the most enduring and valuable of the numerous 'schools' of literary criticism which have flourished (some would say with too great variety) in Brazil since the sixties. Its hallmark is the undogmatic analysis of literature and literary history in its social context. Schwarz has never been sparing in his admiration for his teacher: more importantly, he is in some senses the critic who has brought the *Formação* to its logical conclusion, by including into its argument the greatest literary figure of nineteenth-century Latin America, Machado de Assis. 1872 is the date of Machado's first novel, but although he was a very active writer in the 1860s (when he was in his twenties), Candido excluded him from systematic consideration in his book, and in fact has published only one (excellent) essay on him.[5] It was obviously a deliberate omission; a kind of invitation or challenge to a younger critic, and Schwarz was the one to take it up.

In order to carry on Candido's work, Schwarz had to lay out a tighter theoretical framework than is necessary to the *Formação*, and the first two chapters of *Ao vencedor*, translated here as 'Misplaced Ideas' and 'The Importing of the Novel to Brazil and its Contradictions in the Work of Alencar', are dedicated to this task. For this purpose, he had a simple model of Brazilian society at this time, consisting of owners, slaves and, crucially for his purpose, a 'middle' class, which was, however, anything but bourgeois. These were the dependants, many of them ex-slaves or descendants of slaves, who were legally free but in fact utterly subordinate to the owner class – as he says of a character in one of Machado de Assis's early novels, 'he has the whole territory of Brazil to drop down dead in'. It is this form of dependency that underlies the crucial, structural importance of favour in Brazilian nineteenth-century fiction. When called 'favour', it may seem too accidental or capricious a thing to have the role so expressive of a society's very structure which Schwarz attributes to it. Capricious it certainly is, but it is also expressive, first, of the way in which power operates, something which has increasingly concerned Brazilian intellectuals in recent years; also, perhaps, when it is called 'dependency', we can see that in some largely unspoken way the experience of this 'class' reflects that of the nation as a whole in its relations with the developed world – it is certainly no accident that the crucial structural role attributed to favour emerged at the same time as dependency theory. It is partly because it appears so random in its operation and because it can continue to function under the guise of the free relationship between equals posited by liberal ideology, that 'favour' is so important to the self-esteem of both masters and dependants. Such ambiguities, pretences and repressions are evidently the stuff of literature: most obviously in eighteenth-century Europe, which repeatedly, and in some of its greatest masterpieces, explores the relationships between masters, dependants and servants (in *Pamela*, in *Mansfield Park*, *Le Mariage de Figaro* ...).

In the long and careful essay on José de Alencar and his part in the process without which Machado de Assis could not have existed, Schwarz is defining the rather strange, contradictory or dialectical tradition in which both writers take their place. Alencar (1829–77) is often regarded as the quintessential Romantic nationalist, who in novels with Indian heroes and heroines, like *O Guarani* [The Guarani Indian] (1857) and *Iracema* (1865) laid down some of Brazil's foundation myths. By concentrating on his urban novels, and especially on his last long work, *Senhora* [A Lady] (1875), Schwarz reveals that Alencar's stubborn refusal to ignore or completely to falsify Brazilian realities was not just unthinking localism, but was a conscious decision, taken with some awareness of the artistic difficulties it inevitably brought in its wake. Here, then, the theory of misplaced ideas is appropriated as an analytical tool in the realm of literary history. In Alencar, there is an involuntary clash between the essentially bourgeois, 'European' dramas of love and money (exemplified in their most obvious form by Balzac), on the one hand, and on the other, 'Brazilian' realities dominated by local value-systems of a less grand status. As Schwarz asks, how could one imagine the moral universe of favour and dependency producing their Kant? – not that such a thing is inconceivable in principle, but it was in nineteenth-century Brazil, where, as Machado de Assis plainly stated, 'there is not, for the moment, in our milieu, the necessary energy for the invention of new doctrines.'[6]

Whereas Alencar is the artistic *victim* of misplaced ideas, producing interesting but uneven novels, Machado learned to exploit this same literary unevenness to positive literary effect, in the interests of a profoundly original realism. Here again, Schwarz is rewriting literary history: if Alencar is conventionally seen as the great nationalist, Machado is, according to the same myth, the writer who transcended national limitations to achieve universal greatness. He certainly is, as no one would dispute, the first truly great novelist to have written in Latin America, possessed of an extraordinary intelligence, wit and capacity for experimentation and adaptation: but he also gives literary expression to the Brazil of his own time quite as much as, say, Jane Austen does to the England of hers. Indeed, as Schwarz hints, this false dichotomy between the 'national' and the 'universal' writer does an injustice to both novelists, and simplifies the complex relationship between them – Machado was an admirer, a friend, even to an extent a protégé of the older novelist, and liked to recall long discussions of literary questions in Garnier's, the publishing house/bookshop they both frequented, but this does not prevent him lampooning him in some of the early scenes of *Memórias póstumas de Brás Cubas*, as Schwarz shows in his most recent book.

Above all, Schwarz reveals Machado as a great and consequent realist, whose novels, in their larger structures and their small details, are conformed by the realities of a slave-owning, favour-ridden, dependent, provincial society. If it seems strange that he should have to 'reveal' this fundamental fact, more than eighty years after Machado's death,[7] the reason lies in the novelist's extraordinarily pervasive and ingenious irony, particularly adept at choosing first-person narrators who seem much more reliable than they are. As he knew his characters, Machado also knew his readers, and loved, as one critic has said, to be misunderstood by them – no doubt this had the added advantage of providing a quiet life, an understandable requirement for a man subject to epileptic fits. Machado, then, may attract readers – and critics – as a kind of nineteenth-century Third World Sterne, and he does in fact invoke the example of *The Life and Opinions of Tristram Shandy*, no doubt partly to protect his experimentalism with illustrious literary forbears. But the digressive, cock-snooking, self-contradictory position of the narrator, who in his first great novel, *Memórias póstumas de Brás Cubas*,[8] is already dead, speaking to us from beyond the grave, is revealed as having its real roots in the irresponsible, insouciant, ideologically eclectic – in the end, contradictory – position of the slave-owning Brazilian upper class.

As the essays on Machado reproduced here show, Schwarz has produced criticism worthy of this great, if deeply pessimistic and apparently eccentric, writer. The biographical sketch and 'Who can tell me this character is not Brazil?', both originally published as prefaces to a Spanish translation of *Quincas Borba*[9] (1891) are admirable introductions to the man, his life and his polemical, problematic position in Brazilian culture: they have been placed first for that reason, and obviate the need for much background information here. But 'Complex, modern, national and negative', a kind of blueprint for *Um mestre na periferia do capitalismo*, takes us deep into the world of the novels themselves. Schwarz is a brilliant analyst of style, whose perception of detail would satisfy the most fastidious New Critic, though his real gift in this regard lies in his attunement to the echoes of varying ideologies and habits of thoughts implied in, woven into Machado's (or Alencar's, or Oswald de Andrade's) shifting language. He is most at home with a literature full of ironies, with no bounden duty to make its message explicit, obedient to Kant's 'purposefulness without a purpose' – but his excitement comes from the fact that everything is at the same time deeply embedded in contemporary thought and reality.

In Brazil, as Schwarz says in 'Beware of Alien Ideologies', there is a relative consistency about the intellectual tradition, which in some respects compares favourably with Spanish America. He is thinking primarily perhaps of literature in the nineteenth century, when Brazilian writers, and in particular Machado, learned from the experiments and even the mistakes of others. In this context, there is no doubt that the basis for this continuity was laid by Brazil's relative political stability during the Empire, which lasted from 1822 to 1889, falling a year and a half after the abolition of slavery. But critics have also become aware of a longer-lived tradition with roots in the Brazilian social system itself, above all since the publication in 1970 of an article by Antonio Candido, to which Schwarz refers more than once: 'Dialética da malandragem' ['The Dialectics of Roguery'][10], on the novel by Manuel Antônio de Almeida, *Memórias de um sargento de milícias* (1852–3). For Candido, this apparently innocent romp, set in the lower-class Rio of the early nineteenth century, is an early expression of the point of view of the urban 'middle' class of dependants, who, because of their relative freedom (and awareness of its limitations) were able to see Brazilian society both from inside and out; in the twentieth century, its satirical irreverence and 'trivial' realism has surfaced over and over again, in one form or another (often in 'minor' genres, like popular song). Machado de Assis is obviously a perfect, if a rather sophisticated and self-conscious representative of this tradition: his own origins lay in a family of retainers, and he rose to be a distinguished civil servant – a kind of retainer on a national scale, one might say. To some degree, a radical reorientation of the class point of view of Brazilian criticism has taken place over the last two decades, which has allowed a whole series of re-evaluations. This is part of a much wider process taking place in the culture as a whole, which began in the twenties and thirties, but has widened and deepened since 1950. What had been, with a few notable exceptions, largely the preserve of the oligarchy, and was even in its sceptical moments instinctively elitist, gradually shifted to see that other points of view were possible, in creative literature as much as in criticism. Such undertakings as the anthology of essays on the poor in Brazilian literature, which Schwarz himself organized, and to which he contributed 'The Poor Woman and Her Portraitist', are an important part of this democratizing process.

One can see elements of this tradition in the essays on such twentieth-century figures as Oswald de Andrade (1890–1954), by no means a retainer, but still a contradictory figure, a member of a wealthy family who became a communist, the author, most famously, of the *Anthropophagist Manifesto* (1928) which proclaimed that Brazilians, in the fine tradition of their Indian forebears, ought to 'digest' European culture. He is the subject of another magnificent exercise of stylistic and ideological analysis in 'The Cart, the Tram and the Modernist Poet'. The title, I think, has general implications: Oswald is being taken as *the* modernist, the representative of this important literary movement of the twenties in Brazil. Schwarz is arguing for a more rigorous historical and social appraisal of a movement too often seen either as purely poetic or (more frequently) as comfortingly nationalist.[11] As always with him, literary criticism is undertaken both for its own sake and as a way of revising our general understanding of the past, in the face of established, unexamined 'truths'. Here his implicit opponents are, first, the official co-option of an often rebellious and iconoclastic modernist movement by the media since 1970, and, second and more interestingly, the revaluation of Oswald in the 1960s by Haroldo de Campos, one the leading Concretist poets, long accepted as definitive. Schwarz would be the first to recognize the importance of Campos' rescue of an important writer from the oblivion to which he had been consigned by an earlier domestication of modernism. At the very least, he ensured a permanent place for his poetry, his experimental novels, and his drama in the canon. But for Schwarz, the radicalism Campos attributes to Oswald is too purely aesthetic, too obviously modelled on a European avant-garde to which the Concretists themselves (in the 1950s) aspired to belong. The ideas, the forms, the artistic aims of the avant-garde in Europe might look the same as those of the Brazilians who were influenced by them, but Schwarz is careful to put the ideas, and the forms, back into place, and to see them in their own context (see especially pp. 119–21) – which has the enjoyable result of making the poetry itself seem fresher and more comprehensible. What this essay also gives perhaps more vividly than any other is the sense of the pursuit of an elusive quarry in the determination to catch the precise nature of Oswald's humour -- is it, after all, liberating or condescending, marked by the poet's origins, or by his allegiances? If Schwarz feels most attracted to works of art which explore the ironies and ambiguities of a historical situation, it is not out of love of irony for its own sake, but because it is in that way that contradictions are best revealed. It is no accident that the two films he writes about – *The Guns* and *A Man Marked Out To Die* – each contain different styles of filming, and so force the spectator to reflect on the differences, the conditions of production, and thus the social function of the cinema itself.

Perhaps the inevitable consequence of such subterranean arguments as that carried on in the article on Oswald was that they would reach the surface in one of those public polemics which mark Brazilian cultural history from time to time: Schwarz himself refers to the argument between Alencar and Joaquim Nabuco in the 1870s (and Alencar's career began in the 1850s with another), and to Silvio Romero's extremely aggressive and blinkered attack (in the 1890s) on Machado de Assis, who himself had always tried to practise moderation in criticism, though he had mistakenly tried to combine it with honesty. 'Beware of Alien Ideologies' is a reply to the (relatively civilized) criticism of the notion of misplaced ideas by the historian Maria Sylvia de Carvalho Franco.

In 1985, however, motivated by a poem, 'Póstudo' ('Post-everything'), which is itself a kind of self-justifying manifesto, Schwarz launched a sharp, though also very elegant and well argued, attack on the Concretist poet Augusto de Campos, reproduced here as 'A Historic Landmark'. The Concretist movement began in the 1950s as a salutary reaction to the stuffy formalism of the so-called '1945 generation', and proposed something much more adventurous in its experiments with word-pictures and non-linear poetry, its invocation of such central figures as Mallarmé and Pound, whose revolutions, they said, must be incorporated into Brazilian poetry. It had very widespread influence, even on mature poets like Carlos Drummond de Andrade and Manuel Bandeira – though they perhaps liked to show that they could turn their hand to a concretist poem as well as the next man. It had its heyday in the late fifties and early sixties, a moment of national enthusiasm, of the foundation of Brasília, to which the Concretists explicitly compared their project, and of the international acclaim for the bossa nova, which they also supported with enthusiasm. What was less healthy was the imperialist manner – the adjective is not too strong – in which, in later years, the Concretist poet/critics, especially the Campos brothers, decided that they were the legitimate avant-garde, that they could dictate taste, decide who should be read and who rejected, who revalued (one or two of their choices were much more questionable than that of Oswald). Schwarz's demolition, which is deliberately personal only to the minimum degree demanded by the subject, and does the poem the honour of a serious 'reading', nevertheless focuses on the Concretists' hubristic desire to assure themselves a place in history. When looked at in this light, the Concretists themselves, with their internationalist aspirations to write 'poetry for export', are revealed as the victims of misplaced ideas. Those who try to ignore, or too consciously to bypass, the fact that Brazil is on the periphery, is to that extent a cultural province, in fact condemn themselves to being provincial.

It would be easy to see Roberto Schwarz as a pessimist. He certainly is unwilling to ignore the brute facts of mass poverty and exploitation which have plagued Brazil's past and continue to plague its present. One can feel his anger at those who try to argue, with singularly contorted logic and deafness to the calls of common sense, that things are better because they are worse: because Brazilians have always imitated, but are now told there is no reason to think that imitations are inferior to the things they copy, they are suddenly in the vanguard. The fact that the theory used to 'prove' this is that of French philosopher (Derrida) only sharpens the irony. Such logic might seem too far-fetched to be taken seriously, but it is not a million miles away from Borges's assertion that Latin Americans belong to all the literatures of Europe because they belong to none. Suddenly, the periphery becomes the centre. Haroldo de Campos plays another, similar, sleight of hand (see p. 195). Such false optimism is certainly not for Schwarz: but it would be better not to describe him in such terms at all. He himself, I suspect, would prefer to be called an enlightened materialist, who recognizes what he calls a 'difficult state of affairs', and reveals it for what it is.

John Gledson

Notes

1. Eça de Queirós, *Os Maias*, Lello, Oporto 1965, p. 142.

2. *Um mestre na periferia do capitalismo: Machado de Assis*, Duas Cidades, São Paulo, 1990, p. 13.

3. Quoted from an interview with the 'Idéias' section of the *Jornal do Brasil*, January 16 1991. I am most grateful to Elmar and Hilda Pereira de Mello for sending me a copy of this, which I have used more than once in this introduction.

4. The title of *Ao vencedor as batatas* is taken from Machado's second great novel, *Quincas Borba* (1891; see note 9): it is the summary of the extreme social Darwinist views of the madman who gives the book its title.

5. 'Esquema de Machado de Assis' in *Vários escritos*, Duas Cidades, São Paulo, 1970, pp. 13-32.

6. See 'A nova geração' [The New Generation], *Obra completa*, Aguilar, Rio de Janeiro, 1962, Vol. III, p. 810.

7. Another basic contribution to the understanding of Machado in his social context is Raymundo Faoro's detailed and complete study *A pirâmide e o trapézio*, Editora Nacional, São Paulo, 1974. My own contributions to this process - which postdate Schwarz, and are in part motivated by his interpretations, are *The Deceptive Realism of Machado de Assis: A Dissenting Interpretation of* Dom Casmurro, Francis Cairns, Liverpool, 1984, and *Machado de Assis: Ficção e História*, Paz e Terra, São Paulo, 1986.

8. This novel is most familiar in English as *Epitaph of a Small Winner*, Vintage Press, London, 1991.

9. Published as *The Heritage of Quincas Borba* in Britain (Allen Lane, London, 1954), and as *Philosopher or Dog?* in the United States (most recently, Avon, New York, 1986). The translation, by Clotilde Wilson, is the same.

10. 'Dialética da malandragem (Caracterização das *Memórias de um sargento de milícias*)' in *Revista do Instituto de Estudos Brasileiros*, 8 (1970); a Spanish translation can be found as the prologue to the edition of the novel in the Biblioteca Ayacucho, Caracas, 1977.

11. As he explains in note 20 to this essay: Davi Arrigucci's important contribution to the reconsideration of Manuel Bandeira, *Humildade, Paixão e Morte*, which has been published since (Ática, São Paulo, 1990) is a prime example of what he is arguing for.

ONE

Brazilian Culture:

Nationalism by Elimination

We Brazilians and other Latin Americans constantly experience the artificial, inauthentic and imitative nature of our cultural life. An essential element in our critical thought since independence, it has been variously interpreted from romantic, naturalist, modernist, right-wing, left-wing, cosmopolitan and nationalist points of view, so we may suppose that the problem is enduring and deeply rooted. Before attempting another explanation, let us assume that this malaise is a fact. Its everyday manifestations range from the inoffensive to the horrifying. Examples of inappropriateness include Father Christmas sporting an eskimo outfit in a tropical climate and, for traditionalists, the electric guitar in the land of samba. Representatives of the 1964 dictatorship often used to say that Brazil was not ready for democracy, that it would be out place here. In the nineteenth century people spoke of the gulf between the empire's liberal façade, copied from the British parliamentary system, and the actual reality of the system of labour, which was slavery. In his 'Lundu do Escritor Dificil' Mário de Andrade[1] ridiculed his fellow countrymen whose knowledge spanned only foreign matters. Recently, when the São Paulo state government extended its human rights policy to the prisons, there were demonstrations of popular discontent at the idea that such guarantees should be introduced inside prisons when so many people did not enjoy them outside. In this perspective even human rights seem spurious in Brazil. These examples, taken from unrelated spheres and presupposing in-compatible points of view, show how widespread the problem is. They all

I

involve the same sense of contradiction between the real Brazil and the ideological prestige of the countries used as models.[2]

Let us examine the problem from a literary point of view. In twenty years of teaching the subject I have witnessed a transition in literary criticism from impressionism, through positivist historiography, American New Criticism, stylistics, Marxism, phenomenology, structuralism, post-structuralism, and now Reception theories. The list is impressive and demonstrates our university's efforts to overcome provincialism. But it is easy to see that the change from one school of thought to another rarely arises from the exhaustion of a particular project; usually it expresses the high regard that Brazilians feel for the newest doctrine from America or Europe. The disappointing impression created, therefore, is one of change and development with no inner necessity and therefore no value. The thirst for terminological and doctrinal novelty prevails over the labour of extending knowledge and is another illustration of the imitative nature of our cultural life. We shall see that the problem has not been correctly posed, although we may start by accepting its relative validity.

In Brazil intellectual life seems to start from scratch with each generation.[3] The hankering for the advanced countries' latest products nearly always has as its reverse side a lack of interest in the work of the previous generation of Brazilian writers, and results in a lack of intellectual continuity. As Machado de Assis noted in 1879: 'A foreign impetus determines the direction of movement.' What is the meaning of this passing over of the internal impulse, which is in any case much less inevitable than it was then? You do not have to be a traditionalist or believe in an impossible intellectual autarky to recognize the difficulties. There is a lack of conviction, both in the constantly changing theories and in their relation-ship to the movement of society as a whole. As a result little importance is attached to work itself or to the object of investigation. Outstanding analyses and research on the country's culture are periodically cut short and problems that have been identified and tackled with great difficulty are not developed as they deserve. This bias is negatively confirmed by the stature of such few outstanding writers as Machado de Assis,[4] Mário de Andrade and now Antonio Candido. None of them lacked information or an openness to contemporary trends, but they all knew how to make broad and critical use of their predecessors' work, which they regarded not as dead weight but as a dynamic and unfinished element underlying present-day contradictions.

It is not a question of continuity for the sake of it. We have to identify a set of real, specific problems – with their own historical insertion and duration – which can draw together existing forces and allow fresh advances to be made. With all due respect to the theoreticians we study in our faculties, I believe we would do better to devote ourselves to a critical assessment of the ideas put forward by Silvio Romero,[5] Oswald and Mário de Andrade, Antonio Candido, the concretists and the CPCs.[6] A certain degree of cultural density arises out of alliances or disagreements between scientific disciplines, artistic, social and political groups, without which the idea of breaking away in pursuit of the new becomes meaningless. We should bear in mind that to many Latin Americans Brazil's intellectual life appears to have an enviably organic character, and however incredible it may seem, there may be some relative truth in this view.

Little remains of the conceptions and methods that we have passed under review, since the rhythm of change has not allowed them to attain a mature expression. There is a real problem here, part of that feeling of inappropriateness from which we started out. Nothing seems more reasonable, for those who are aware of the damage, than to steer in the opposite direction and think it is enough to avoid copying metropolitan trends in order to achieve an intellectual life with greater substance. This conclusion is illusory, as we shall see, but has strong intuitive support. For a time it was taken up by both right and left nationalists, in a convergence that boded ill for the left and, through its wide diffusion, contributed to a low intellectual level and a high estimation of ideological crudities.

The search for genuine (i.e. unadulterated) national roots leads us to ask: What would popular culture be like if it were possible to isolate it from commercial interests and particularly from the mass media? What would a national economy be like if there were no admixture? Since 1964 the internationalization of capital, the commodification of social relations, and the presence of the mass media have developed so rapidly that these very questions have come to seem implausible. Yet barely twenty years ago they still excited intellectuals and figured on their agenda. A combative frame of mind still prevailed – for which progress would result from a kind of *reconquista*, or rather from the expulsion of the invaders. Once imperialism had been pushed back, its commercial and industrial forms of culture neutralized, and its allied, anti-national section of the bourgeoisie isolated, the way would be clear for the flowering of national culture, which had been *distorted by these elements as by an alien body*. This correct emphasis on the mechanisms of US domination served to mythologize the Brazilian community as object of patriotic fervour, whereas a class analysis would

3

have made this much more problematic. Here a qualification is necessary: such ideas reached their height in the period of the Goulart government, when extraordinary events, which brought about experimentation and democratic realignments on a large scale, were taking place. The period cannot be reduced to the inconsistencies of its self-image - indicative though they are of the illusion inherent in populist nationalism that the outside world is the source of all evil.

In 1964 the right-wing nationalists branded Marxism as an alien influence, perhaps imagining that fascism was a Brazilian invention. But over and above their differences, the two nationalist tendencies were alike in hoping to find their goal by eliminating anything that was not indigenous. The residue would be the essence of Brazil. The same illusion was popular in the last century, but at that time the new national culture owed more to diversification of the European models than to exclusion of the Portuguese. Opponents of the romantic liberal distortion of Brazilian society did not arrive at the authentic country, since once French and English imports had been rooted out, the colonial order was restored. And that was a Portuguese creation. The paradox of this kind of purism is apparent in the person of Policarpo Quaresma, whose quest for authenticity led him to write in Tupi, a language foreign to him.* The same goes for Antonio Callado's *Quarup***, in which the real Brazil is found not in the colonial past - as suggested by Lima Barreto's hero — but in the heart of the interior, far from the Atlantic coast with its overseas contacts. A group of characters mark the centre of the country on a map and go off in search of it. After innumerable adventures they reach their destination, where they find ... an ants' nest.

The standard US models that arrived with the new communications networks were regarded by the nationalists as an unwelcome foreign presence. The next generation, however, already breathing naturally in this air, considered nationalism to be archaic and provincial. For the first time, as far as I know, the idea spread that it was a worthless enterprise to defend national characteristics against imperialist uniformity. The culture industry

---

*Policarpo Quaresma is the hero of the novel *Triste fim de Policarpo Quaresma* (1915) (translated as *The Patriot* [London: Peter Owen, 1978], by Afonso Henriques de Lima Barreto [1881-1922]. The hero is a caricature patriot, if a sympathetic character, who gradually becomes disillusioned with the state of Brazil.

**For a brief description of this novel, published in 1967, see pp. 157-8 below.

would cure the sickness of Brazilian culture – at least for those who were willing to delude themselves.

In the 1960s nationalism also came under fire from those who thought of themselves as politically and artistically more advanced. Their views are now being taken up in the context of international mass media, only this time without the elements of class struggle and anti-imperialism. In this 'world' environment of uniform mythology, the struggle to establish an 'authentic' culture appears as a relic from the past. Its illusory nature becomes evident, and it seems a provincial phenomenon associated with archaic forms of oppression. The argument is irrefutable, but it must be said that in the new context an emphasis on the international dimension of culture becomes no more than a legitimation of the existing mass media. Just as nationalists used to condemn imperialism and hush up bourgeois oppression, so the anti-nationalists invoke the authoritarianism and backwardness of their opponents, with good reason, while suggesting that the reign of mass communication is either emancipatory or aesthetically acceptable. A modern, critical position, perhaps, but fundamentally conformist. There is another imaginary reversal of roles: although the 'globalists' operate within the dominant ideology of our time, they defend their positions as if they were being hunted down, or as if they were part of the heroic vanguard, aesthetic or libertarian, of the early twentieth century; they line up with the authorities in the manner of one who is starting a revolution.

In the same order of paradox, we can see that the imposition of foreign ideology and the cultural expropriation of the people are realities which do not cease to exist just because there is mystification in the nationalists' theories about them. Whether they are right or wrong, the nationalists become involved in actual conflicts, imparting to them a certain degree of visibility. The mass media modernists, though right in their criticisms, imagine a universalist world which does not exist. It is a question of choosing between the old and the new error, both upheld in the name of progress. The sight of the Avenida Paulista is a fine illustration of what I mean: ugly mansions, once used by the rich to flaunt their wealth, now seem perversely tolerable at the foot of modern skyscrapers, both for reasons of proportion and because of that poetry which emanates from any historically superseded power.

Recent French philosophy has been another factor in the discrediting of cultural nationalism. Its anti-totalizing tendency, its preference for levels of historicity alien to the national milieu, its dismantling of conventional literary scaffolding such as authorship, 'the work', influence, originality, etc. - all these destroy, or at least discredit, that romantic correspondence between individual heroism, masterly execution and collective redemption which imbues the nationalist schemas with their undeniable knowledge-value and potential for mystification. To attack these coordinates can be exciting and partially convincing, besides appeasing national sensibility in an area where one would least expect this to be possible.

A commonplace idea suggests that the copy is secondary with regard to the original, depends upon it, is worth less, and so on. Such a view attaches a negative sign to the totality of cultural forces in Latin America and is at the root of the intellectual malaise that we are discussing. Now, contemporary French philosophers such as Foucault and Derrida have made it their speciality to show that such hierarchies have no basis. Why should the prior be worth more than the posterior, the model more than the imitation, the central more than the peripheral, the economic infrastructure more than cultural life, and so forth? According to the French philosophers, it is a question of conditioning processes (but are they all of the same order?) - prejudices which do not express the life of the spirit in its real movement but reflect the orientation inherent in the traditional human sciences. In their view, it would be more accurate and unbiased to think in terms of an infinite sequence of transformations, with no beginning or end, no first or last, no worse or better. One can easily appreciate how this would enhance the self-esteem and relieve the anxiety of the underdeveloped world, which is seen as tributary to the central countries. We would pass from being a backward to an advanced part of the world, from a deviation to a paradigm, from inferior to superior lands (although the analysis set out to suppress just such superiority). All this because countries which live in the humiliation of having to imitate are more willing than the metropolitan countries to give up the illusion of an original source, even though the theory originated there and not here. Above all, the problem of mirror-culture would no longer be ours alone, and instead of setting our sights on the Europeanization or Americanization of Latin America we would, in a certain sense, be participating in the Latin Americanization of the central cultures.[7]

It remains to be seen whether this conceptual break with the primacy of origins would enable us to balance out or combat relations of actual subordination. Would the innovations of the advanced world suddenly become dispensable once they had lost the distinction of originality? In order to use them in a free and non-imitative manner, it is not enough simply to divest them of their sacred aura. Contrary to what the above analysis might lead us to believe, the breaking down of cultural dazzlement in the underdeveloped countries does not go to the heart of a problem which is essentially practical in character. Solutions are reproduced from the advanced world in response to cultural, economic and political needs, and the notion of copying, with its psychologistic connotations, throws no light whatsoever on this reality. If theory remains at this level, it will continue to suffer from the same limitations, and the radicalism of an analysis that passes over efficient causes will become in its turn largely delusive. The inevitability of cultural imitation is bound up with a specific set of historical imperatives over which abstract philosophical critiques can exercise no power. Even here nationalism is the weak part of the argument, and its supersession at the level of philosophy has no purchase on the realities to which it owes its strength. It should be noted that while nationalism has recently been almost absent from serious intellectual debate, it has a growing presence in the administration of culture, where, for better or worse, it is impossible to escape from the national dimension. Now that economic, though not political, space has become international – which is not the same as homogeneous – this return of nationalism by the back door reflects the insuperable paradox of the present day.

In the 1920s Oswald de Andrade's 'anthropophagous' Pau-Brazil programme also tried to give a triumphalist interpretation of our backwardness.[8] The disharmony between bourgeois models and the realities of rural patriarchy is at the very heart of his poetry – the first of these two elements appearing in the role of absurd caprice ('Rui Barbosa*: A Top Hat in Senegambia'). Its true novelty lies in the fact that the lack of accord is a source not of distress but of optimism, evidence of the country's innocence and the possibility of an alternative, non-bourgeois historical development. This *sui generis* cult of progress is rounded out with a technological wager: Brazil's innocence (the result of Christianization and *embourgeoisement* barely scraping the surface) plus technology equals utopia; modern material progress will make possible a direct leap from pre-bourgeois society to paradise. Marx himself, in his famous letter of 1881 to Vera Zasulich, came

---

*Rui Barbosa (1849–1923) was a prominent liberal politician, and regarded as a model of culture, linguistic purity and erudition in the early twentieth century: he achieved an almost mythical status, known as 'The Eagle of the Hague' for his diplomacy at an International Conference there in 1906. In this phrase, obviously, it is the incongruity of such false representatives of high culture in Brazil which is underlined.

up with a similar hypothesis that the Russian peasant commune would achieve socialism without a capitalist interregnum, thanks to the means made available by progress in the West. Similarly, albeit in a register combining jokes, provocation, philosophy of history and prophecy (as, later, in the films of Glauber Rocha), Anthropophagy set itself the aim of leaping a whole stage.

Returning once more to the idea that Western culture has been inappropriately copied in Brazil, we can see that Oswald's programme introduced a change of tone. Local primitivism would give back a modern sense to tired European culture, liberating it from Christian mortification and capitalist utilitarianism. Brazil's experience would be a differentiated cornerstone, with utopian powers, on the map of contemporary history. (The poems of Mário de Andrade and Raúl Bopp[9] on Amazonian slothfulness contain a similar idea.) Modernism therefore brought about a profound change in values: for the first time the processes under way in Brazil were weighed in the context of the present-day world, as having something to offer in that larger context. Oswald de Andrade advocated cultural irreverence in place of subaltern obfuscation, using the metaphor of 'swallowing up' the alien: a copy, to be sure, but with regenerative effect. Historical distance allows us to see the ingenuousness and jingoism contained in these propositions.

The new vogue for Oswald's manifestoes in the 1960s and particularly the 1970s appeared in the very different context of a military dictatorship which, for all its belief in technological progress and its alliance with big capital both national and international, was less repressive than expected in regard to everyday habits and morality. In the other camp, the attempt to overthrow capitalism through revolutionary war also changed the accepted view of what could be termed 'radical'. This now had no connection with the provincial narrowness of the 1920s, when the Antropófago rebellion assumed a highly libertarian and enlightening role. In the new circumstances technological optimism no longer held water, while the brazen cultural irreverence of Oswald's 'swallowing up' acquired a sense of exasperation close to the mentality of direct action (although often with good artistic results). Oswald's clarity of construction, penetrating vision and sense of discovery all suffered as greater value was attached to his primal, 'de-moralizing' literary practices. One example of this evolution is the guiltlessness of the act of swallowing up. What was then freedom against Catholicism, the bourgeoisie and the glare of Europe has become in the eighties an awkward excuse to handle uncritically those ambiguities of mass culture that stand in need of elucidation. How can one fail to notice that the *Antropófagos* – like the nationalists – take as their subject the abstract Brazilian, with no class specification; or that the analogy with the digestive process throws absolutely no light on the politics and aesthetics of contemporary cultural life?

Since the last century educated Brazilians – the concept is not meant as a compliment but refers to a social category – have had the sense of living among ideas and institutions copied from abroad that do not reflect local reality. It is not sufficient, however, to give up loans in order to think and live more authentically. Besides, one cannot so much as conceive of giving them up. Nor is the problem eliminated by a philosophical deconstruction of the concept of copy. The programmatic innocence of the Antropófagos, which allows them to ignore the malaise, does not prevent it from emerging anew. 'Tupi or not Tupi, that is the question!' Oswald's famous saying, with its contradictory use of the English language, a classical line and a play on words to pursue the search for national identity, itself says a great deal about the nature of the impasse.

The problem may appear simpler in historical perspective. Silvio Romero, despite many absurdities, made a number of excellent remarks on the matter. The following extract is taken from a work on Machado de Assis, written in 1897 to prove that this greatest Brazilian writer produced nothing but a literature of Anglomania, incompetent, unattuned, slavish, etc.

> Meanwhile a kind of absurdity developed ... a tiny intellectual elite separated itself off from the mass of the population, and while the majority remained almost entirely uneducated, this elite, being particularly gifted in the art of learning and copying, threw itself into political and literary imitation of everything it found in the Old World. So now we have an exotic literature and politics, which live and procreate in a hothouse that has no relationship to the outside temperature and environment. This is the bad side of our feeble, illusory skill of mestizo southerners, passionate, given to fantasy, capable of imitation but organically unsuited to create, invent or produce things of our own that spring from the immediate or remote depths of our life and history.
>
> In colonial times, a skilful policy of segregation cut us off from foreigners and kept within us a certain sense of cohesion. This is what gave us Basilio,* Durão,

---

*The names of a group of the so-called Minas group of Arcadian poets who flourished in the interior, gold-mining area of the country in the latter half of the eighteenth century.

Gonzaga, Alvarenga Peixoto, Claudio and Silva Alvarenga, who all worked in a milieu of exclusively Portuguese and Brazilian ideas.

With the first emperor and the Regency, the first breach [opened] in our wall of isolation by Dom João VI grew wider, and we began to copy the political and literary romanticism of the French.

We aped the Charter of 1814 and transplanted the fantasies of Benjamin Constant; we mimicked the parliamentarism and constitutional politics of the author of *Adolphe*, intermingled with the poetry and dreams of the author of *René* and *Atala*.

The people ... remained illiterate.

The Second Reign*, whose policy was for fifty years vacillating, uncertain and incompetent, gradually opened all the gates in a chaotic manner lacking any criteria or sense of discrimination. Imitation, mimicking of everything – customs, laws, codes, verse, theatre, novel – was the general rule.

Regular sailings assured direct communication with the old continent and swelled the inflow of imitation and servile copying....

This is why, in terms of copying, mimickry and pastiches to impress the gringos, no people has a better Constitution on paper ... , everything is better ... on paper. The reality is appalling.[10]

Silvio Romero's account and analysis are uneven, sometimes incompatible. In some instances it is the argument that is interesting, in others the ideology, so that the modern reader will want to examine them separately. The basic schema is as follows: a tiny elite devotes itself to copying Old World culture, separating itself off from the mass of the population, which remains uneducated. As a result, literature and politics come to occupy an exotic position, and we become incapable of *creating things of our own that spring from the depths of our life and history*. Implicit in this demand is the norm of an organic, reasonably homogeneous national culture with popular roots – a norm that cannot be reduced to a mere illusion of literary history or of romanticism, since in some measure it expresses the conditions of modern citizenship. It is in its opposition to this norm that the Brazilian configuration – Europeanized minority, uneducated majority – constitutes an *absurdity*. On the other hand, in order to make the picture more realistic, we should remember that the organic requirement arose at the same time as the expansion of imperialism and organized science – two tendencies which rendered obsolete the idea of a harmonious and auto-centred national culture.

---

*That of the Emperor Pedro II, which lasted from 1840 to 1889.

The original sin, responsible for the severing of connections, was the copy. Its negative effects already made themselves felt in the social fissure between *culture* (unrelated to its surroundings) and *production* (not springing from the depths of our life). However, the disproportion between cause and effects is such that it raises some doubts about the cause itself, and Silvio Romero's own remarks are an invitation to follow a different line of argument from the one he pursues. Let us also note in passing that it is in the nature of an absurdity to be avoidable, and that Romero's argument and invective actually suggest that the elite had an obligation to correct the error that had separated it from the people. His critique was seeking to make the class gulf intolerable for *educated people*, since in a country recently emancipated from slavery the weakness of the popular camp inhibited the emergence of other solutions.

It would seem, then, that the origins of our cultural absurdity are to be found in the imitative talent of mestizo southerners who have few creative capacities. The *petitio principii* is quite transparent: imitativeness is explained by a (racial) tendency to that very imitativeness which is supposed to be explained. (The author's argument, we should note, itself imitated the scientific naturalism then in vogue in Europe.) Today such explanations can hardly be taken seriously, although it is worth examining them as an ideological mechanism and an expression of their times. If the Brazilians' propensity for copying is racial in origin, why should the elite have been alone in indulging it? If everyone had copied, all the effects of 'exoticism' (lack of relation to the environment) and 'absurdity' (separation between elite and people) would have vanished as if by magic, and with them the whole problem. It is not copying in general but *the copying of one class* that constitutes the problem. The explanation must lie not in race but in class.

Silvio Romero goes on to sketch how the vice of imitation developed in Brazil. Absolute zero was in the colonial period, when writers 'worked in a milieu of exclusively Portuguese and Brazilian ideas.' Could it be that the distance between elite and people was smaller in that epoch? Or the fondness for copying less strong? Surely not – and anyway that is not what the text says. The 'cohesion' to which it refers is of a different order, the result of a 'skilful policy of segregation' (!) that separated Brazil from everything non-Portuguese. In other words, the comparison between stages lacks an object: the demand for homogeneity points, in one case, to a social structure remarkable for its inequality, and in the other case to the banning of foreign ideas. Still, if the explanation does not convince us, the observation that it seeks to clarify is accurate enough. Before the nineteenth century, the copying of the European model and the distance between educated people and the mass did not constitute an 'absurdity'. In highly schematic terms, we could say that educated people, in the colonial period, felt solidarity towards the metropolis, Western tradition and their own colleagues, but not towards the local population. To base oneself on a foreign model, in cultural estrangement from the local surroundings, did not appear as a defect – quite the contrary! We should not forget that neo-classical aesthetics was itself universalist and greatly appreciated respect for canonical forms, while the theory of art current at that time set a positive value on imitation. As Antonio Candido acutely observed, the Arcadian poet who placed a nymph in the waters of the Carmo was not lacking in originality; he incorporated Minas Gerais into the traditions of the West and, quite laudably, cultivated those traditions in a remote corner of the earth.[11]

The act of copying, then, did not begin with independence and the opening of the ports*, as Silvio Romero would have it. But it is true that only then did it become the insoluble problem which is still discussed today, and which calls forth such terms as 'mimickry', 'apeing' or 'pastiche'. How did imitation acquire these pejorative connotations?

It is well known that Brazil's gaining of independence did not involve a revolution. Apart from changes in external relations and a reorganization of the top administration, the socio-economic structure created by colonial exploitation remained intact, though now for the benefit of local dominant classes. It was thus inevitable that modern forms of civilization entailing freedom and citizenship, which arrived together with the wave of political emancipation, should have appeared foreign and artificial, 'anti-national', 'borrowed', 'absurd' or however else critics cared to describe them. The strength of the epithets indicates the acrobatics which the self-esteem of the Brazilian elite was forced into, since it faced the depressing alternative of deprecating the bases of its social pre-eminence in the name of progress, or deprecating progress in the name of its social preeminence. On the one hand, there were the slave trade, the latifundia and clientelism – that is to say, a set of relations with their own rules, consolidated in colonial times and impervious to the universalism of bourgeois civilization; on the other

---

*In the wake of his flight to Brazil, to escape Napoleon's invasion of Portugal in 1807-8, in which he was escorted by the British fleet, King João VI opened the ports of the colony for the first time to non-Portuguese (largely British) shipping.

hand, stymied by these relations, but also stymying them, there was the Law before which everyone was equal, the separation between public and private, civil liberties, parliament, romantic patriotism, and so on. The ensuring of the stable coexistence of these two conceptions, in principle so incompatible, was at the centre of ideological and moral preoccupations in Brazil in the nineteenth century. For some, the colonial heritage was a relic to be superseded in the march of progress; for others, it was the real Brazil, to be preserved against absurd imitations. Some wanted to harmonize progress and slave labour, so as not to have to give up either, while still others believed that such a reconciliation already existed, with deleterious moral results. Silvio Romero, for his part, used conservative arguments with a progressive intent, focusing on the 'real' Brazil as the continuation of colonial authoritarianism, but doing so in order to attack its foundations. He scorned as ineffectual the 'illusory' country of laws, lawyers and imported culture: 'No people has a better Constitution on paper ... ; the reality is appalling.'

Silvio Romero's list of 'imitations', not to be allowed through customs, included fashions, patterns of behaviour, laws, codes, poetry, drama and novels. Judged separately against the social reality of Brazil, these articles were indeed superfluous imports which would serve to obscure the real state of impoverishment and create an illusion of progress. In their combination, however, they entered into the formation and equipping of the new nation-state, as well as laying the ground for the participation of new elites in contemporary culture. This modernizing force – whatever its imitative appearance and its distance from the daily course of things – became more inseparably bound up with the reality of Brazil than the institution of slave labour, which was later replaced by other forms of forced labour equally incompatible with the aspiration to enlightenment. As time passed, the ubiquitous stamp of 'inauthenticity' came to be seen as the most authentic part of the national drama, its very mark of identity. Grafted from nineteenth-century Europe on to a colonial social being, the various perfections of civilization began to follow different rules from those operating in the hegemonic countries. This led to a widespread sense of the indigenous pastiche. Only a great figure like Machado de Assis had the impartiality to see a peculiar mode of ideological functioning where other critics could distinguish no more than a lack of consistency. Sérgio Buarque de Holanda remarked: 'The speed at which the "new ideas" spread in the old colony, and the fervour with which they were adopted in many circles on the eve of independence, show quite unequivocally that they had the potential to satisfy an impatient desire for change and that the people were ripe for such change. But it is also clear that the social order expressed in these ideas was far from having an exact equivalent in Brazil, particularly outside the cities. The articulation of society, the basic criteria of economic exploitation and the distribution of privileges were so different here that the "new ideas" could not have the same meaning that was attached to them in parts of Europe or ex-English America.'[12]

When Brazil became an independent state, a permanent collaboration was established between the forms of life characteristic of colonial oppression and the innovations of bourgeois progress. The new stage of capitalism broke up the exclusive relationship with the metropolis, converting local property-owners and administrators into a national ruling class (effectively part of the emergent world bourgeoisie), and yet retained the old forms of labour exploitation which have not been fully modernized up to the present day. In other words, the discrepancy between the 'two Brazils' was not due to an imitative tendency, as Silvio Romero and many others thought; nor did it correspond to a brief period of transition. It was the lasting result of the creation of a nation-state on the basis of slave labour – which, if the reader will forgive the shorthand, arose in turn out of the English industrial revolution and the consequent crisis of the old colonial system. That is to say, *it arose out of contemporary history.*[13] Thus Brazil's backward deformation belongs to the same order of things as the progress of the advanced countries. Silvio Romero's 'absurdities' – in reality, the Cyclopean discords of world capitalism – are not a historical deviation. They are linked to the finality of a single process which, in the case of Brazil, requires the continuation of forced or semi-forced labour and a corresponding cultural separation of the poor. With certain modifications, much of it has survived to this day. The panorama now seems to be changing, thanks to the desegregationist impulse of mass consumption and mass communications. These new terms of cultural oppression and expropriation have not yet been much studied.

The thesis of cultural copying thus involves an ideology in the Marxist sense of the term – that is, an illusion supported by appearances. The well-known coexistence of bourgeois principles with those of the ancien régime is here explained in accordance with a plausible and wide-ranging schema, essentially individualist in nature, in which effects and causes are systematically inverted.

For Silvio Romero imitation results in the lack of a common denominator between popular and elite culture, and in the elite's low level of permeation by the national. But why not reverse the argument? Why should the imitative character of our life not stem from forms of inequality so brutal that they lack the minimal reciprocity ('common denominator') without which modern society can only appear artificial and 'imported'? At a time when the idea of the nation had become the norm, the dominant class's *unpatriotic* disregard for the lives it exploited gave it the feeling of being alien. The origins of this situation in colonialism and slavery are immediately apparent.

The defects normally associated with imitation can be explained in the same way. We can agree with its detractors that the copy is at the opposite pole from originality, from national creativity, from independent and well-adapted judgements, and so on. Absolute domination entails that culture expresses nothing of the conditions that gave it life, except for that intrinsic sense of futility on which a number of writers have been able to work artistically. Hence the 'exotic' literature and politics unrelated to the 'immediate or remote depths of our life and history'; hence, too, the lack of 'discrimination' or 'criteria' and, above all, the intense conviction that all is mere paper. In other words, the painfulness of an imitative civilization is produced not by imitation – which is present at any event – but by the social structure of the country. It is this which places culture in an untenable position, contradicting its very concept of itself, and which nevertheless was not as sterile, at that time, as Silvio Romero would have us believe. Nor did the segregated section of society remain unproductive. Its modes of expression would later acquire, for educated intellectuals, the value of a non-bourgeois component of national life, an element serving to fix Brazilian identity (with all the evident ambiguities).

The exposure of cultural transplantation has become the axis of a naive yet widespread critical perspective. Let us conclude by summarizing some of its defects.

1. It suggests that imitation is avoidable, thereby locking the reader into a false problem.

2. It presents as a national characteristic what is actually a malaise of the dominant class, bound up with the difficulty of morally reconciling the advantages of progress with those of slavery or its surrogates.

3. It implies that the elites could conduct themselves in some other way which is tantamount to claiming that the beneficiary of a given situation will put an end to it.

4. The argument obscures the essential point, since it concentrates its fire on the relationship between elite and model whereas the real crux is the exclusion of the poor from the universe of contemporary culture.

5. Its implicit solution is that the dominant class should reform itself and give up imitation. We have argued, on the contrary, that the answer lies in the workers gaining access to the terms of contemporary life, so that they can re-define them through their own initiative. This, indeed, would be in this context a concrete definition of democracy in Brazil.

6. A copy refers to a prior original existing elsewhere, of which it is an inferior reflection. Such deprecation often corresponds to the self-consciousness of Latin American elites, who attach mythical solidity -in the form of regional intellectual specialization - to the economic, technological and political inequalities of the international order. The authentic and the creative are to the imitative what the advanced countries are to the backward. But one cannot solve the problem by going to the opposite extreme. As we have seen, philosophical objections to the concept of originality tend to regard as non-existent a real problem that it is absurd to dismiss. Cultural history has to be set in the world perspective of the economics and culture of the left, which attempt to explain our 'backwardness' as part of the contemporary history of capital and *its advances*.[14] Seen in terms of the copy, the anachronistic juxtaposition of forms of modern civilization and realities originating in the colonial period is a mode of non-being or even a humiliatingly imperfect realization of a model situated elsewhere. Dialectical criticism, on the other hand, investigates the same anachronism and seeks to draw out a figure of the modern world, set on a course that is either full of promise, grotesque or catastrophic.

7. The idea of the copy that we have been discussing counterposes national and foreign, original and imitative. These are unreal oppositions which do not allow us to see the share of the foreign in the nationally specific, of the imitative in the original and of the original in the imitative. (In a key study, Paulo Emilio Salles Gomes refers to our 'creative lack of competence in copying'.[15]) If I am not mistaken, the theory presupposes three elements - a Brazilian subject, reality of the country, civilization of the advanced nations - such that the third helps the first to forget the second. This schema is also unreal, and it obscures the organized, cumulative nature of the process, the potent strength even of bad tradition, and the power relations, both national and international, that are in play. Whatever its unacceptable aspects - unacceptable for whom? - Brazilian cultural life has elements of dynamism which display both originality and

lack of originality. Copying is not a false problem, so long as we treat it pragmatically, from an aesthetic and political point of view freed from the mythical requirement of creation *ex nihilo,*

Notes

1. *Mário de Andrade* (1893-1945), novelist, poet and critic, was the acknowledged leader of the modernist movement in Brazil and bore the brunt of the initial scandal that it caused. The language of his *Macunaíma: The Hero without Any Character* (1928) synthesizes idioms and dialects from all the regions of Brazil. | *Trs.* |

2. For a balanced and considered opinion on the subject, see Antonio Candido, 'Literatura e subdesenvolvimento', *Argumento* No. 1, São Paulo, October 1973.

3. This observation was made by Vinicius Dantas.

4. *Joaquim Maria Machado de Assis* (1839-1908) is regarded as the greatest of all Portuguese-language novelists. He wrote nine novels and two hundred short stories, including *Epitaph of a Small Winner* (1880), *Dom Casmurro* (1990) and *Esau and Jacob* (1904), which are considered to be far ahead of their time. | *Trs.* |

5. *Sílvio Romero* (1851-1914) wrote the first modern history of Brazilian literature, a work which is still of interest today, despite the scientist language of the period. | Trs. |

6. The *Centro Popular de Cultura* (CPC) was established in 1961 at the start of the social ferment that ended with the military coup in 1964. The movement was created under the auspices of the National Union of Students, which wanted to fuse together artistic irreverence, political teaching and the people. It produced surprisingly inventive cinema, theatre and other stage performances. Several of its members became major artistic figures: Glauber Rocha, Joaquim Pedro de Andrade and Ferreira Gullar among others. The convergence of the student and popular movements gave rise to completely new artistic possibilities. | *Note supplied by Ana McMac* |.

7. See Silviano Santiago, 'O Entre-lugar do discurso latino-americano', in *Uma literatura nos trópicos*, São Paulo 1978; and Haroldo de Campos, 'Da razão antropofágica: diálogo e diferença na cultura brasileira', *Boletim Bibliográfico Biblioteca Mário de Andrade*, vol 44, January–December 1983.

8. *Oswald de Andrade* introduced European avant-garde ideas into Brazil. He espoused extreme primitivism (anthropophagy) and his *Manifesto da Poesia Pau-Brasil* (1924) and *Manifesto Antropofágo* (1928) are the most daring writings of the 'modern movement' which emerged in 1922, attacking academic values and respectability and seeking poetry written in the Brazilian vernacular. | *Trs.* |

9. The greatest achievement of Raúl Bopp (b. 1898) was his 'cannibalist' poem 'Cobra Norato' (1921), an exploration of the Amazon jungle. | *Trs.* |

10. Silvio Romero, *Machado de Assis*, Rio de Janeiro 1897, pp. 121-3.

11. Antonio Candido, *Formação da literatura brasileira*, São Paulo 1969, vol. 1, p. 74.

12. Sergio Buarque de Holanda, *Do império à republica*, II, São Paulo 1977, pp. 77-78.

13. Emilia Viotti da Costa, *Da monarquia à república: Momentos decisivos*, São Paulo 1977, Chapter 1; Luis Felipe de Alencastro, 'La traite negrière et l'unité nationale brésilienne', *Revue Française de l'Histoire de l'Outre-Mer*, vol. 46, 1979; Fernando Novais, 'Passagens para o Novo Mundo', *Novos Estudos Cebrap* 9, July 1984.

14. See Celso Furtado, *A Pre-Revolução Brasileira*, Rio de Janeiro 1962, and Fernando H. Cardoso, *Empresario industrial e desenvolvimento económico no Brasil*, São Paulo 1964.

15. Paulo Emilio Salles Gomes, 'Cinema: trajetória no subdesenvolvimento', *Argumento* No. 1, October 1973.

TWO

Misplaced Ideas: Literature and Society in Late-Nineteenth-Century Brazil

Every science has principles on which its system is based. Free labour is one of the principles of Political Economy. Yet in Brazil the 'unpolitical and abominable' fact of slavery reigns.

This argument – the summary of a liberal pamphlet, by a contemporary of Machado de Assis[1] – places Brazil outside the system of science. We fell short of the reality to which science refers; we were rather an 'unpolitical and abominable' moral fact. All this was a degradation, when we think that science was Enlightenment, Progress, Humanity, etc. As for the arts, Joaquim Nabuco expresses a comparable feeling when he protests against the subject of slavery in the plays of Alencar: 'If it is horrible to the foreigner, how much more does it humiliate the Brazilian!'[2] Other authors of course came to opposite conclusions. Since the science of economy and other liberal ideologies did not concern themselves with our reality, they are what is abominable, irrelevant to political life, foreign and foolish. 'Better have good Negroes from the African coast, for our happiness and theirs, notwithstanding the Briton, with his morbid philanthropy, which makes him forget his own home and allows his poor white brother to die from hunger, a slave without a master to pity him; the hypocritical and stupid Briton, who weeps over the destiny of our happy slave and thus exposes himself to the ridicule of true philanthropy.'[3]

These authors, each in his own way, reflect the disparity between the slave society of Brazil and the principles of European liberalism. Shaming some, irritating others who insist on their hypocrisy, these principles – in which neither one nor the other of the opposing parties can recognize Brazil – are the unavoidable frame of reference for everybody. In sum, an ideological comedy is set up, *different from the European*. Of course, free labour, equality before the law and, more generally, universalism were also an ideology in Europe; but there they corresponded to appearances and hid the essential – the exploitation of labour. Among us, the same ideas would be false in a different sense, so to speak, in an original way. The Declaration of the Rights of Man, for instance, transcribed in part in the Brazilian Constitution of 1824, since it did not even correspond to appearances, could not deceive, and indeed cast the institution of slavery into a sharper light.[4] This professed universality of principles throws the same sharp light on the general practice of *favour* and transforms it into scandal. Under these conditions, what was the value of the grand bourgeois abstractions that we used so often? They didn't describe life – but ideas do not live by that alone. Thinking in a similar direction, Sérgio Buarque remarks: 'By bringing from distant lands our forms of life, our institutions, and our vision of the world and by striving to maintain all that in an environment sometimes unfavourable and hostile, we were exiles in our own land.'[5] This inadequacy in our thinking, no accident as we shall see, was in fact continually present, impregnating and rendering awkward the ideological life of the Second Reign, even down to its smallest detail. Sometimes inflated, sometimes trivial, very seldom on the right note, the literary prose of the time is one of the many witnesses of this fact.

Although the causes of this state of affairs are commonplaces of our historiography, their cultural effects have been insufficiently studied. As is well known, we were an agrarian and independent country, divided into latifundia, whose productivity depended on the one hand on slave labour and on the other on a foreign market. The peculiarities we have already mentioned arise more or less directly from this. For instance, bourgeois economic thinking – the priority of profit with all its social implications – was inevitable for us, since it prevailed in international trade, toward which our economy was directed. The constant practice of such trade taught this way of thought to more than a few. Moreover, we had become independent not long ago in the name of French, English and American liberal ideas, which were therefore part of our national identity. On the other hand, with equal necessity, this ideological ensemble had to be at war with slavery and its defenders and yet live with them.[6] In the realm of belief, the incompatibility between slavery and liberalism is clear, as we have seen. But at the practical level it could also be felt. Inasmuch as he was property, a slave could be sold, but not fired. In this respect, the free worker gave more freedom to his employer, and immobilized less capital. This is one reason, among others, why slavery set limits to the rationalization of production. Commenting on what he saw on a plantation, a traveller wrote: 'there is no specialization of labour because they try to make economic use of their hands.' After quoting this passage, F. H. Cardoso remarks that here 'economic' does not stand for reducing work to a minimum, but for stretching it to a maximum amount of time. Work had to be made to fill and discipline the day of the slave. In short, the opposite of what was modern. Based on violence and military discipline, slave production could not be ordered around the idea of efficiency.[7] The rational study and continual modernization of the processes of production, with all the prestige that went with the revolution they were causing in Europe, made no sense in Brazil. To make things more complex, the slave latifundium had been an enterprise of commercial capital from the very beginning, and therefore profit had always been its pivot. However, profit as a subjective priority is common to early forms of capitalism and to more modern ones. So that, up to the time when slave labour became less profitable than wage labour, the 'uncultivated and abominable' slaveowners who sought profit were in fact more thoroughly capitalistic than our defenders of Adam Smith, as capitalism for the latter meant only freedom. In short, the lines of intellectual life were bound to be hopelessly entangled. In matters of rationality, roles were shuffled: economic science became fantasy and morality, obscurantism equalled realism and responsibility, technical considerations were not practical, and altruism sought to bring about the exploitation of labour, etc. And, more generally, in the absence of the point of view of the slaves, who were not organized, the confrontation between humanity and inhumanity, in which no doubt there was a question of justice, ended up in a more earthbound way as a conflict between two modes of investment. Of course, one of the parties found the more spiritual version of this opposition more suitable.[8]

Challenged at every turn by slavery, the liberal ideology – the ideology of the newly emancipated nations of America – was derailed. It would be easy to deduce the resulting incongruities, many of which stirred the mind and conscience of nineteenth-century Brazil. We have already seen some examples. However, they remained oddly inessential. The test of reality did not seem important. It was as if the coherence and generality of thought was of little importance, or rather as if the criteria by which culture was judged were different – but in what way? By its sheer presence, slavery revealed the inadequacy of liberal ideas; but this does not mean to say that they affected or changed their orientation. Slavery was indeed the basic productive relationship, and yet it was not the social relation directly at work in ideological life. The key lay elsewhere. To find it, we must take up again the country as a whole. To schematize, we can say that colonization, based on the monopoly of the land, produced three classes of population: the proprietor of the latifundium, the slave and the 'free man', who was in fact dependent. Between the first two, the relation is clear. Our argument will hinge on the situation of the third. Neither proprietor, nor proletarian, the free man's access to social life and its benefits depended, in one way or another, on the favour of a man of wealth and power.[9] The caricature of this 'free man' was the *agregado*.[10] Favour was, therefore, the relationship by which the class of free men reproduced itself, a relationship in which the other member was the propertied class. The field of ideological life is formed by these two classes, and it is governed, therefore, by this relationship.[11] Thus, under a thousand forms and names, favour formed and flavoured the whole of the national life, excepting always the basic productive relationship which was secured by force. Favour was present everywhere, combining itself with more or less ease to administration, politics, industry, commerce, the life of the city, the court, and so on. Even professions, such as medicine, or forms of skilled labour, such as printing, which in Europe were on the whole free of favour, were among us governed by it. As the professional depended on favour to exercise his profession, so the small proprietor depended on it for the security of his property, and the public servant for his position. Favour was our quasi-universal social mediation – and being more appealing than slavery, the other relationship inherited from colonial times, it is understandable that our writers based their interpretation of Brazil upon it, thereby unwittingly disguising the violence that had always been essential to the sphere of production.

Slavery gives the lie to liberal ideas; but favour, more insidiously, uses them, for its own purposes, originating a new ideological pattern. The element of arbitrariness, the fluid play of preferences to which favour subjects whatever it touches, cannot be fully rationalized. In Europe, when attacking such irrationalities, universalism had its sights on feudal privilege. In opposing this, bourgeois civilization had postulated the autonomy of the individual, universality of law, culture for its own sake, a day's pay for a day's work, the dignity of labour, etc., against the prerogatives of the *Ancien Régime*. Favour in turn implies the dependency of the individual, the exception to the rule, ornamental culture, arbitrary pay and the servility of labour. However, Brazil was not to Europe as feudalism was to capitalism. On the contrary, we were a function of European capitalism, and moreover, had never been feudal, for our colonization was the deed of commercial capital. In face of the European achievement, no Brazilian could have had the idea nor the strength to be, let us say, the Kant of favour, giving universality to this social form.[12] In this confrontation, the two principles were not of equal strength: in the sphere of reasoning, principles the European bourgeoisie had developed against arbitrariness and slavery were eagerly adopted; while in practice, sustained by the realities of plantation life, favour continually reasserted itself, with all the feelings and notions that went with it. The same is true of institutions, bureaucracy and justice, for example, which although ruled by patronage affirmed the forms and theories of the modern bourgeois state. As well as the predictable debates, therefore, this antagonism produced a stable coexistence between the two views which is of interest to study. *Once the European ideas and motives took hold, they could serve, and very often did, as a justification, nominally 'objective', for what was unavoidably arbitrary in the practice of favour.* Real as it was, the antagonism vanished into thin air, and the opposing positions walked hand in hand. The effects of this displacement of function were many, and deeply touched our literature, as we will see. Liberalism, which had been an ideology well grounded in appearances, came to stand for the conscious desire to participate in a reality that appearances did not sustain. When he justified arbitrariness by means of some 'rational' reason, the beneficiary consciously exalted himself and his benefactor, who, in turn, had no motive to contradict him, rationality being the highest value of the modern world. Under these conditions, which side believed in the justification? To what appearance did it correspond? But this was not a problem, for what was important was the commendable intention which governed both patronage and gratitude. The symbolic compensation was perhaps a little out of tune, but not ungrateful. Or, we might say, this use of justification was out of harmony with liberalism, but quite in tune with favour, which was, of course, all important. And how better to give lustre to individuals and to the society they establish, than through the most illustrious ideas of their time, which in this case were European? In this context, ideologies do not describe reality, not even falsely, and they do not move according to a law of their own; we shall therefore call them 'ideologies of the second degree'. Their law of movement is a different one, not the one they name; it honours prestige, rather than a desire for system and objectivity. The reasons for this were no secret: the inevitable 'superiority' of Europe, and the demands of the moment of expression, of self-esteem and fantasy, which are essential to favour. In this way, as we have said before, the test of reality and coherence did not seem to be decisive, notwithstanding its continuous presence as a requirement, recalled or forgotten according to circumstances. Thus, one could methodically call dependence independence, capriciousness utility, exceptions universality, kinship merit, privilege equality, and so on. By linking itself to the practice of what, in principle, it should criticize, liberalism caused thought to lose its footing. Let us not forget, however, the complexity of this step: inasmuch as they became preposterous, these ideas also ceased to mislead.

This was not the only way in which favour and liberalism could meet. However, it was the most complex, all-embracing, and striking of the possible combinations, and in our ideological climate, decisive. For the moment, let us consider but a few aspects of it. We have seen that in this combination, the ideas of the bourgeoisie, ideas whose sober grandeur goes back to the civic and rational spirit of the Enlightenment, take on the function of providing ... ornament and aristocratic style; they attest and celebrate participation in a majestic sphere, in this case the European world in the process of ... industrialization. There could not be a stranger relation between name and function. The historical novelty lies not in the ornamental character of knowledge and culture, part of the colonial and Iberian tradition, but in the extraordinary dissonance created when 'modern' culture is used to this purpose. Is it as impractical as a trinket? Or does it confer distinction upon those who wear it? Could it be our panacea? Should it shame us before the eyes of the world? What is for sure is that in the comings and goings of argument and interest, all these aspects would show up, so that in the minds of the more attentive they were inextricably linked and mixed. Ideological life degraded and elevated its participants all at once, and this was often well known. For this reason, it was an unstable combination which could easily degenerate into the most bitter and hostile criticism. In order to maintain itself, it needed a permanent complicity, a complicity which the practice of favour tended to guarantee. At the moment of the exchange of favours, with its aspect of mutual personal recognition, it was not in the interest of either party to denounce the other, although both had the wherewithal to do so. This ever-renewed complicity had, moreover, heavy implications of class: in the Brazilian context, favour assured both parties, especially the weaker one, that neither was a slave. Even the most miserable of those given favour saw his freedom recognized in this act. All this transformed these exchanges, even if very modest, into a ceremony conferring social superiority, and therefore valued in itself. Ballasted by the infinite duress and degradation of slavery which it seeks to conjure away, this recognition sustains an extraordinary complicity, made even worse by the adoption of the bourgeois vocabulary of equality, merit, labour and reason. Machado de Assis will be the master of these complexities. Yet there is another side to it. Immersed as we are, still today, in the universe of capital, which did not take classical form in Brazil, we tend to see this combination as being only disadvantage. It may well not have had any advantage, but in order to appreciate it in its complexity, we should keep in mind that the ideas of the European bourgeoisie, initially aimed at privilege, had become apologetic from 1848 on: the wave of social struggles in Europe showed that universality hid class antagonisms.[13] Therefore, to catch its peculiar tone, we must consider that our improper discourse was hollow even when used properly. We can note in passing, that this pattern will be repeated in the twentieth century, when we have several times sworn fealty to its most bankrupt ideologies on the world stage – in full belief that we are quite up-to-date. In literature, as we shall see, something singular results, an emptying out of what is already hollow. Here again, Machado will be the master.

In short, if we insist upon the extent to which slavery and favour twisted the ideas of the times, it is not in order to dismiss them, but to describe them *qua* twisted – not in line with their own demands. They are recognizably Brazilian in their peculiar distortion. Hence, stepping back from the search for causes, we are still left with that experience of incongruity which was our point of departure: the impression that Brazil gives of ill-assortedness – unmanageable contrasts, disproportions, non-sense, anachronisms, outrageous compromises and the like – the sort of combination which the art of Brazilian Modernism, and later on, Tropicalism, as well as political economy, have taught us to appreciate.[14] Examples abound. Let us look at some, not for the purpose of analysis but to suggest the ubiquity of what we have described and the variation of which it is capable. In the magazines of the time, the statement of purpose in the first issue, whether serious or bantering, is written for bass and falsetto: first, the redeeming purpose of the press is asserted, in the combative tradition of the Enlightenment; the great sect founded by Gutenberg calls for action in the face of indifference; at the heights, youth and the condor, rejecting the past and its prejudices, look toward the future, while the purifying torch of the press banishes the darkness or corruption. Second, accommodating themselves to circumstances, the magazines declare their goodnaturedness, their eagerness to 'provide all classes, and particularly honest families, a means of delightful instruction and agreeable recreation.' The redeeming intention joins with puzzles, calls for the unity of all Brazilians, dress patterns, practical hints and serial novels.[15] The light verse that serves as the epigraph to *The Marmot in the Court* [During the Empire, the city of Rio was known as the 'Court'] is an unintended caricature of this sequence: 'Here is the marmot/In his variety/He is ever-liked/And by all/He speaks the truth/Says what he feels/Loves and respects/Everyone.' If, in another realm, we scrape our walls a little, we find the same conjunction: 'The change in architecture was superficial. European wallpaper was pasted or hung on slave-built walls of earth, or paintings were hung, in order to create the illusion of modern interiors, like those of industrial Europe. In some cases, the pretence reached the absurd: The painting of Greco-Roman architectural motifs – pilasters, architraves, colonnades, friezes, etc., often done to deceive, suggested a neoclassic setting that could never have been built with the techniques and materials available in Brazil. In other cases, windows were painted on the walls with views of Rio de Janeiro or Europe, suggesting an exterior world quite distant from the real one of slave quarters and slave labor.'[16] This text describes rural homes in the Province of São Paulo in the second half of the nineteenth century. As for the Court: 'Here changes responded to new habits, which included the use of objects of greater refinement – crystal, china and porcelain – and in the adoption of more formal behavior, as in the serving of meals. At the same time these architectural changes gave an appearance of veracity to the whole, which tried to reproduce the life of European homes. The social strata that benefited the most from a slave-system exclusively based on agricultural production, attempted to create an illusion for their own use of an ambience with urban and European characteristics ... thus everything or almost everything had to be imported.'[17] This comedy lives in the remarkable opening chapters of *Quincas Borba*. Under the pressure of opinion, Rubião, a recent heir, must exchange his black slave for a French cook and a Spanish servant, with whom he is not at ease. Besides gold and silver, the metals that speak to his heart, he now buys statuettes of bronze as well – a Faust and a Mephistopheles. A graver matter, but equally under the imprint of the times, is the wording of our hymn to the Republic, written in 1890 by Medeiros e Albuquerque, a self-proclaimed 'decadent' poet. It was progressive and altogether unconvincing. 'We cannot believe that of yore/slaves could have existed in our noble land.' ('Of yore' was but two years before, abolition having occurred in 1888.) A declaration of the revolutionary government of Pernambuco made many years earlier (1817), sounds just as off, but for opposite reasons: 'Patriots, your properties, even those most repugnant to the ideals of justice, will be held sacred.'[18] It refers to rumours of emancipation, which had to be denied to reassure the owners. The life of Machado de Assis is an example as well; in it, the militant journalist (enthusiastic about 'the workingman's intelligence'), the author of a humorous column and of serious quatrains (the latter commemorating the wedding of the imperial princesses), and the Chevalier of the Order of the Rose follow one another in rapid succession.[19] Against all this Silvio Romero will take the field. 'It is necessary to lay the foundations of a national spirit, conscious of its merits and defects, of its strength and its infirmities, and not concoct a pastiche, a kind of stuffed puppet, which only serves to shame us in the eyes of the foreigner. There is but one way to achieve this desideratum, we must immerse ourselves in the life-giving current of naturalistic and monistic ideas which are transforming the old world.'[20] From afar, this substitution of one pastiche for another is so obvious it makes us smile. But it is also dramatic, since it points out to what extent our desire for authenticity had to express itself in an alien language. The romantic pastiche was only superseded by another, this time Naturalism. In sum, in the magazines, in behaviour, in the setting of the home, in national symbols, in revolutionary proclamations, in theory and in everything else, always the same 'harlequin' composition, to use Mário de Andrade's word: the dissonance between representations, and what, upon consideration, we know to be their context.

The combination of latifundia and unfree labour, given durability by its important role in the international market, and later, by internal politics, stood firm through Colony, Emperors and Regencies, through Abolition, the First Republic, and even now is a matter of debate and bullets.[21] Our ideological life, no less determined by national dependency, did vary: at a distance, it followed in the steps of Europe. (Let us point out that it is only the ideology of independence which turns this into a problem; foolishly when it insists on an impossible cultural autonomy; profoundly, when it reflects upon what was truly possible.) The tenacity of the basic social relationships and the ideological volatility of the 'elite' were both a part of the dynamics of capitalism as an international system, the part that it was ours to live out. The latifundia, little changed, saw the baroque, neoclassic, romantic, naturalist and modernist cultures pass by, cultures which in Europe reflected immense transformations in its social order. We could well suppose that here they would lose their point, which in part did occur. But this loss, to which we were condemned by the working of the international system of colonialism, condemned the working of that very system itself. We say this to indicate its more-than-national significance.

All this was no secret, although not worked out theoretically. For the arts, as opposed to theory, making something of it was easier since there was always a way to adore, quote, ape, sack, adapt or devour these manners and fashions, so that they would reflect, in their defectiveness, a cultural embarrassment in which we would recognize ourselves. Let us go back for a moment. Liberal ideas could not be put into practice, and yet they could not be discarded. They became a part of a special practical situation, which would reproduce itself and not leave them unchanged. Therefore, it does not help to insist on their obvious falsehood. We should rather observe their dynamics, of which this falsehood was a true component. Faced with these ideas, Brazil, the outpost of slavery, was ashamed – for these were taken to be ideas of the time – and resentful, for they served no purpose. But they were also adopted with pride, in an ornamental vein, as a proof of modernity and distinction. And, of course, they were revolutionary when put in the service of Abolitionism. Subordinate to the demands of place, and not losing their original claims, they circled, governed by a peculiar rule whose merits and faults, ambiguities and deceptions were peculiar as well. To know Brazil was to know these displacements, experienced and practised by everyone as a sort of fate, for which, however, there was no proper name, since the improper use of names was part of its nature. Widely felt to be a defect, well-known but little reflected upon, this system of displacement certainly did debase ideological life and diminished the chances for genuine thought. However, it made for a scepticism in matters of ideology which could be both thorough and effortless, and compatible, besides, with a good deal of talk. Pushed a bit further, it will produce the astonishing force of Machado de Assis' vision. Now, the ground of this scepticism surely lies not in the reflective exploration of the limits of liberal thought. It rather lies in an intuitive starting point, which spared us this effort. Embedded in a system they did not describe, even in appearance, the ideas of the bourgeoisie saw everyday life invalidate their pretension to universality from the very beginning. If they were accepted, they were so for reasons they themselves could not accept. Instead of functioning as the horizon of thought, they appeared on a vaster background which rendered them relative: the back-and-forth of arbitrariness and favour. The ground of its claims to universality was shaken. Thus, what in Europe was a great critical feat, could among us be ordinary incredulity. Utilitarianism, egoism, formalism, and the like, were clothes to be worn on occasion, perhaps fashionable, but uncomfortably tight Thus we see that this world is of consequence to the history of culture: when in its peculiar orbit, the most prestigious ideology of the West was bound to cut the ludicrous figure of a mania among manias. In such wise, our national oddities became world-historical. Perhaps this is comparable to what happened in Russian literature. Faced with the latter, even the greatest novels of the French realism seem naïve. And why? In spite of their claims to universality, the psychology of rational egoism and the ethics of Enlightenment appeared in the Russian Empire as a 'foreign' ideology, and therefore, a localized and relative one. Sustained by its historical backwardness, Russia forced the bourgeois novel to face a more complex reality. The comic figure of the Westernizer, Francophile or Germanophile (frequently under an allegorical or ridiculous name), the ideologies of progress, of liberalism, of reason, all these were ways of bringing into the foreground the modernization that came with Capital. These enlightened men proved themselves to be lunatics, thieves, opportunists, cruel, vain and parasitical. The system of ambiguities growing out of the local use of bourgeois ideas – one of the keys to the Russian novel – is not unlike the one we described for Brazil. The social reasons for this similarity are clear. In Russia, too, modernization would lose itself in the infinite extent of territory and of social inertia, and would clash with serfdom or its vestiges – a clash many felt as a national shame, although it gave others the standard by which to measure the madness of the individualism and progressomania that the West imposed and imposes on the world. The extreme form of this confrontation, in which progress is a disaster and backwardness a shame, is one of the springs of Russian literature. Whatever the difference in stature, there is in Machado – for the reasons that I have pointed out – something similar, something of Gogol, Dostoyevsky, Goncharov and Chekhov.[22] Let us say, then, that the very debasement of thought among us, of which we were so bitterly aware, and which today stifles the student of our nineteenth century, was a sore spot of the world-historical process and for this reason a valuable clue to it.[23]

In the process of reproducing its social order, Brazil unceasingly affirms and reaffirms European ideas, always improperly. In their quality of being improper, they will be material and a problem for literature. The writer may well not know this, nor does he need to, in order to use them. But he will be off-key unless he feels, notes, and develops – or wholly avoids – this aspect. And although there is an indefinite number of solutions to the problem, violations are palpable and definite. Their non-artistic names are ingenuousness, loquacity, narrow-mindedness, aping, provinciality, etc., the specific and local effects of an alienation with long arms – the consequences of the lack of social transparency, imposed, first, by our colonial situation and later on by our dependency. For all that, the reader has learned very little about Brazilian history, literary or general, and we have not placed Machado de Assis. What is then the use of what has been said so far? Instead of a literary history set within a social 'panorama', a construction always suggestive and true to a certain extent, but necessarily vague, I have tried a different solution. I have sought to specify a social mechanism in the form in which it became an internal and active element of our culture: the inescapable difficulty which Brazil forced upon its cultivated men in the very process of its social reproduction. In other words, an analysis of the ground of intellectual experience. I have tried to see in the movement of our ideas something that made us singular, starting from the common observation, almost a feeling, that in Brazil ideas were off-centre in relation to European usage. And I have presented a historical explanation for this displacement, an explanation which brought in relations of production and parasitism in Brazil, our economic dependency and its counterpart, the intellectual hegemony of Europe, revolutionized by capital. In short, in order to analyse a national peculiarity, sensed in everyday life, we have been driven to reflect on the colonial process, which was international. The constant interchange of liberalism and favour was the local and opaque effect of a planetary mechanism. Now, the everyday movement of ideas and practical perspectives was the obvious and natural material for literature, once the fixed forms had lost their validity in the arts. It was, therefore, the point of departure for the novel, even more so, the realistic novel. Thus, what we have described is the manner in which the movement of world history, in its cryptic and local results, repeated again and again, passes into writing, which it now determines from the inside – whether or not the writer knows or wills it. In other words, we have defined a vast and heterogeneous, but structured, field, which is a historical *consequence*, and can be an artistic *origin*. While studying it, we saw that it differs from the European field, although using the same vocabulary. Therefore, difference, comparison and distance are part of its very definition: sometimes reason is on our side, sometimes it belongs to others, but it always appears in an ambiguous light. The result is an equally singular chemistry the affinities and antipathies of which we have described to some extent. It is only natural that such material should propose original problems to the literature that depends on it. As a final observation, let us only say that, contrary to what is generally thought, the material of the artist turns out not to be shapeless: it is historically shaped and in some way registers the social process to which it owes its existence. In shaping it, in turn, the writer superimposes form upon form, and the depth, force, and complexity of the artistic results will depend upon the success of this operation, of this relation to the pre-formed material in which the energies of history lie. The match of forms is not obvious. And, one more variation of the same theme, let us conclude by saying that even when dealing with the most modest matters of everyday life, the subject matter of our novelists has always been world-historical. This they shaped as well as they could, but it would not have been their subject, had they dealt with it directly.

Notes

1. A. R. de Torres Bandeira, 'A liberdade do trabalho e a concorrência, seu efeito, so prejudiciais à classe operária?', in *O Futuro*, No. IX, 1-15-1863. Machado was a frequent contributor to this magazine.

2. *A Polêmica Alencar-Nabuco*, organization and introduction by Afrânio Coutinho, Tempo Brasileiro, ed., Rio de Janeiro, 1965, p. 106.

3. Deposition of a commercial firm, M. Wright & Cia., regarding the financial crisis of the 1850s. Cited by Joaquim Nabuco, *Um Estadista do Império*, São Paulo, 1936, Vol. I, p. 188, and again by S. B. de Holanda, *Raízes do Brasil*, J. Olympio, Rio de Janeiro, 1956, p. 96.

4. E. Viotti da Costa, 'Introdução ao estudo da Emancipação política,' in C. G. Mota ed., *Brasil em Perspectiva*, Difusão Européia do Livro, São Paulo, 1968.

5. Holanda, *Raízes do Brasil*, p. 15.

6. E. Viotti da Costa, 'Introdução'.

7. F. H. Cardoso, *Capitalismo e Escravidão*, Difusão Européia do Livro, São Paulo, 1962, pp. 189-91 and 198.

8. As Felipe de Alencastro remarks in an as yet unpublished work, the true national question of our nineteenth century was the defence of the slave traffic in the face of English pressure. A question that could not be less attractive to intellectual enthusiasm.

9. For a more complete discussion of the subject, see Maria Sylvia de Carvalho Franco, *Homens Livres na Ordem Escravocrata*, Instituto de Estudos Brasileiros, S. P., 1969.

10. *Agregado* roughly means a man of no property, totally dependent upon a family with property, but still not a slave.

11. On the ideological effects of latifundia, see Chapter III of *Raízes do Brasil*, 'A herança rural'.

12. As Machado de Assis remarks in 1879, 'the external impact determines the direction of our movement; for the time being in our environment, the force necessary for the creation of new doctrines is lacking.' Cf. 'A nova geração', *Obra Completa*, Aguilar, Rio de Janeiro, 1959, Vol. III, pp. 826-7.

13. G. Lukács, 'Marx und das Problem des Ideologischen Verfalls', in *Probleme des*

Realismus; Werke, Vol. 4, Luchterhand, Neuwied.

14. Dealt with in a different manner, the same observation can be found in Sérgio Buarque: 'We may construct excellent works, enrich our humanity with new and unforeseen aspects, bring to perfection the type of civilization we represent: still, what is certain is that the consequences of both our efforts and of our laziness seems to take part in a system proper to another climate and a different landscape' (*op. cit.*, p. 15).

15. See the 'prospecto' in *O Espelho*, a weekly magazine of literature, fashion, crafts and the arts, Typographia de F. de Paula Brito, R. J., 1859, No. 1, p. 1; 'Introdução' in *Revista Fluminense*, a weekly for news, literature, science, pastimes, etc., Year 1, No. 1, November 1868, pp. 1 and 2; *A Marmota na Corte*, Typographia de Paula Brito, No. 1, 7 September, 1840, p. 1; *Revista Ilustrada*, published by Angelo Agostini, Rio de Janeiro, 1 January, 1876, No. 1, 'Apresentação' in *O Bezouro*, a humorous and satiric periodical, Year 1, No. 1, 6 April, 1878: 'Cavaco', in *O Cabrião*, No. 1, Typ. Imperial, São Paulo, 1866, p. 2.

16. Nestor Goulart Reis Filho, *Arquitetura Residencial Brasileira no Século XIX*, manuscript, pp. 14-15.

17. Ibid., p. 8.

18. Viotti da Costa, 'Introduçao'.

19. Jean-Michel Massa, *A juventude de Machado de Assis*, Civilização Brasileira ed., Rio de Janeiro, 1971, pp. 265, 435, 568.

20. S. Romero, *Ensaios de Crítica Parlamentar*, Moreira, Maximino & Cia., Rio de Janeiro, 1883, p. 15.

21. For the reasons for this inertia, see Celso Furtado, *Formação econômica do Brasil*, Companhia Editora Nacional, São Paulo, 1971.

22. For an exacting analysis of our ideological problems, in a manner somewhat different from my own, see Paula Beiguelman, *Teoria e Ação no Pensamento Abolicionista, Vol. 1, in Formação Politica do Brasil*, Livraria Pioneira ed., S. Paulo, 1967. In her book there are several quotations which seem to come from Russian novels. For example, the following from Pereira Barreto: 'On one side are the abolitionists, riding upon a sentimental rhetoric and armed with a revolutionary metaphysics, pursuing abstract types in order to turn them into social formulas; on the other side are the land-owners, silent and humiliated, in the attitude of those who recognize their guilt or meditate an impossible revenge.' P. Barreto was the proponent of a scientific agriculture – in the avant-garde of coffee cultivation – and he believed that abolition should be an automatic consequence of agricultural progress. Besides, he considered negroes to be an inferior race; it was a disgrace to depend upon them, *op. cit.*, p. 159.

23. Antonio Candido offers suggestive ideas on this matter. He tries to identify a tradition rooted in the social type we call 'Malandro' (rogue) in our literature. See his 'Dialética da Malandragem,' in *Revista do Instituto de Estudos Brasileiros*, São Paulo, 1970, No. 8, and the paragraphs on 'anthropophagy,' an ironic theory of the 1920s concerning Brazil's incorporation of foreign cultures, in 'Digressão sentimental sobre Oswald de Antrade', in *Vários Escritos*, Livraria Duas Cidades, São Paulo, 1970, p. 84 et seq.

THREE

Beware of Alien Ideologies

An Interview with *Movimento**

In your opinion, what is the importance of external influence in the direction taken by ideological life in Brazil?

Its importance was and is enormous. But first of all the question must be looked at broad-mindedly. Not everything Brazilian is good, not everything foreign is bad, foreign ideas can help us to understand our own world, and native things can serve as a cover for the worst kind of dependence. Thus, for example, nothing was more open to foreign influences than the Modernism of 1922, which however also transformed the everyday reality of the people into an active element of Brazilian culture. While this was happening, programmatic nationalism was burying itself alive in picturesqueness, quite unintentionally proclaiming as 'authentic' those aspects of our life which were the results of our position as a banana republic.

Having said that, the answer to the question differs according to the sphere of culture it is applied to. Some time ago I had the pleasure of discussing the matter with Maria Sylvia de Carvalho Franco.** In her opinion, the notion of external influence is superficial and idealist, since

---

Movimento was the first weekly of a strongly democratic and oppositional nature to be published (at personal risk, by Fernando Gasparian), after the hardening of the military regime in 1968.

**In an essay entitled 'As idéias estão no lugar' ('Ideas are in place'), published in *Cadernos de Debate*, No. 1, 1976, Maria Sylvia de Carvalho Franco, the author of *Homens livres na ordem escravocrata* (São Paulo: Ática 1976) argued that modern ideas have their origins within the country, and do not come from outside.

ideas do not travel, except in the brain of those who believe in 'diffusionism' (an anthropological theory, which gives a great deal of importance to the process of cultural diffusion). According to Maria Sylvia, ideas *are a social product*. For my part, I'm not going to deny that, but I still think they travel. As far as Brazilian literature in the nineteenth century is concerned, I even think they travelled by ship. They came from Europe every fortnight, by steamship, in the form of books, magazines and newspapers, and everyone went down to the harbour to wait for them. Anyone who deals with literary history – or, to give another example, with the history of technology – cannot escape the notion of external influence, because these are areas in which the history of Brazil always appears as something backward, as a continuous process of keeping up.

It is true that the backwardness and the attempts to keep up have internal causes, but it is also true that forms and techniques – literary and other – that are adopted at times of modernization were created out of social conditions very different from ours, and that their importation produces a maladjustment which is a constant trait of our civilization. From an internal perspective, this maladjustment is the mark of backwardness. In a world perspective, it is the effect of the unequal, cumulative effect of capitalism, of which it reveals essential aspects: from this springs its 'universal' significance. In other words, we didn't invent Romanticism, Naturalism, Modernism, or the car industry, none of which prevented us adopting them. But adopting them did not imply that we reproduced the social system of their countries of origin. So, without losing their original form, literary and scientific schools and Volkswagens expressed local aspirations, whose dynamic, however, was quite different. That is why there is an indirect relationship, the maladjustment referred to above, which is a specific problem for anyone who studies the literature of underdeveloped countries. You have to have an ear, and a sense of reality to see the differences, and above all to interpret them. For example, Araripe Jr observed that our Naturalism was not pessimistic as the European movement was, Antonio Candido notes that the first Brazilian Baudelaireans were healthy young men rebelling against the hypocrisy of sexual mores, and Oswald de Andrade and tropicalists put this same maladjustment at the centre of their artistic technique and their conception of Brazil.* These are problems which should be faced in an unprejudiced way:

---

*Araripe Jr, 'Naturalismo e pessimismo', *Obra critica*, Vol. 1, pp. 469–87; Antonio Candido, 'Os primeiros baudelaireanos' *A educação pela noite e outros ensaios*, Atica, São Paulo 1987, pp. 23–38; for Oswald de Andrade and the Tropicalists see essays 9 and 10.

on one level it is obvious that the maladjustment makes us inferior, and that the relative organicity of European culture is an ideal. But, on the another level, this does not mean that the cultural forms that we appropriate in a more or less imperfect fashion may not also be negative in their place of origin, or that they may be negative there, but positive here, in their maladjusted form. It is something which should be analysed case by case. Thus, there is no doubt that ideologies are produced socially, but this does not prevent them travelling and being taken over in contexts which have very little to do with their original matrix. Coming to our own day, look at structuralism, whose 'internal' philosophical cause was the coup of 1964, which put Marxism out of fashion; Marxism is also an 'exotic' ideology, as right-wing people like to say – they are, of course, quite convinced of the autochthonous origins of Fascism. And who can say that as they were naturalized in Brazil, these ideas did not somewhat change direction also? It's an interesting question, for anyone who likes investigating hornets' nests. When he studied 'The Present Generation' ['A nova geração', 1879], Machado de Assis said that 'it is external influence that determines the direction of movement; so far, there is not sufficient strength in our milieu for the invention of new doctrines'. In other words, this is a young country, and external influences help to civilize it and bring it up to date. Many years before, apropos of the project for a History of Brazil with which the German von Martius* had won the prize from the Institute for Brazilian History and Geography, an anonymous gentleman wrote to the *Ostensor Brasileiro* in 1846: 'Europe, which sends us back our cotton spun and woven ... is even telling us the best way to write the history of Brazil.' (I owe this quotation to Luiz Felipe de Alencastro.) The nexus between economic exploitation (i.e. the export of raw materials and import of manufactures) and ideological subordination was beginning to dawn in our consciousness. In other words, external influence has a political dimension, pointing up unequal relations. From the point of view of our elites, both evaluations are correct, even though they are contradictory. External influence is indispensable to progress, at the same time as it subordinates us and gets in the way of that same progress. These are the contradictions of under-development: the country is capitalist, and is necessarily measured by the yardstick of capitalist progress, but this progress itself is beyond its grasp,

---

*Philip von Martius (1794–1868); a botanist who, in the company of the zoologist J. B. Spix, travelled around Brazil between 1817 and 1820, in the service of the King of Bavaria. Their account of their journey is a vital source of information about Brazil at this period.

for the international division of labour gives it another role, a role which seems unacceptable in the light of this same urge for advancement.

Taking up the thread of our argument again: the basic documentation for Maria Sylvia's research is lawsuits in Guaratinguetá [a small town in the province of São Paulo: Ed. note] in the nineteenth century, material linked to the most static area of Brazilian society (the poor man in the area dominated by the large plantation), in which the ideological influence of contemporary Europe would not be a decisive element. Thus, vast theoretical differences can originate, at least in part, in the quite accidental differences between the subjects that people specialize in. However that may be, it is clear that the problem is posed differently in different domains of social life.

Anyone who uses the words 'external influence' is thinking in terms of Brazilian versus foreign and, in our context, it is probable that they are thinking of the cultural alienation that goes with economic and political subordination. These are undeniable facts. However, if they are translated merely into the language of nationalism, they delude and can bring quite different results from those desired. In the strict sense, it is, of course, true that independence in the economic, political or cultural spheres not only does not exist, but is practically inconceivable. What exist in fact are different forms of interdependence, as Marshal Castello Branco said with other aims in mind* – forms which naturally interest different layers of the population. It is true that nationalism gives rise to a great deal of pugnacious enthusiasm, but it is no less true that it is more discreet when it comes to specifying and analysing social interests. In my opinion, this is the most important failing of our critical writing. The problem therefore is not whether one is for or against external influence, but to consider it (and the national tradition) in a popular perspective.

In any case, external influence takes on a look of caricature, above all when this perspective is lacking.

Has there been a significant change, between the nineteenth century and now, in terms of the way external ideological influences and our capitalist practice adjust to each other?

---

*Soon after the coup, Marshal Castello Branco said that the era of independence was over, and that of interdependence had begun. This expression became a symbol of the military regime's alliance with the United States.

Certainly there has, but I am unable to define it with any brevity. And there are continuities too. It was impossible, in the second half of the nineteenth century, to give a brilliant and enthusiastic defence of slavery, which was, however, an institution fundamental to our economy. There was a skeleton in the cupboards of our intellectuals, whose mental universe, to a greater or lesser extent, was defined by the French Revolution. For similar reasons, any panegyric on the system as it exists now can only be technocratic, cynical or childish.

In the classical era of European capitalism, ideology was termed 'false conscious-ness' and its role was to hide the true mechanism of social life. In these terms, what was the role of ideology in the Brazilian case?

Ideology, in this definition of the word, is a fact of the bourgeois era. It is an apparently true account of the social process as a whole, which, however, puts forward the interests of one class as being everyone's. The most perfect example is the liberal ideology of the nineteenth century, with its formal equalities. Note that ideology in this sense has to be convincing as far as appearances are concerned, to such an extent that even the losers can see their own place within it. In other words, by its very existence ideological life presumes that people are integrated into social life by means of considered convictions, and not by brute force (which makes it a blessing, as well as an illusion). Now, it is clear that slaves were not integrated into social life by means of ideas, and that in this sense, the ideological universalization of the interests of the owners was superfluous. That is the reason for the ornamental aspects of our ideological life, its superfluous role and its relatively restricted sphere. In our own day, the situation is different, but not that much so. Along with the Frankfurt School, I believe that the principal ideology of modern capitalism lies in the mass of available goods, and in the organization of the productive process, while ideas properly so-called have taken a back seat. Well, if it is true that in Brazil the consumerist ideology exists, it is even clearer that it's not this ideology that keeps those who do not consume quiet. In a very disagreeable sense, there is less ideology and more truth.

Does reflection on countries on the periphery have any advantages for the criticism of capitalism in general?

In the first place, it does, in the obvious sense that underdevelopment is a part of the system. Then, because the inorganic and secondary character of modernization on the periphery makes the development of productive forces appear in another light. The social process in which large-scale industry was created is one thing: the more or less deliberate transplanting of its *results* is something else. My impression is that the most interesting novelty of the last few years has been the critical analysis of the modern productive (economic, technical, scientific) system, whose supposed political neutrality is being questioned. These are ideas which have already affected our understanding of the advanced countries, and which owe their world-wide repercussions to an extremely backward country, which is searching for another path to industrialization, different from the one created by classical capitalism. We have got used to thinking of the mass of workers from the point of view of industrialization, something which corresponds to present-day power relations. However, in a case where the size of that mass goes far beyond the possibilities of industry, and above all in the case where its power can be made to be felt effectively, it should be the turn of industrialization to be thought of from the point of view of the mass. This argument opens up a new area of problems and a different analytical perspective: forms designed to dominate nature are not progress pure and simple, they are also forms of social domination. It is interesting to note that this same analysis of the centralizing and authoritarian ideological function of large-scale industry – i.e. the ideology of productivism – had been already carried out (with much less repercussion, of course) by the Frankfurt School, who, as politicized people like to say, have no contact with reality. Naturally, Brazil's course is a different one. Anyone who reads Brazilian newspapers after some time out of the country, is in for a shock: one half is progress, the other half accidents and their victims. There is an immortal classic waiting to be written by some Brazilian so inclined: a courageous and well analysed enquiry into the barbarism of these years of progress.

In the populist period, Brazilian intellectuals were much more concerned with the impasses of capitalism on the periphery than with possible ways of transforming it. In your opinion, does this situation still persist?

It does persist, and it is natural. What is not natural is that when we speak of transformation we should speak only in generalities. We must go into detail, submit theories to the test of reality, to the test of the monstrous and extremely varied inequalities of the country. If there is no solution in sight, that is one more reason to imagine it: and we should do this, basing ourselves not on general arguments, but on the most inimical facts presented to us by reality itself.

Could not a naive reading of your essay 'Misplaced Ideas' lead to the conclusion that any ideology, even a libertarian one, would be out of place in peripheral countries?

That problem does exist. Ideas are in place when they represent abstractions of the process they refer to, and it is a fatal consequence of our cultural dependency that we are always interpreting our reality with conceptual systems created somewhere else, whose basis lies in other social processes. In this sense, libertarian ideologies themselves are often ideas out of place, and they only stop being so when they are reconstructed on the basis of local contradictions. The best-known example is the transposition of the slavery-feudalism-capitalism sequence to Brazil, a country born in the orbit of capital, and yet whose social order is very different from the European. But the problem goes further than that. Even when used with supreme skill, a method does not represent the same thing in two different circumstances. For instance, when in Europe, in the nineteenth century, the critical theory of society was being elaborated, it generalized a class experience which was in movement, criticized a science (Political Economy) that was at the peak of its glory, gave continuity to certain literary and philosophical traditions, etc. In other words, the theory of the union of theory and practice was part of a powerful movement going in this direction. However complicated its most important works may be, they never lose contact with the spontaneous – and with the critical – ideologies of their period, a contact which is after all one of the distinctive criteria of real, concrete analysis. Coming to Brazil, look at the fundamental historical works in our tradition. Even when they are excellent, their contact with the social process is of an entirely different order. The circumstances are different. These are aspects of the matter which should be taken into account, since from the materialist point of view, theory is also part of reality, and its insertion into the real process is a part of what it concretely is.

Might not the use of parody as a privileged mode of expression in our culture risk leading to an excessively contemplative position?

I don't see why it should. Parody is one of the most combative of literary forms, so long as that is its intention. And anyway, a little contemplation never did anyone any harm. Aside from which, in countries where culture is imported, parody is almost a natural form of criticism: it simply makes explicit unintentional parodies which are in any case inevitable (look at the 'Letter to the Icamiabas'). Besides, in our times ideological bankruptcy is extraordinary and more or less generalized, a situation which is also conducive to parody. Proust, Joyce, Kafka, Mann, Brecht were all consummate parodists. In Brazil, Machado, Mário, Oswald, and today Glauber and Caetano."

Is it necessary to be right up to date with what is happening in the hegemonic centres to understand the toings and froings of our socio-cultural life?

Naturally it depends on the object of study. It's that that defines the limits of what has to be known. However, as the importation of forms is a constant part of our cultural process, of course it is not enough to know the Brazilian context. It is also necessary to know the original context, to appreciate the difference, which is an objective presence, even if a somewhat elusive one, in our ideological life. For that reason, our historiography has to be comparative. It would be interesting for example if some public-spirited, well-read person laid out a programme of comparative studies necessary for the proper knowledge of Brazilian literature. This, in the placid realm of university research. On the level of the interpretation of contemporary society, which after all is the most important thing, nowadays it is much easier to be up to date with the international bibliography than with the reality of Brazil. This latter difficulty is not just an academic one. If the historical experience of entire sectors of the country has been shattered and doesn't add up, how can we know what it means? Just to remain with a secondary aspect of the question, it makes us all stupid.

---

*A satirical letter written in flowery and over-correct Portuguese which is one of the chapters of Mário de Andrade's *Macunaíma*.

**Glauber Rocha: the most important Brazilian avant-garde cinema director, whose most famous movies were made in the 1960s: he made *Deus e o diabo na terra do sol* (*Black God, White Devil*, 1963), *Terra em transe* (*Land in Anguish*, 1967), *Antônio das Mortes*, 1969, etc. On Caetano Veloso, see 'Culture and Politics in Brazil, 1964-1969', pp. 140-42.

FOUR

The Importing of the Novel to Brazil and its Contradictions in the Work of Alencar

The novel had existed in Brazil before there were any Brazilian novelists.[1] So when they appeared, it was natural that they should follow the European models, both good and bad, which had already become entrenched in our reading habits. An obvious statement, perhaps, but one which has many implications: our imagination had become focused on an artistic form whose presuppositions, in the main, either did not apply to Brazil at all, or applied in altered circumstances. Which was at fault: the form – the most prestigious of the period – or the country? One example of this ambivalence, which occurs particularly in peripheral nations, was provided at the time by the American Henry James, whose interest in the imaginative possibilities of England's social structure led to his emigration there.[2] Let us look at the matter more closely. To adopt the novel was to accept the way in which it dealt with ideologies. It has already been noted [in 'Misplaced Ideas'] that these became displaced in the context of Brazilian life, although they retained their original names and their standing remained the same. The discrepancy was an involuntary one and can be regarded as the practical result of our social development. To achieve harmony with reality, the writer would have to repeat this dislocation on a formal level if he was to keep up with the objective complexity of his material – no matter how closely he followed the example of the masters. This would be the great achievement of Machado de Assis. In brief, that same global dependency which forces us to think in inappropriate categories, led us to produce a literature in which that misfit between ideology and reality had no means of surfacing. Or, to put it another way, and to anticipate my argument: instead of acting as a constructive principle, the disparity was bound to surface in an involuntary and undesired way, surreptitiously and as a defect. This is a literary instance of the inferior intellectual level referred to in 'Misplaced Ideas'.

Recalling his formative years, Alencar* writes of the literary *soirées* of his childhood, in which he would read aloud to his mother and other female relatives, leaving them all in tears.[3] The books involved were *Amanda and Oscar, Saint-Clair das Ilhas, Celestina* and others.** He also mentions the lending-libraries, the Romantic reading-matter of his fellows in the student 'republics' [fraternities] of São Paulo – Balzac, Dumas, Vigny, Chateaubriand, Hugo, Byron, Lamartine, Sue and, later, Scott and Cooper – besides describing the impression left on him by the success of Macedo's first novel, *A Moreninha.**** Why should he not also attempt to write? 'What regal crown can be compared to that halo of enthusiasm that surrounds the name of a writer?'[4] There was no shortage of great figures to emulate but, more important than this or that individual reputation, was the prestige of the general model, and the patriotic desire to enrich one's country with yet another product of the modern spirit.[5] However, the implantation of the novel, and of its realist strand in particular, would be no easy matter. No one had any difficulty in making a mental visit to the *soirées* and barricades of Paris. But it did not seem quite right to bring the whole cortège of sublime viscountesses, ruthless parvenus, illustrious criminals, witty ministers, idiot princes and visionary scientists to the drawing-rooms and streets of Brazil, even if we limited ourselves to the transportation of their

---

*José de Alencar (1829–77) The most important Brazilian Romantic novelist. He wrote some twenty novels in a relatively short life, as well as being an important politician (Minister of Justice 1868–70). He is perhaps most famous for his Indianist novels, especially *O Guarani* (*The Guarani Indian*) (1857), which made his reputation when he originally published it as a feuilleton, and the shorter, more lyrical, and carefully constructed *Iracema* (1865). Both fictionalize (and sentimentalize) the encounter between the Portuguese colonists and the indigenous peoples of Brazil. His aim was the establishment of a national literature, intended to cover all aspects of the country's history and present society, somewhat on the model of Balzac. *Senhora* (*A Lady*) (1875), the novel with which this essay is primarily concerned, was among the last to be completed, and is one of a group, along with *Diva* (1864), *A pata da gazela* (*The Gazelle's Foot*) (1870) and others, intended to represent urban life. *O tronco do ipê* (1871) (*The Ipê Trunk*) and *Til* (1872) deal with the life of the interior.

**These novels are all mentioned by Alencar in 'Como e porque sou romancista'. They are popular romances by forgotten authors, usually British and female, which were widely read in translation in Brazil between about 1820 and 1860. More information can be found in the excellent article by Marlyse Meyer cited in the author's note 1.

***Published in 1844, this sentimental novel set in Rio was the first popular success of its author, Joaquim Manuel de Macedo (1820–82).

problems and of their general atmosphere. Could the novel, however, exist without them? How would those great energizing themes in which the novel was anchored – social climbing, the corrupting power of money, the clash between the aristocratic and bourgeois ways of life, the antagonism between love and marriages of convenience, between vocation and the need to earn a living – how would these work out in Brazil? They would be modified, of course. But they did exist in our active imaginations, with the real existence that the body of European ideas held for us. However, the means of modifying them were not apparent, still less the effects of any such modification on literary form. These had yet to be elaborated and discovered, just as the above-mentioned themes had not always been present, awaiting the appearance of the European novel to be given concrete form. They emerged, or took on modern form, in the soil of the – continent-wide, age-long – transition from feudal times to the capitalist era. In Europe too, it was necessary to explore, isolate and combine these themes, until a kind of literary repertoire had been formed upon which all writers, good, bad and indifferent, could draw. It was, by the way, this cumulative and collective aspect of literary creativity, even at the level of the individual, which would permit the appearance of the large number of efficient, second-rate novels that were produced by Realism. Riding on the crest of a wave of contemporary ideas and solutions, these books give the impression of being complex, even when they are not particularly profound in their treatment of modern themes, and are thus able to sustain our interest. Just like a good modern film. This was a kind of accumulation that was difficult for Brazilian literature to adopt, since its stimuli came and continue to come from outside the country. A position of disadvantage, perhaps, but one which today has its advantages, since it has quite naturally coincided with the bankruptcy of the Western literary tradition, something which European intellectuals have some difficulty in accepting, and that has led to what may be regarded as one of the most symptomatic features of our times – namely, a cultural discontinuity and arbitrariness that in Brazil has always existed, albeit against our will.

As a reflective and gifted writer, Alencar responded to this situation in various, and often profound, ways. His work is one of the treasure-stores of Brazilian literature, and looks forward in some ways to Modernism, although this is not immediately apparent. Something of *Iracema* came down to *Macunaíma*: the long journeys between adventures, the geographical representation of Brazil, the mythological material, Indian place-names juxtaposed with the history of the white man; something of *Grande*

Sertão was already present in *Til,* in the pace of João Fera's exploits; our imaginative iconography, with its innocent maidens, its Indians and forests owes much of its social definition to his work; and finally, on a more general level, and so as not to lengthen the list, the inventive and peculiarly Brazilian ease of Alencar's prose remains as capable of inspiring us as ever. However, one has to admit that his books are never truly successful, that they display a certain imbalance and even, when it comes down to it, a kind of silliness. Even so, it is interesting to note that these weaknesses become strengths when looked at from another angle. They are not accidental, nor do they result from a lack of talent; on the contrary, they provide us with proof of intelligence and coherence. They reveal to us the points at which the European model, as it combined with local colour (of which Alencar was a fervent supporter), led to incongruity. Such points are critical for Brazilian life and letters since they reveal the objective conflicts – the ideological incongruities – that occurred as a result of the transplantation of the novel and of European culture to our country. In order to identify these conflicts, we shall be studying them as they appear in Alencar's urban novels and then go on to show how they are resolved by Machado de Assis."

Interestingly, Nabuco," the pro-European who clearly observed and detested these same impasses, made a curious comment on them in his famous dispute with Alencar. Contrary to popular belief, the quarrel – referred to by Afrânio Coutinho as a *tête-à-tête* between giants – is short on ideas and lacking in substance; they even squabble about who knows the more French. But it does at least record a particular situation. Nabuco hated Alencar's realism for two reasons: for not keeping up appearances, on the one hand, and on the other for not satirizing those same appearances with

---

'*Grand sertão: veredas* (*The Devil to Pay in the Backlands*) (1956) is the greatest achievement of João Guimarães Rosa (1908-67). In plot it is somewhat like a cowboy story, and is set in the wild Brazilian outback: however, its language and its themes make it one of the great modern experimental novels.

"In the book, *Ao vencedor as batatas* (*The Winner Gets the Potatoes*) of which 'Misplaced Ideas' is the first chapter, and this essay the second, the final chapters deal with Machado de Assis' early novels, written in the 1870s. The full resolution of the contradictions present in Alencar's work would only be resolved, however, in *Memórias póstumas de Brás Cubas* (1880). See especially essays 5 and 6.

'''Joaquim Nabuco (1849-1910) was one of the leading writers and politicians of the late nineteenth century in Brazil, most famous for having been one of the leaders of the movement for the abolition of slavery. In 1873, he engaged in a polemic with Alencar which originated in the failure of the latter's drama *O jesuíta*, but which extended to take in a critique of his novelistic production also.

the knowing and acceptable licence of French novels. He reacts like a man who, having spent some time away, returns to his home town, where he is horrified by the existence of a brothel, and shocked by its lack of chic. In Nabuco's eyes, Alencar's young women, with all their airs and graces, are both improper and idiotic, neither romantic nor naturalist – a perceptive observation, even though he sees only the negative results of the mixture.[6] The same is true of his comments on the topic of slavery and on the Brazilianization of the language. If Alencar were to have accepted such criticisms, he would have written either morally edifying or totally European novels. Nabuco puts his finger on real weaknesses, but only because he wants to conceal them; Alencar, however, stubbornly continued to insist on such weaknesses, guided as he was by his sense of reality, which allowed him to feel at those precise points of weakness new topics and a Brazilian flavour. By defining these areas without resolving them, he established and laid out the elements of the great literature that he failed to produce – providing us with yet another example of how tortuous the process of literary creation can be.

In a study of Macedo, whose novels mark the beginning of the Brazilian tradition, Antonio Candido has observed that his work is a combination of detailed realism, 'sensitive to the social conditions of the period', and the machinery of the Romantic plot. These are two aspects of a single conformity, which ought to be distinguished: one being a pedestrian adherence 'to the humanly and socially limited milieu of the carioca bourgeoisie'; and the other, 'which we could call poetic, and which makes use of typically Romantic ideas and models, as has just been suggested: tears, darkness, betrayal, conflict'. As a result, Macedo's works are lacking in verisimilitude: 'So much so that we wonder how such pedestrian characters could possibly become involved in the agonizing situations to which Macedo submits them'.[7] The same judgement applies, with a slight adjustment, to the analysis of Alencar's urban novels, as we shall see in due course. Let us look first of all, however, at their basic elements. The detailed realist style and the local colour expected of the novels of the period, provided the characters and anecdotes of our everyday Brazilian world with literary respectability and status. The plot, however – the real principle of composition – drew its energy from the ideologies of romantic destiny which came either in the form of the serialized love story (in Macedo and some of Alencar) or in its realist version in Alencar's more powerful urban novels. As is noted in 'Misplaced Ideas', everyday life in Brazil was regulated by the mechanics of favour, which were incompatible – in a sense which will be specified at a later point – with the melodramatic plots of a Realism that had been heavily influenced by Romanticism. By submitting itself to everyday reality and literary convention at the same time, the Brazilian novel set off on two diverging routes, and it was inevitable that it should stumble in its own fashion, in a way that French works did not, since the social history upon which the latter were based could be thoroughly explored in them by means of those very same plots. Looked at from the point of view of *origins*, the disparity between plot and realist observation is evidence of the juxtaposition of a European model and a local setting (the fact that this setting had itself been transformed into literary material under the influence of Romanticism is of little importance in this context). If we then proceed from the question of geographical origin to the ideas that belong to those places of origin, we will have returned, and with a clearer idea of the underlying forces involved, to the real problem of *composition*. In this context, Romantic ideologies which, whether they were liberal or aristocratic in tendency, constantly implied a mercantilization of life – are used as the master-key with which one can gain entry into the universe of favour. By remaining faithful to observable (Brazilian) reality and the accepted (European) model, the writer unwittingly replays a central incongruity in Brazilian intellectual life, leaving it unresolved. It should be added that there is no simple consequence to be drawn from such a dualism; in a culturally dependent country like ours, its presence is inevitable, and its results can be either good or bad. Each case must be judged on an individual basis. Literature is not a matter of rational judgement, but of imaginative form; the movements of a reputable key which actually opens nothing at all may well be of great literary interest. When we come to look at Machado de Assis we shall see how the key is opened by the lock.

Senhora is one of Alencar's most carefully constructed books, and its composition will serve as a useful starting-point. It is a novel whose tone varies considerably. One could say that the periphery of the novel is far more relaxed than its core: Lemos, the unscrupulous and calculating uncle of the heroine, is 'as round as a Chinese vase' and looks like a piece of popcorn; old Camargo is a gruff, bearded landowner, rough-hewn but honest; dona Firmina, the personal maid and errand woman, gives great smacking kisses to her young mistress, and when she sits down accommodates 'her half-century of corpulence'.[8] In other words, what we have here is a simple and familiar milieu, which has the potential for suffering and conflict, without itself being called into question, since it is legitimized by the natural and appealing ability of the characters to get by on the day-to-day level. The businessmen are rascals, little sisters are self-effacing, relatives are on the make; vices, virtues and defects are calmly acknowledged and described in such a way that the prose retains its sense of proportion. It is neither conformist, since it does not set out to justify, nor is it critical as such, since there is no desire to transform. The register changes, however, once we move into the more sophisticated social circle. It is restricted to a group of marriageable young people – a fact that is not without its interest, as we shall see. This domain is ruled by the power of money and appearances, as well as by the course of love. The combination of hypocrisy, complex by definition, of the ethical pretensions that are peculiar to this sphere, and the spontaneity that is typical of Romantic sentiment, result in a language that is saturated with moral implications. The reader is inevitably obliged to reflect on the text in a normative way, at the expense of enjoying the simple pleasures of the evocation of the characters and their milieu. The salons and the prose of Balzac provide a distant source. Finally, at the centre of this centre, the voltage hits the ceiling each time Aurelia, the heroine of the novel, enters the scene. For this beautiful, intelligent and much-courted heiress, money is no more than an accursed intermediary: as far as she is concerned, all men and all things are under suspicion of having their price. Her sense of purity is equally excessive, and is expressed in the most conventionally moral terms. Throwing herself from one extreme to the other – from purity to degradation, one of which may be feigned, the other of which is intolerable – Aurelia gives rise to a dizzying motion which has immense ideological import, in as much as it deals with money, that 'modern god' – but is also somewhat banal, since, at its extremes, it lacks complexity. The problem of wealth is reduced to one of virtue and corruption, and is inflated to the point where it dominates the whole scene. The result is a prose at one and the same time thick with moral disgust and with a profound conformism – righteous indignation, in fact – a combination that is not exclusive to Alencar. It was a mixture that was typical of his century, the hallmark of Romantic melodrama, of the future radio soap-opera, and could even be observed only a short time ago in UDN speeches on the corruption of modern times.*

---

*The UDN (União Democrática Nacional) was the party of liberal constitutionalism (i.e. respectable conservatism) of the period 1945-64, between the end of the rule of Vargas and the Estado Novo, and the military coup.

But let us go back and adjust the distinction made earlier between the contrasting tones of the peripheral and central characters. The question is not one of degree, but of kind. In the case of the former, Alencar makes the most of commonly perceived character traits, which are local in nature and very often burlesque, presenting them exactly as they have been fashioned by the forces of tradition, habit and affection. This world is what it is, and does not point to some other different universe into which it might be transformed or, to put it another way, it is unproblematic: there is no place here for the universalist and normative purpose of the Romantic-liberal prose of Aurelia's level of the novel. The tonality is the same as that of one of the important novels in Brazilian literature, the *Memórias de um sargento de milícias*.* And it should be noted that these features are also grounded in a literary tradition of their own. In the case of the central characters, however, Alencar tries to perceive the present as a problem, as a state of affairs that cannot be tolerated. This accounts for the greater importance or 'seriousness' attached to these passages - although in literary terms it is always a relief when Alencar returns to his other manner of composition, which produces a much greater degree of wit and narrative vigour. However, it is by means of this *second* style, heavy with 'principles', polarized between the sublime and the shameful, that he affiliates himself to the central tradition of the Realism of his time, dedicated precisely to showing the present in all its contradictions; rather than presenting local difficulties, their interest lay in the universal tensions and conflicts of bourgeois civilization. This was the style that would prevail. By way of summary we could say that serious commentary in *Senhora* is limited to the worldly sphere of money and social climbing, which, as a result, takes priority in the narrative. Like the great protagonists of the *Comédie Humaine*, Aurelia lives out her torment and, in trying to express it, transforms it into both an intellectual element of her everyday existence and a formal element - as we shall see when we come to look at the plot - which is responsible for the tight structure of the novel. However, that

---

*The only novel of Manuel Antônio de Almeida (1831–61), it was originally serialized in 1852–3. In tone, plot and setting it is completely different from the other fiction of the time. It concerns the exploits of a rascal, Leonardo, in the lower-class Rio of the early part of the nineteenth century. Its importance as a precursor to much of the less serious, but none the less critical literature of the twentieth century was pointed out by Antonio Candido in his seminal article 'Dialética da malandragem (The Dialectics of Roguery)', *Revista do Instituto de Estudos Brasileiros* (São Paulo) 8 (1970), pp. 67–89.

reflective and questioning tone, though well elaborated in and of itself, is not entirely convincing, and does not live happily with the other. It feels pretentious, somewhat inappropriate, and could do with being analysed in greater detail.

First of all, it ought to be noted that in *Senhora* the formal dominance and the social importance of the characters do not coincide. If it is natural that the 'sophisticated' world should form a contrast with life in the provinces and the world of poverty, it is odd that it should include petty civil servants and the daughters of not so well-off businessmen. And it is even odder that it should exclude adults: the mothers who attend parties in Rio are never anything more than respectable ladies who watch over their daughters and never tire of criticizing Aurelia's daring ways, 'unseemly in a well-bred young woman'.[9] The same is true of the men, who are all caricatures, unless they are young. In other words, the up-to-date tone is reserved for the nubile and respectable young men and women, and is used in an ornamental way, rather than as a means of synthesizing the social experience of a certain class, besides being dubious in itself if taken too far. Its rule does not run among those characters who may be serious in their own right, but are excluded from the literary spotlight and from the movement of ideas that has the task of carrying the novel through to its conclusion. The composition of the book is thus limited by frontiers of frivolity, to the detriment of its ambitious structure. The original literary model did not contain any such discrepancy; one need only recall the importance of adultery, of politics, of the arrogance of power, etc., in Balzac's world to feel the difference. Alencar keeps the same tone and several of the same techniques, all of which, however, are displaced by the local setting demanded by verisimilitude. We will return to this difference at a later point.

For the time being let us consider the different, complex aspects of this cultural borrowing. First of all, we must rid ourselves, though not entirely, of the pejorative connotations of the concept of borrowing itself. Consider what it meant, in terms of its modernity and audacity, for a character, and a female one at that, to grapple freely with the contemporary, or at least recent, issues of European Realism. In one very obvious sense, this was in itself an achievement, whatever its literary results. It could be compared, for the benefit of the present younger generation [i.e. in 1977: *Ed. note*], to the jump made in the sixties from reading the standard philosophy and sociology manuals in Spanish to the works of Foucault, Althusser and Adorno. For the truly cultivated person, the choice between an old and a new form of alienation is not hard to make. Leaving a small-scale and complacent imitation behind, the novelist forced himself to conceptualize his world and impose a contemporary structure on his thought processes. The novel was approaching the seriousness that Romantic poetry had attained some time before.* Finally, the actual process of this imitation ought to be considered, since it is more complex than it appears. In the preface to *Sonhos d'Ouro*, Alencar writes: 'To accuse these books of being of foreign confection is, begging critics' pardon, to reveal a profound ignorance of carioca society, which is right here, showing off its Parisian bows and frills, and speaking the universal tongue, the language of progress, a jargon littered with French, English, Italian and now German terms. How can we hope to photograph this society without copying down its features?'[10] Thus, the first step is taken by society, not literature, which in effect imitates an imitation.[11] But inevitably, progress and Parisian frills took on a different meaning in Brazil; to repeat an expression used in 'Misplaced Ideas', they represent a second-degree ideology.[12] The novelist, himself a part of this fashionable movement of society, arrives on the scene and not only copies these new features, which have already been copied from Europe, but copies them in a European way. Now, this second copy disguises, though not completely, the true nature of the first, which is unfortunate as far as literature is concerned, since it accentuates its tendency towards the ornamental. In adopting the form and tone of the realist novel, Alencar accepts its tacit understanding of the world of ideas. Herein lies the problem: he treats as serious those ideas which take on a different form in Brazil; he deals with second-degree ideas as if they were of first degree. All of which adds up to a style that is bombastic and uncritical – despite its scandalous subject matter – and which lacks the venom without which a modern style of writing cannot deal with Brazilian historical experience. Once again we have come to the knot that Machado de Assis will untie.

In sum, foreign debt is as inevitable in Brazilian letters as it is in any other field, and is not simply an easily dispensable part of the work in which it appears, but a complex feature of it. It makes a significant contribution to our general body of culture, producing varying degrees of benefit, and

---

*Above all, in the works of such writers as Antônio Gonçalves Dias (1823-64), the first Indianist poet of stature, and other Romantics such as Manuel Antônio Alvares de Azevedo (1831-52), sometimes called the Brazilian Byron.

borrowings can quite easily be morally, politically and aesthetically audacious as well as artistically inappropriate. Which of these contexts is most important? Nothing, apart from professional deformation, speaks in favour of a purely aesthetically-based judgement. We are attempting to focus on a given moment of deprovincialization, on the reasoning that lies behind the dominant tone of *Senhora*, without, however, neglecting to point out the novel's negative aspects, or reveal its structural weakness. To go back a step: the tone of the novel, in its aims at least, is bold and aggressive, it would like to be regarded as modern and up-to-date; its position in the whole composition, however, goes against its profound intentions and relegates it to the level of a mere social accomplishment. In the final analysis it is this ornamental aspect which predominates. For some reason or other, which we should by now be beginning to understand, the harsh moral dialectic of money is used to describe the gallantries of frivolous young men and women but does not affect the rich landowner, the businessman, the bourgeois mothers, or the poor governess, whose lives are ordered by the laws of favour, or of brutality pure and simple. However, it is people like this that give the novel its variety. Though they are secondary characters, they make up the social framework within which the central figures circulate, and they determine its importance. In other words, our procedure so far has been as follows: we linked the essential structure of the plot – after characterizing it – to the restricted circle it describes, always using the same terms in which the novel operates. Then we saw how this circle fits into the fictional social sphere, where it is considered in relative terms, in terms of the place given to it in the Brazilian social milieu, itself also fictional. What authority does this discourse have? The deciding factor is the ebb and flow of the second aspect (that of the minor characters), which undermines the fundamental tone of the book and its central purpose. Style and structure run at cross-purposes, which is exactly the opposite of what happens in the original model: Balzac's sensationalist and generalizing style, so tightly and artificially constructed, goes hand in hand with an extraordinary sense of *concentration*, to the point where this style becomes less and less uncomfortable as we begin to convince ourselves of its essential continuity with countless casual and 'peripheral' figures that displace, reflect upon, invert, modify – in other words, play their part in – the central conflict, in which they are all involved, in one way or another.[13] Take, for example, the discourse of any of his great female protagonists, disillusioned in tone and vitally 'central' to the novel: just like that of any character who appears 'casually' on the scene – the criminal, the seamstress, the pederast, the banker, the soldier – we find them all equally by turns rebellious, meddlesome, vulnerable, calculating and intrepid. The furious movement of the plot is far from being natural, and comes close to being ridiculous, but somehow manages to retain its link with reality – on an abstract level – due to the overwhelming weight of *savoir faire* and of experience, which is beyond the scope of the individual, and is not simply a literary phenomenon: it is the sum total of a reflective social process, seen through the eyes of a genius. This is the experienced and sociable fifty year old whom Sartre has identified as the narrator of French Realism.[14] We shall be looking at the historical presuppositions of this form later on. For the present it is sufficient for us simply to understand that this artistic elaboration had its roots in a real process, one which was new, as furious as the prose it produced and not at all 'natural', which was turning the whole of European society inside out, and was doing the same in Brazil, but without actually managing to transform the core of that society: what we are talking about is the diffusion – together with its innumerable effects – of the market as a form, of money as the basic nexus of all social relationships. It is the immense magnitude of this movement, which was both global and localized at the same time, that sustains the variety and the overtly theatrical mobility of Balzac's work, allowing him to move freely through vast and apparently disparate areas of society and experience. When Brazilians came into possession of the novel, then, we inherited more than it alone; we also acquired a posture and a diction that were not in harmony with local circumstances, but rather struck a note of discord. Machado de Assis would take full advantage of this disagreement, naturally in a comic vein. To be plain, the main thrust of our argument is as follows: what is peripheral and localist in Alencar becomes the central subject-matter of Machado's novels; this displacement affects 'European' motifs and the serious grandiloquence that is central to Alencar's work, so that they do not disappear completely but take on a grotesque tone. In Machado, then, the problem is solved.

But let us get back to *Senhora*. Our argument may seem somewhat arbitrary: how can a few secondary characters, who take up a minor portion of the novel, play such a decisive role in its general tone? Indeed, if they were taken away, the dissonance would disappear. But we would be left with a French novel. That is not what the author intended, who on the contrary wanted the novel to become a national genre. However, his small, secondary world, introduced into the novel as local colour rather than as an active, structural element – a decorative edging, but one without which the book would not be set in Brazil – dislocates the intended effect and importance of the action as it develops in the foreground. What matters is this: if the local soil is rich enough for the novel to take root in it, then it ought also to be able to sustain a stable diction. For reasons that we have already considered and for others that we shall go on to look at, the diction of the Brazilian novel did not immediately acquire this stability. In other words, the roots of our artistic problem, one of formal unity, lay in the unusual nature of our ideological grounding and ultimately, at the bottom of this, in our dependent–independent position in the concert of nations – even if these things were not specifically addressed in Alencar's book. It is a literary expression of the difficulties we had in trying to integrate both localist and European tonalities, controlled by the ideologies of favour and of liberalism respectively. Not that the novel could actually eradicate this opposition; but it had to discover some arrangement by which these elements, instead of producing an incongruent form, would become part of a regulated system, with its own logic and its own – our own – problems, dealt with on their own appropriate level.

Rather than explain, what we have done so far is to make certain attributions: one tone is ours, another theirs, the plot is European, the peripheral anecdotes are Brazilian, etc. To escape the accidental element of paternity, however, the contingency of geographical origin needs to be substituted by the sociological presuppositions of the forms, which are essential and irremovable. To be more precise, let us say that, out of the more or less contingent body of conditions in which a form is born, this form retains and reproduces some – it would make no sense if it did not – *which then become its literary effect*, its 'reality effect', the world they represent.[15] The vital point is this: a part of the original historical conditions reappears, as a sociological form, first with its own logic, but this time also on the fictional plane and as a literary structure. In this sense, forms are the abstract of specific social relationships, and that is how, at least in my opinion, the difficult process of transformation of social questions into properly literary or compositional ones – ones that deal with internal logic and not with origins – is realized. We could say, for example, that there are two dictions in *Senhora*, and that one prevails over the other when it ought not to. The sensible reader will probably recognize, because he can notice certain similarities, that one of these dictions comes from European Realism, while the other is closer to a familiar and localist tone. As an explanation, however, this recognition does not really address the problem. Why shouldn't the two styles be compatible, if incompatibility is a question of form and not of geography? And why can't the form adopted by European Realism become Brazilian? This final question turns our perspective on its head: though we have seen that one cannot sustain an argument on the basis of origin, we can also see that in real terms its contribution is decisive. Thus, my main topics for discussion are: some important formal borrowings, with some indication of the presuppositions on which they are based, and which eventually were transformed into their 'effect'; a description of the material to which the form was applied; and finally, the literary results of this displacement.

To begin with, let us look at how the story unfolds. Aurelia, an extremely poor and virtuous young woman, loves Seixas, a modest and rather weak-minded young man. Seixas asks her hand in marriage, but then spurns her for another who is able to offer a dowry. Aurelia suddenly inherits a fortune. She would have forgiven Seixas for his inconstancy, but she cannot forgive his financial motives. Without revealing her identity, she invites her former fiancé to marry her in secret, promising a massive dowry, but requesting a receipt. The young man, who is up to his neck in debt, accepts the offer. It is here that the main plot begins in earnest. In order to humiliate her lover and avenge herself, but also to test his mettle and for sadistic reasons – something of all three – Aurelia begins to treat her recently purchased husband as a piece of property: she reduces the marriage of convenience to its mercantile aspect, and the implications of this will aggressively dominate the plot – to such a degree that the four stages of the story are entitled *The Price, Discharged from Debt, In Possession, Ransomed.* As the rigorous structure imposed on the conflict indicates, the plot and its characters are in the tradition of Balzac. With much self-analysis and suffering they play out one of the great ideological themes of the period to its improbable logical conclusion (though there is a reconciliation at the end, which we shall look at later on). Aurelia is fashioned in the iron-clad, unyielding mould of the avengers, the alchemists, the money-lenders, the artists, the social climbers, etc., of the *Comédie Humaine;* like them she grasps an idea – one of those that had caught the imagination of the century – and from then on, without it, her life has no meaning. As a result, the logic and the historical destiny of an important contemporary issue become determining elements in the organization of the plot, attaining the status of a formal principle – among other things. Not that the characters involved represent some abstract notion, in the way that Harpagon had represented avarice for Molière. Rather we are dealing with an abstraction – one that will be combined with all sorts of particular aspects of biology, psychology and social position – that, once the choice is made, tilts the balance in their personalities in crucial ways: it decides their destiny for them. Like a flash of light in the night sky, these reflective and emphatic characters make their mark on the social scene, and leave behind them, apart from the violence of their whirlwind movements, the implacable outline of the contradictions that arise from the conflict between their ideals and society. If we pick up on this theme, we can observe that we are dealing with a narrative model whose material necessarily includes first-degree ideologies – unquestioned ideals such as equality, the republic, the redeeming power of science and art, romantic love, the acknowledgement of merit and the possibility of social mobility, ideas which, after all, in nineteenth-century Europe, gave meaning to life in a very real way.[16] In this sense, the Realist novel was a great dream-destroying machine. To understand its importance, one needs to look at it as a whole, as an active movement which crossed national boundaries, paying no respect to the existing hierarchy of topics: one by one it set up the most fervently held ideals of the period, attached them to the stronger and more gifted characters, and allowed them to be destroyed – during the course of the plot – by the implacable mechanism of money and of social class. This explains the intellectual importance of the movement, its bold posture as the friend of truth, which is taken up anew by Alencar. Once again we come to the old problem that was mentioned earlier on: Brazil was importing a model, whose involuntary effect was to raise the profile of these ideas and extend their compass – to give them echoes, energy, critical force – in a way which was at variance with Brazilian experience. Or, from a compositional point of view: in a way which did not include the secondary characters, who were responsible for providing local colour, in the general structure of things. What message did Aurelia's universalizing and polemical discourse have for these characters, whose main interest lies in survival? In such circumstances, the very boldness of the realist approach has its meaning transformed, as we shall see.

As another example of the same thing, take Aurelia's 'Machiavellianism', i.e. the ease with which she takes advantage of this society's mode of operation. Having been lucky enough to inherit a small fortune, the young woman is disgusted at first by the venality of her suitors. Then, after giving some thought to the matter, she hatches a plot and ends up buying the husband of her choice. The victim of money learns the lesson of money, and surrenders her happiness to it – and to its hateful mechanisms. She thus takes her place alongside the illustrious group of 'superior' beings who escape the rule of fortune and social mobility in as much as they were able to understand it and manoeuvre it in their own interests. At the right time and in their proper place, such figures, of which realist fiction is full, had the weight of reality. They were ridding themselves of obsolete traditions, they had no illusions about morality, and they paid for their clear vision with the hardening of their hearts. It is one of the basic situations of the nineteenth-century novel: the whims of love and of social position, made possible by the bourgeois revolution, collide violently with inequality, which, though transformed, remains a fact of life; such desires have to be put off to another time, compromises have to be reached, by means of the effective manipulation of one's energies and those of other people ... until finally, after wealth and power have been acquired, it is discovered that the hopeful young man of the earlier chapters no longer exists. With a thousand and one variations, this three-act formula was absolutely fundamental. Placed between the eager hopes of the early chapters and the disillusionment of the ending, there was always the same interlude, in which the principles of modern life were allowed unrestricted play: the machinery of money and of 'rational' self-interest goes about its business, anonymously and effectively, and leaves a contemporary stamp on the odyssey of trials that has been the destiny of heroes since time immemorial. Such are the consequences, from the point of view of bourgeois individualism, of the general victory of exchange-value over use-value – a victory also known as alienation – which becomes the touchstone for the interpretation of the period. The literary effect and the social pre-suppositions of this plot, springing from the moment of greed which is its lever, lie in the autonomy – perceived as a dehumanization of the emotions, a reification – of the economic and political spheres, which appear to function separately from the others, according to an inhuman and mechanical rationale. As far as economic matters are concerned, the reasons for this lie in the automatic nature of the market, where objects and the workforce are regarded as one and the same thing, and which, from the point of view of personal merit, is as arbitrary as a roller-coaster. As for politics, in the historical period that began with the establishment of the modern state, according to the teaching of Machiavelli, its rules of behaviour have nothing to do with moral norms. In both spheres, as in the area of social mobility, which is in some senses an intermediate one, social life is seen as an apparently negative and implacable thing, and the only way to maintain any dignity is to confront it.[17] It is against this background, and no other, that the Romantic conflict, exhilarating at times, sinister at others, between the individual and the social order can be called poetic. Solitary, free and obsessed, the protagonists of the novel draw up their financial, amorous or social plans. Some triumph through their intelligence and toughness, others through marriage or crime, still others fall, and finally there are those symbolic figures who make a pact with the devil. All possess a certain grandeur, which could be termed satanic, but which stems from their radical loneliness and their firm determination to use their brains to achieve happiness. Even Seixas, a distant grandson of Rastignac, makes a calculation of this nature: realizing that he is being treated like a piece of merchandise, he accepts the part, and plays it with such rigour that Aurelia, exasperated and finally defeated by his obedience, ends up begging him to start behaving like a human being again. Stated in the terms of our problem: these are fables which owe their symbolic force to a world which had not existed in Brazil. Its form is the underlying metaphor of the society that has been demythologized (*entzaubert*, to use Max Weber's word) and mystified as a result of bourgeois rationality, that is, by the gradual spread of the concept of mercantile exchange.

Having said all this, the direct confrontation between a literary form and social structure can only occur in theory, since the latter, being both impalpable and real, cannot appear in person between the covers of a book. The truly literary experience is a different matter, and must be addressed by any good theory: theoretical competence in any field can be judged by the measure of agreement or disagreement between the form and the material to which that form is applied. Such material does bear the mark of and is formed by real social forces, and becomes their – more or less awkward – representative within a work of literature. Therefore, it is the form which this material takes on which interests us, so that we can compare it with the material that surrounds it. How, then, can we identify these formal embryos, that guarantee fidelity to the local scene and form a contrast to the certainties upon which the model of the European novel – imitated by Brazilian writers – was based? Some pages back, we talked about 'a more relaxed tone'. Let us return to the problem, this time with reference to the plot.

The initial section of the novel, entitled 'The Price', ends in suspense and climax, on the very night of the wedding: Seixas 'was singing his song of love, that sublime poetry of the heart', when Aurelia interrupts him and declares, receipt in hand, that he is a 'bought man'. Here we have 'the chaste first fruits of sacred conjugal love' and the intolerable 'one hundred *contos*' of the dowry face to face. Within the limits of the vibrant black-and-white oppositions consecrated by Romantic ideology, the antagonism between ideals and money could not be more highly-charged.[18] End of chapter. The second part of the novel opens simply and in an unconstrained manner, in a different register, and benefits greatly from the contrast. The narrator takes us back in time so that he can recount Aurelia's story and that of her family, from their modest origins to the thousand-*conto* inheritance. Leaving behind the elegant sphere of polite society, we enter scenes of poverty, set in the suburbs or the countryside. It will be seen that in this setting the stories – subplots which play no decisive role in determining the form of the book – are of a different kind. Pedro Camargo, for example, is the illegitimate son of a rich landowner, whom he fears more than death itself. He comes to Rio to study medicine. He falls in love with a poor young girl, cannot summon the courage to tell his father, and marries her in secret. In leaving home, she too is escaping the opposition of her family, since the young lad is not officially recognized as the landowner's son and therefore might not inherit. Their marriage produces two children: Aurelia and a 'weak-minded' boy.[19] Still fearing to tell all to his father, the student returns to the plantation, where he eventually dies. He leaves his wife and children in Rio, in the awkward position of being a family with no known father. The mother and daughter sew for a living, the son takes on such jobs as shop assistant, etc. Notice, in this brief summary, how, though they are undoubtedly present, the elements of the Realist novel are dealt with in a completely different way: the grandfather – from whom Aurelia will go on to inherit a fortune – is not presented as a despicable figure for having had illegitimate children, nor is the son condemned in the name of Love for having failed to move mountains, or in the name of Medicine, which he rejected as a vocation, nor is his wife thought any less of for having had scant respect for her family and for tradition, nor can her family, which after all was large and poor, be condemned for not taking in a penniless student. In other words, love, money, family, decency, and profession are not presented as a secular priesthood, in that absolute sense that had been conferred upon them by bourgeois ideology, and whose necessary presence dramatizes and raises the tone of the major portion of the novel. They do not constitute a first degree ideology. The formal consequences of this fact are many. First, the tension is lowered, losing both its normative stridency and its central position as the dividing line between what is acceptable and what is not. Since it is not an obligatory and collective moment of destiny, the ideological conflict does not centralize the economy of the narrative, in which it plays a circumstantial and incidental part. It does not permit the combination of individualism and the Declaration of Human Rights, which the classic plot of the Realist novel depends upon for its vibrancy. The solutions it proposes are not based on principle, but on convenience, and are in accord with their immediate circumstances. Arrangements that in the bourgeois world would have been regarded as degrading, are looked upon in this sphere as facts of life. Note also the episodic nature of the story, the way in which its conflicts are spread out: indeed, these conflicts presuppose the above-mentioned 'relaxed tone', without which the poetry of its erratic movement, so Brazilian in style, would be clouded over with moralism. As far as the prose is concerned, its literary quality does not consist in its critical force and its ability to address a problem, but is admirable in terms of its verbal facility, its quick sketches, its movement, all of which are direct mimetic virtues, and which remain in sympathetic, effortless contact with everyday speech and with trivial ideas. It is a stream of events, described with great artistic skill and capable of being prolonged indefinitely, which in the end turns into something like the repertoire of possible destinies in this world we live in. This brings us close to the oral tradition and, possibly, to the 'yarn', simpler in structure than the novel, but tuned into the dreams – which are also individualistic – of our social universe. It is the literary correlative to the ideological predominance of favour: the lack of normative absolutes reflects, if we can put it this way, the arbitrariness of the will, to which everybody must conform. This explains the modern preference for this narrative style, in which the Absolute values, which still today drain us of our energy and morale, are relativized, because they are linked to the shifting, human – illusory, it is worth repeating – basis of interpersonal relations. To get an idea, then, of the ideological distance travelled in this shift of register, we could say that it cuts across or short circuits the fetishism that belongs to the civilized world of Capital; a fetishism that isolates and makes absolute the so-called 'values' (Art, Morality, Science, Love, Property, etc., and above all economic value), and which, as it separates them from social life as a whole, makes them irrational in substance, at the same time as it makes them, for the individual, the depositaries of all available rationality: a kind of insatiable exchequer, to which we owe and conscientiously pay for our existence.[20]

One novel, but two reality-effects, incompatible and superimposed – that is what we are talking about. Aurelia is out of the ordinary: her trajectory will be the curve of the novel, and her reasons, which in order to be serious presuppose the classic order of the bourgeois world, are transformed into a formal principle. Around her, however, the atmosphere is one of patronage and protection. Old Camargo, Dona Firmina and Sr

Lemos, the decent Abreu and the honest Dr Torquato, Seixas' family, the ease with which Seixas is able to arrange a sinecure for himself – all these are characters, lives, styles which imply an entirely different order of things. Formally, the structure of the plot dominates the novel. Artistically, however, this same domination is not carried through, because Alencar does not complete the formal predominance of bourgeois values with criticism of the rule of favour, of which he is both a friend and an admirer. Thus, not only does the form not reach its full potential, but its force is also restricted: the sign of negation that logically and in more implicit ways it should present to the aspects of the novel opposed to it loses its authority, counterbalanced merely by fine words. *That is, alternation between incompatible ideological presuppositions breaks the fictional spine of the book.* They result in a divided base, which will be accompanied on the literary plane by incoherence, a false tone and, above all, by lack of proportion. If Balzac's middling characters stare, petrified, into the Medusa-like features of his radical characters, who represent a concentrated form of everyone's truth – they are the 'types' of which Lukács speaks – in Alencar, they look in shock at Aurelia, whose vehemence seems extravagant nonsense to some, to others a mere social accomplishment. To both it looks like imported literature. The programmatic nature of her sufferings, which ought to guarantee her a dignity above personal considerations, seems like an isolated caprice, a young girl's whim. When love and money or appearance are not absolute and exclusive, it is entirely reasonable that she should take them (and other things) into account when she gets married; the conflict that makes them absolute seems unnecessary and unnatural. The same goes for the prose, which seems exaggerated. And even from the point of view of linear coherence there are difficulties, because, although she is a good, compassionate and unselfish young woman, Aurelia spits out flames of satanic heat and is rigorous in applying the ethics of her contract. It may be thought that this is dialectical: what we have here is Shylock and Portia in a single character. Not so, since, although there is some movement between the two terms, furious at times, the process does not transform either of them – Alencar holds on to them both, out of a respect for local morality on the one hand, and an attachment to modernity on the other – so that these things leave the book in exactly the same state as they began it. Note also in this context the uncertain weight of Aurelia's disillusioned remarks: if they were justifiable (as they would be if they worked in the formal context of the book), those women who criticize them, on the grounds of impropriety, would be made to look like hypocrites; but they are not, they are well-meaning mothers. The fashionable young men, who find them piquant and are not offended, are accused of moral insensitivity. At the end of the novel, Seixas, who had romantically agreed to humble himself in order to win the esteem of his beloved, includes among the reasons for his obedience ... commercial integrity, and thus returns approval to the commercial nexus upon which the whole critical force of the plot is targeted.[21] One can see how much damage is done to the very fabric of the prose by looking at the opening pages of the novel. Rio's polite society is referred to successively as elegant, backward and wicked, without any attention being drawn to the contradiction. Also, the narrator himself does not remain the same. Sometimes he speaks with the complicity of the social chronicler, on other occasions he speaks like a wise commentator on the nature of the human heart and the laws of social intercourse, at other times he is a strict moralist, or an educated man who is well aware of Brazil's provincial status, or, finally, he is a respecter of local social practices. For the purposes of the novel, where does the truth lie? Add a little humour and self-criticism and these incoherent points of view would be transformed into the vertiginous inconstancy of Machado's narrative stance.

Similar discrepancies arise in a more naive fashion in *A pata da gazela* and in *Diva*. In the latter book, which begins amusingly, the general atmosphere – like that of *Senhora* – is that of the family, of social niceties, parties and little romantic flirtations. Then the plot suddenly takes off: the heroine's prudish and timid inclinations, quite normal and convincing at the beginning, are extended to breaking-point, and expressed in the most inappropriate and exaggerated Romantic rhetoric, which speaks of purity, doubt and total disillusionment, with the whole thing ending in marriage. Between the banality of social life and the movement of the plot, there lies an abyss. They are talking at cross-purposes. Even so, though it never reaches the level that only artistic coherence can provide, the plot does have a certain energy: there is something crude and blunt about its development, despite its conformism, something peculiar to violent, wordy fictions, full of delicious punishments and disgusting triumphs, by means of which the humiliated imagination compensates for its resentment and for the vicissitudes of life.

The lack of proportion that we find in *A pata da gazela* occurs in the reverse fashion: instead of the Romantic intensification of minor conflicts, here we witness the rapid emptying out of the initial Romantic situation, despite the fact that it is the book's main focus of interest. Horacio, a dissolute man-about-town, is placed in stark contrast with Leopoldo, a young man who is modest on the outside, virtuous and idealistic within – so much so that his eyes are phosphorescent. The former says to the latter: 'you love a woman's smile, I love her feet', which can be taken both figuratively and literally.[22] Indeed, materialism and illicit fixations are opposed to the love of moral beauty – all with reference to a foot. If the foot is pretty, Horacio could not care less who it belongs to; for Leopoldo, if the woman concerned spoke directly to his soul, he would marry her even if her foot were a 'deformity', an 'elephant's foot', 'covered in lumps like a tubercle', or a 'joint of meat, a stump!'[23] However, the perverse and cruel components are gradually removed, leaving the arena to the safe contrast between the frivolous young man and the sincere one, with its predictable ending. Imperceptibly – not even that imperceptibly – the question at issue changes. The boldness of the ideological conflict is like a false beam which holds the attention of the reader but, in the final analysis, it fails to support the narrative. Since they are not metaphors for Brazilian society as a whole, perversion, the elegant social whirl, ennui, the fashionable tailors and shoemakers that appear take on the role of ornamentation, superimposed without much skill on the daily routine of our real life, which somehow needed their prestige. Not that it was lacking in depth – as Machado de Assis would prove. But it would be necessary to provide it with a proper structure. Getting back to the point, once again we have returned to the situation we looked at earlier: the up-to-date tone provides the narrative with breadth and an air of modernity, only for that same narrative to render it useless: it is neither necessary nor superfluous. Or rather, it is necessary for narrative literature to be *presentable*, but is out of proportion when it comes to the incorporation of the local element.[24] The same goes for the conflict between moral ideologies, which at one moment is daring and serious, *à la* Balzac, at another complete and utter affectation, deliberately humorous at times, at others unintentionally so. It should be obvious that each of these sudden turns destroys the web of credibility that has been woven by the previous context. The good literary material that remains, of which there is a fair amount, owes its existence, once again, to the author's grasp of mimetic techniques, which survives the incongruities of his composition. Even the question of the foot, made into a legitimate literary topic by Romanticism's satanic side, works within its own unexpected, petty, direct but lively sphere, in a similar manner to that noticed in the development of *Diva*. Not only does it originate an insipid debate between the body and the soul; it also gives rise to more intimate, spontaneous thoughts, expressed, for example, in the names given to the physical defect or the way in which its discovery affects the lover. So amid the generalizing blandness, a certain piquancy filters through, which forms part of a Brazilian literary tradition, the tradition - if it can be put in this way - of crass vulgarity, carefully planned in some cases, spontaneous in others. To document its historical existence one need only recall the incident of the haemorrhoids in Macedo's *A moreninha;** the strange sensation experienced by the hero of *Cinco minutos,* Alencar's first story, when it occurs to him that the veiled and mysterious night traveller, on whose shoulder he had placed 'his ardent lips', at the back of an omnibus, might have been an ugly old woman; the terrible chapters on Eugenia, the lame girl in the *Memórias postumas de Brás Cubas*; the multitude of barbarities produced by the Parnassian-Naturalists, a combination which has its own kind of vulgarity; and in our own day and age the jokiness of Oswald de Andrade, the deliberate rottenness of Nelson Rodrigues, the petty, miserable atmosphere of Dalton Trevisan, as well as a vast, well-established tradition in popular music.*

Alencar's Realist fiction is inconsistent at its core; but its inconsistency merely repeats in a purified and developed form the essential dilemma of our ideological position in Brazil, and is its effect and restatement. It is an inconsistency which is not at all incidental: on the contrary it has great substance. From the point of view of theory, when one repeats an ideology, even when it is done in a concise and lively manner, all that happens is that an ideology has been repeated, and nothing else. But from the point of view of literature, which is imitation - at least at this level of the process - and not a matter of rational judgement, this inconsistency takes us halfway down the road. To get from this stage to the conscious, critical representation of social reality, is only a single step. Though we have concentrated so far on one particular aspect, our analysis reveals that there are two sides to

---

*In *A moreninha*, Ch. 3, the hero, a medical student, in enquiring after the health of a respectable mature woman, and being given various euphemistic descriptions, tells her that she has haemorrhoids.

**Chapters 30–3 of *Memórias póstumas* deal with the hero's passing fancy for a sixteen-year-old illegitimate girl; the Parnassian-Naturalist poets flourished in the latter part of the nineteenth century - Schwarz is probably thinking of such bizarre poets as Augusto dos Anjos (1884–1914); for Oswald de Andrade see essay 8; Nelson Rodrigues (1913–80), Rio dramatist, who focusses on the seamy side of the petty-bourgeois existence in Rio; Dalton Trevisan (b. 1925), in his short stories, deals with rather similar subjects, though in the provincial city of Curitiba.

the coin. Let us move on to its more positive side. It is more than likely that Alencar himself sensed something of what we have been trying to put across here with reference to *Senhora*, and to the figure of Seixas. When the latter was attacked for his lack of moral stature, Alencar replied by explaining that he 'models his characters to accord with the true measure of Rio society', and then boasts 'precisely of ... that national stamp'. 'Your colossal figures', he tells his critic, 'would look like stone guests in our (Brazilian) world.'[25] It all depends on what he means by that reduced scale, 'the measure of Rio', the one that bears the Brazilian trade-mark. Why must a social climber in Rio be smaller than his Parisian equivalent, or risk looking like a mere shadow? If we look into the matter more closely, it becomes evident that the stature of Alencar's major figures does not remain stable. Are they mediocre? Or do they stand out from the mass? First one thing, then another. They oscillate between the titanic and the familiar, according to the dramatic necessities of the European and localist features of the plot respectively. Thus we have Aurelia, who lives in a world of the most severe absolutes – in which she is as sensual as a salamander, belts out arias from *Norma* and tramples on society 'as if it were a poisonous reptile' – asking Dona Firmina whether she is prettier than Amaralzinha, her constant companion at parties and functions; later on, when the author wants to underline her intelligence, she is complimented on her knowledge of arithmetic. Similarly, Seixas is referred to, for Romantic purposes, as a 'predestined' and a 'superior' being, while the rest of the time he is a very ordinary young man.[26] In *Diva*, Medicine is a priestly office, but the doctor spends his time courting a girl who refuses him.[27] Also, it does not take long for the rather heterodox admirer of women's ankle-boots, in *A pata da gazela*, to be revealed as a respectful young man, who feels 'outpourings of contentment' when his beloved's father welcomes him into their home.[28] In reality, then, the 'measure of Rio' is the result of the unresolved alternation of two opposing ideologies. Restated in the terms of our argument, it is a consequence of the fact that in Brazil European ideas are degraded, emptied of their effectiveness one might say, due to their displacement by the mechanics of our social structure.

That's as far as reality is concerned. When we come to the fiction, Alencar's expression must be regarded with some caution, with a careful distinction being made between the constructive plan and its actual artistic effect, i.e. between degrees of intention. We have already seen how these characters – contrary to the author's own statements – are not lacking in extremes, particularly in *Senhora*; their stature is determined, to the detriment of their intended grandeur, by the network of secondary relationships, which weakens, and consequently relativizes, the position and the basis of the central conflict. This explains the sense of disproportion, of formal duality, that we have attempted to point out, which is the aesthetic effect of these books, and which also constitutes their profound harmony with Brazilian experience. Having been excluded from the façade of the composition, which is determined by the uncritical adoption of the European model, our national peculiarities come back in through the backdoor, in the shape of a literary inviability, *which Alencar nevertheless gives value to because of its mimetic accuracy*. Thus the tribute paid for the inescapable lack of authenticity of Brazilian literature is acknowledged, its price fixed, and is then capitalized upon and turned into a positive advantage. It is this transition from an involuntary reflex action to a careful elaboration, from incongruity to artistic truth, that must be studied. Here we have the beginnings of a new and different dynamic for the composition of the Brazilian novel. Notice, however, that the problem is as follows: what we have identified as a *compositional defect* is regarded by Alencar as an *imitative success*. Indeed, the formal flaw that we have been highlighting, and which Alencar, guided by his sense of the 'measure of Rio', continued to reproduce, is of immense mimetic value, and there is nothing more Brazilian than this half-baked literature. In this case, then, the difficulty is only an apparent one: all literary forms have a mimetic aspect, just as an imitation will always contain the germ of a literary form; it is possible for a frustrated construction to be an imitative accomplishment (as we have just observed is the case here) which, though it cannot redeem the work, can give it artistic relevance, either as the basic material for a future form, or as material for further consideration.

Let us see in what sense this is true. Alencar does not stress the contradiction between the European form and the local social scene, but he does insist on juxtaposing them – all this as a member of his class, who could appreciate progress and the cultural novelties of his day, to which he had right of access; but who also appreciated the traditional social relationships, since they justified his privileged position. It was not a case of indecision, but rather of simultaneous adhesion to two entirely heterogeneous terms of reference, incompatible in their principles – but harmonized within the practice of our 'enlightened paternalism'. We are now in the presence of the initial pattern for conservative modernization, whose story has not yet reached its conclusion.[29] We are back to the problem outlined in the previous chapter: wherein lies the logic of this weird, though very real, combination? By repeating the interests of his class, without criticizing them, Alencar thus reveals a crucial fact of Brazilian social life – the reconciliation of clientelism and liberal ideology – while at the same time denying its problematic nature, which explains his failure when it comes to another kind of conformism, that of common sense. His literary incoherence is the symptom of his failure in this regard. In other words, we could say that the European form and the local social scene are taken as raw material, with skill but without being reworked. Placed face to face, in the narrow, logical space of a novel, they contradict each other as a matter of principle, while this same contradiction is not expanded upon because of … a sense of reality. Being neither reconciled, nor in conflict, they do not make the vital reference to each other that would enable them to rid themselves of their conventionality and gain artistic integrity: the former lacks verisimilitude, the latter is made insignificant, and as a result the whole is stunted and unbalanced. It was a whole, however – and this is the most surprising thing – in which there is real imitative achievement, the 'national stamp' which led Alencar to repeat his recipe, and stabilize its form within our national literature. This represents his most profound legacy to the tradition of Brazilian Realism.

Formal breakdown and mimetic force, then, are linked in *Senhora*. The reader will understand that we are re-reading the book through a different prism. Inconsistency is not now being regarded as a weakness in a particular work or of a specific author – that is, as a repetition of ideologies – but as the imitation of an essential aspect of reality. It is not the final effect, but a necessary transition to another, more complete artistic effect. This is a 'second-degree' reading, which recovers the sometimes unintentional truths of the 'measure of Rio' for the purposes of further consideration. One must also note that in this perspective the formal defect is an ingredient, just as are the very ingredients which produced the defect itself. Having constituted itself as form, the inconsistency becomes itself material, something to be turned into form in its turn. So much so that instead of the combination of two elements – the European form and the local material – which turns out to be unstable, we have a three-fold combination: the instability that results from a combination of European form and local material, which turns out to be funny. In the place of Alencar's unintentional effects, which can now be seen merely as a constituent element of something more complex, another very different and more relaxed effect appears, whose humour lies in the awkwardness of the first. Clearly, the intellectual and artistic fruits of this second effect are almost completely absent in Alencar. It would be necessary to wait until the second phase of Machado de Assis' career fully to appreciate its benefits. Nevertheless, this second effect is the very substance — yet to be developed – of the 'measure of Rio'. To give the argument its abstract form: if the contradictory effect is an initial and intentional part of the construction, it ought to determine and qualify the elements that produce it, as well as defining the way they relate to each other. It ought to relativize the emphatic presentation of European themes, remove the marginality and the innocence of the local body of themes, and give the sudden shifts of the narrative tone, which mark the contradictory nature of the postulates contained in the book, a carefully calculated and comic meaning. One can recognize here, I hope, the characteristic tone of Machado de Assis.

My argument becomes even more convincing if we take into account a question of scale: if the imitative power of Alencar's novel is the result of a break within the construction of the work, which is thus weakened by being split, the reading of the work will be tedious and frustrating (as, in fact, is the case) and someone has made a mistake of literary construction. To make the most out of the end result, it needs to be concentrated, so that its presence is felt at all points in the narrative; its large-scale structural effect needs to be transformed into the minute chemistry of composition. And in fact, Machado's prose is dependent upon a kind of miniaturization of qualities that had occurred previously within limited zones of Alencar's novels; it explores this same ideological space in almost every phrase, inconsistencies included. Having been reduced, regulated and stylized into a single rhythmic pattern, the difference in proportion between the grand bourgeois ideas and the fluctuating movements of favour is transformed into a diction, into a music that is both sardonic and surprisingly familiar. From a formal inconsistency to a humorous, deliberate incoherence, the literary effect has become a cause, made of much more complex material, which another form will go on to explore. I am not hereby suggesting that Machado's novels are the simple product of the criticism of Alencar's. Literary tradition does not run on a separate course to life in this way. Clearly, Alencar's problems, with very little adjustment, were the problems of the time in which he lived, as can be easily documented by contemporary parliamentary speeches and in the press, which contain the same contradictions and betray the same lack of proportion. Machado could have been correcting the faults of any of these sources. But it is not really a case of influences, although these did exist and are not difficult to find. What needs to be looked at more closely here is the formation of a literary substratum which is of sufficient historical density to support the creation of a literary masterpiece.

Let us go back a step to the mimetic power of the formal impasse. According to our analysis, the reason for this same impasse lies in the uncritical adoption of an ideological combination, common in Brazil – which is subjected to the need for unity demanded by the Realist novel and by modern literature. Because it repeats ideologies, which are themselves the repetitions of appearances, literary is also an ideology. In the next, second, stage of the process, the impasse is regarded as being characteristic of the Brazilian way of life. Consequently, it becomes a consciously desired effect, which is the same as saying that the combination of ideologies and forms that produces it are relativized, once these begin to lose their intrinsic worth and are appreciated instead for the dubious results of their contact with each other. *The ideological repetition of ideologies is interrupted*, in the cause of mimetic fidelity. This little hiatus can thus be given the title 'measure of Rio'; it may not be a complete rupture but it is sufficient to redistribute certain emphases, reorganize certain perspectives, and make possible the emergence of a whole new literary field which does not simply reconfirm well-established illusions – that is the step Machado would make. As far as he himself was concerned, there may have been many motives for this modification. But from an objective point of view, which is what matters at present, the shift has the virtue of incorporating *as something in its own right*, a specific moment of incongruity in our adoption of European ideology into the context of Brazilian letters.

In other words, the process is a complex variant of the so-called dialectic of form and content: our literary material only achieves sufficient density when it takes in, at the level of content, the unsuitability of the European form, without which we cannot be complete. Obviously, there still remains the problem of finding the right form for this new material, an essential part of which is the uselessness of the forms that we were obliged to adhere to. However, before the form could appear, the raw material itself had to be produced, now enriched through a process of degradation of the European formal universe. With reference to this operation, it ought to be noted that its moving force is entirely one of mimesis. Likeness to reality, then, is not merely a superficial feature. The work of adjusting the imitation, limited, at first sight, by the haphazard nature of appearances, lays down, as it were, the course of a new river. The consequences it holds for composition, determined as they are by the logical – i.e. historical – demands of the material that is being used because of its likeness to reality, infinitely exceed the restricted sphere of mimesis, although it is the latter that brings them to light. In this sense, and for the purposes of any author, 'the measure of Rio' could be a vague nationalistic and imitative principle which needed no further definition; in objective terms, however, it gives rise to what could be called an amplification of the internal space of the literary material, a space which will from now on always have the means of referring to European ideologies, something which will both add piquancy and a vital element of truth. In other words, in order to construct a truthful novel one needs to use real material. That is, with Brazil being a dependent country, there needs to be a synthesis in which the distinguishing features of our inferior position in the emerging Imperialist system appear in a regular fashion. Because of the need to imitate, to remain faithful to 'national characteristics', the ideologies of favour and of liberal thought will always be forced to cohabit. Together they make up a brain-teaser which, once it is supplied with the necessary logical – as opposed to mimetic – force, will give rise to a new, made-to-measure, picture of our (reduced size) local bourgeoisie. It is a process which, even today, is of great interest to the critic, since it has not yet reached its completion.

All that remains now is for us to look at the most obvious defect in *Senhora*, namely its sugary ending. If the novel had ended in some other fashion, unspoilt by 'the mysterious hymn of sacred conjugal love', it would have had one less defect, but it would not have been better. None of the problems that we have been considering would have been resolved. The rose-tinted, or, at least, morally edifying ending is not specifically linked to Brazilian literature, but rather to the novel of social reconciliation, to Feuillet and Dumas Fils, for example, who were direct influences. They were writers whose work *was* well and truly wrecked by their calculated conformism. If one were to take Feuillet's *Roman d'un jeune homme pauvre*, and sharpen the contradictions that he tries to attenuate, we would be left with a good Realist novel.[30] Like Alencar, Feuillet had inherited a formal tradition which contained the critical presuppositions of the bourgeois revolution. Both *Senhora* and *Roman d'un jeune homme pauvre* encompass the modest garret and the mansion, the city and the provinces, the business-man's office and the lover's garden, the sentiments of the aristocrat and those of the bourgeoisie, etc. In Feuillet's novel, the antagonisms implied in this juxtaposition of narrative areas and themes are mere shadows of doubt and subversion, diluted by the virtue of his positive characters. The victory always belongs to an exemplary league of egalitarian aristocrats and selfless members of the bourgeoisie. However, the problems of the bourgeois revolution were not only being formalized in the workings of the Realist novel, of which Feuillet is a practitioner. More importantly, he was working with reality itself, with the living society of Europe which was the source of material for this literature. In Feuillet's case, then, to speak of disguising social contradictions and of destroying their literary significance is to say one and the same thing. With Alencar, it is quite a different matter, since he only reconciles the situation at the end of the narrative and is non-conformist during its development, where he is bold and positively enjoys contradictions.[31] What can be done about this form, if its opposing principles do not shape the material that they ought to organize? If old Camargo's plantation is not the seat of provincial and aristocratic virtues, but rather of Capital and the immoral habits of the slave population, how does it shape up in the contrast with the greed and frivolity of Rio? Regardless of how this question is answered, it does not fit in with the central plot, and does not even chime in with it. Similarly, when he moves from his modest lodgings to his wife's mansion, Seixas does not strictly speaking move from one social class and, more importantly, from one ideology to another – as the difference would appear to suggest; all he changes is his standard of living, as we would put it these days, which removes the poetic force of the two settings. And so on, and so forth. If the oppositions that define the form being used do not also govern the social environment to which that form is applied, formal rigour will be accompanied by a lack of artistic balance, and the very frankness with which these – supposedly monstrous, but in fact highly respectable – contradictions are related will itself be conformist. All of which explains the strange effect of these novels on the modern reader: though they are set in a contemporary historical context, they leave no impression of any historical rhythm whatsoever. This is because any poetry the latter might convey is dependent upon a genuine periodization, i.e. on the correspondence between conflicts exactly situated in time and the historical contradictions that organize the movement of the work as a whole.

Having demonstrated, then, that Alencar's most useful contribution to the development of the Brazilian novel lies in the weak points of his writing, let us also look at how his weaknesses contain features that can be regarded as real strong-points, features which, when taken in isolation, reveal his true merit as an author. With reference to *Senhora*, Antonio Candido has observed that its main theme – the purchase of a husband – not only gives form to the plot, but also has repercussions on the book's metaphorical system. What we have here is a case of formal consistency, whose effect ought to be looked at.

> The heroine, hardened by her desire to avenge herself, and given the opportunity to do so by her inheritance, rigidifies her soul as if she were the agent of an operation designed to crush another by means of capital, whereby he is reduced to a mere possession. And the images which Alencar uses themselves emphasize the mineralization of her personality, affected as it is by the dehumanization of the capitalist system, until the Romantic dialectic of love recovers its conventional position. So, both in the work as a whole and in specific details of each section, the same structural principles are active in shaping the material.[32]

Indeed, its dramatic movement transforms the rich young woman, surrounded by the 'mob of suitors',[33] into an angry, vehement woman. When she takes the initiative, Aurelia looks at the world through the eyes of money, and intends to repay with interest all the humiliation she has had to endure. The other side of the coin, however, is that when she feels that she herself is being seen with the same eyes, we see her pale, 'marble-like' complexion, her 'icy' lips, her 'jasper-coloured' cheeks, her nervous contractions, her harsh, metallic voice, etc., take over.[34] To this extent we are shown the moral dialectic of money and the harm it can do to people. However, as the mention of marble and jasper suggests, there is a more complex movement at work. The mineralization to which Antonio Candido refers is situated at the meeting points of many levels of the narrative: it is the hardness necessary to manipulate others, the categorical refusal to become a tool of someone else's schemes, it is the idol worship of unconscious material and of the statuesque, it is the rejection of the body, it is the prestige of expensive substances, etc. In other words, the object of the novel's *economic* criticisms has a *sexual* attraction. 'And such is the way of the world, that the satanic glow of this woman's beauty was her main attraction. The depths of her passion could be divined in the bitter vehemence of her rebellious soul; and one could catch a glimpse of the raging sensuality that the love of this Bacchic virgin contained within itself.'[35] The explicit message, then, is that money puts restraints on one's natural emotions; the underlying message, however, is that money, contempt and denial form an eroticized whole, which opens our eyes to horizons which are more exciting than the conventions of everyday life. In other words, money is pernicious because it creates a division between sensuality and the existing domestic framework, but it is also interesting for that very same reason. This gives rise to the convergence, in Alencar's work, of wealth, female independence, sensual intensity and images taken from the world of prostitution. As we have seen, this is developed with considerable boldness and complexity, though it is true that it is heavily influenced by *La Dame aux Camélias*. Thus, the formal logic with which Alencar develops his theme reinforces – rather than eliminates – the formal duality that we have been studying: it places the bourgeois reification of social relationships at the centre of the novel. Where Antonio Candido recognizes a particular virtue in Alencar's work, there is also a defect. The total manipulation of one person by another, and thus the absolute conflict between them, becomes the model for individual relationships in the novel. This is one of the essential consequences of liberal capitalism, and it is one of the merits of the Realist novel to have revealed it in its own structure. However, it was not the formal principle that Brazil was looking for, despite the fact that – as a theme – it was indispensable to us.

Notes

1. See Marlyse Meyer's stimulating study, 'O que é, ou quem foi Sinclair das Ilhas?', in *Revista do Instituto de Estudos Brasileiros*, No. 14, São Paulo 1973.

2. Theobald, an assertive American in 'The Madonna of the Future', 1873, cries: 'We are the disinherited of Art! We are condemned to be superficial! We are excluded from the magic circle. The soil of American perception is a poor little barren, artificial deposit. Yes! we are wedded to imperfection. An American, to excel, has just ten times as much to learn as a European. We lack the deeper sense. We have neither taste, nor tact, nor force, how should we have them? Our crude and garish climate, our silent past, our deafening present, the constant pressure about us of unlovely circumstance, are as void of all that nourishes and prompts and inspires the artist, as my sad heart is void of bitterness in saying so! We poor aspirants must live in perpetual exile.' *The Complete Tales of Henry James*, Rupert Hart-Davis, London 1962, vol. 3, pp. 14-15. Back in America, on a visit to Boston, James writes: 'I am 37 years old, I have made my choice, and God knows that I have now no time to waste. My choice is the old world – my choice, my need, my life.... My work lies there – and with this vast new world, *je n'ai que faire*. One can't do both – one must choose.... The burden is necessarily greater for an American – for he *must* deal, more or less, even if only by implication, with Europe; whereas no European is obliged to deal in the least with America. No one dreams of calling him less complete for doing so. (I speak of course of people who do the sort of work that I do; not of economists, of social science people.) The painter of manners who neglects America is not thereby incomplete as yet; but a hundred years hence – fifty years hence perhaps, he will doubtless be accounted so.' (*The Notebooks of Henry James*, ed. F. O. Mattiessen and K. B. Murdock, Galaxy Books, New York 1961, dated September 1881, pp. 23-4.)

3. José de Alencar, 'Como e porque sou romancista', [How and Why I became a Novelist], *Obra Completa*, ed. José Aguilar, Rio de Janeiro 1959, vol. I, p. 107.

4. *Ibid.*, p. 109.

5. Antonio Candido, 'Aparecimento da Ficção', *Formação da Literatura Brasileira*, Martins, São Paulo 1969, vol. II, ch. 3.

6. Cf. *A Polêmica Alencar-Nabuco*, Tempo Brasileiro, Rio de Janeiro 1978, and especially Nabuco's objections to *Diva*, pp. 153-63.

7. See the chapters in the above-mentioned *Formação da Literatura Brasileira* that deal with the novel. Put together, these sections make up a theory of its development in Brazil, and can be read as an introduction to the work of Machado de Assis. Though he does not form part of the 'formative' phase dealt with in this book, and is only rarely mentioned, Machado is one of its central characters, its main point of disappearance: the tradition of the novel in Brazil is discussed, at least in part, with Machado's future contribution in mind. See pp. 140, 141 and 142 for quotes referred to.

8. José de Alencar, *Senhora, Obra Completa*, vol. I, pp. 958, 966, 979, 1065 and 1066.

9. *Senhora*, p. 952.

10. *Obra Completa*, vol. I, p. 699.

11. The situation can be compared to that of Caetano Veloso singing in English. When attacked by the 'nationalists', he replied that it was not he who had brought the Americans into Brazil. He had always wanted to sing in the language that he had heard on the radio from an early age. Furthermore, the fact that he sings in English with a northern Brazilian accent clearly marks a significant moment in our historical and imaginative development.

12. In his comments on consumer habits in Brazil at the turn of the century, Warren Dean observes that certain goods, which were commonplace in Europe and the United States, were transformed into luxury items by the import trade. Cf. *The Industrialization of São Paulo: 1880-1945*, The University of Texas Press, 1969.

13. 'Balzac's many-sided, many-tiered world approaches reality much more closely than any other method of presentation. But the more closely the Balzacian method approaches objective reality, the more it diverges from the accustomed, the average, the direct, the immediate manner of reflecting this objective reality. Balzac's method transcends the narrow, habitual, accepted limits of this immediacy and because it thus runs counter to the comfortable, familiar, usual way of looking at things, it is regarded by many as 'exaggerated' and 'cumbersome'.... But his wit is not confined to brilliant and striking formulations; it consists rather in his ability strikingly to present some essential point at the maximum tension of its inner contradictions.' (G. Lukács, 'Balzac: *Lost Illusions', Studies in European Realism*, London, Hillway Publishing 1950, pp. 58-9.)

14. J.-P. Sartre, 'Qu'est-ce que la littérature?', *Situations II*, Paris, Gallimard 1948, pp. 176ff. For a comic condensation of Balzac's writing habits, see the incomparable parody of him done by Proust, in *Pastiches et mélanges*. The enjoyable, comforting side of Balzac's generalizations is mentioned by Walter Benjamin, in his study of the figure of the *flâneur*, in *Charles Baudelaire: A Lyric Poet in the Era of High Capitalism*, London, Verso 1973, p. 39.

15. Althusser's expression, though in another philosophical context.

16. See, for example, Lukács' writings on the role of Romanticism in the Realist novel. Since it was an ideology which sprang spontaneously from the non-conformist and anti-capitalist thinking of the nineteenth century, the Romantic dream became, as it were, an indispensable feature of the novel: it was an ideology which bred a certain character type and literary climate, only to undermine them on the level of plot. 'Balzac and Stendhal', op. cit.

17. 'Only by the eighteenth century, in "civil society", do the various forms of social connectedness confront the individual as a mere means towards his private purposes, as external necessity.' Karl Marx, 'Introduction', *Grundrisse (Foundations of the Critique of Political Economy)*, Penguin, Harmondsworth 1973, p. 84. Cf. also Georg Lukács, *The Theory of the Novel*, Merlin, London 1971, pp. 83-222; and Lucien Goldmann, *Pour une Sociologie du Roman*, Gallimard, Paris 1964.

18. *Senhora*, p. 1028, 1029, 1026, 1029.

19. *Ibid.*, p. 1038.

20. For a way of conceptualizing the contrast between pre-capitalist narrative and the novel – though the basis of the argument lies in the transition from craft production to industry, something which does not fit the Brazilian case – see Walter Benjamin's splendid essay on 'The Storyteller' in *Illuminations* (Schocken, New York 1969), pp. 83–110. In an ideal sense, and exaggerating somewhat, we can say that the 'story' in this sense presents its hearers, their experience, and the traditions to which they are connected, with the simplicity of an anecdote. Experience and traditions are in their turn composed of anecdotes, to which this latest one is added no sooner than it has been uttered. The strength of this genre, then, lies in the poetry of a story which stands out against the background of a varied repertoire of everyday wisdom. It is a genre which has no place for conceptual knowledge, any knowledge, that is, which does not have the guarantee of lived experience, or cannot be translated into another anecdote. This is precisely the opposite of what occurs in the novel, whose adventures are imbued with and explained by the commonplace but counter-intuitive mechanisms of bourgeois society. The poetry of the novel lies in the 'modern' and artistically difficult combination of lived experience, naturally expressed by mimetic means, and of abstract and critical awareness, in particular the social dominance of exchange-value, and the thousand-and-one variations on the contradiction between formal equality and real inequality. In the case of the novel, a certain severity and logical consequence are regarded as a sign of quality. We can say, then, that in the novel, incidents are imbued with generalisation, but that the element of generality refers to a particular type of society, or, better, to a historical stage in the development of that same society, encoded in the central conflict. In the 'story', however, incidents are free of explanation, though, however, they will be added to the ahistorical and generic stock of the motivations and destinies of our species, this latter viewed from the perspective of the diversity of human beings and of peoples, as opposed to that of changing social orders and regimes. The story contributes to the 'casuistics' of human situations and of regional traditions: it introduces you to the adult world, and amuses you, if you have ears to hear. The novel, however, which can only disillusion the reader, is committed to telling the truth about life in a specific social context, and is critical in nature even when unintentionally so. The novel is the most historical artistic form of all, into which so-called scientific knowledge – especially history, psychology and economics, accompanied by the aims of portraying an epoch and denouncing its evils – is incorporated, yet it has been instrumental, in Brazil, in stifling the literary conceptualisation of the country. Here lies the paradox. While the story, incomparably less discriminate and bathed in the almost eternal and unspecific wealth of oral narrative, manages to combine an ahistorical basis – the confusions of life – and an uninhibited delight in reproducing events, which allows it to attain a kind of realism, the Realist tradition not only failed to achieve this result in Brazil, but actually hampered it.

However, it is obvious that Alencar is not a true storyteller in this sense, if for no other reason because he is writing. Thanks to one of those happy paradoxes of Romanticism, he combines an authentically popular vein with the modern, nostalgic Romanticism of evocation of the past, whose broad and sustained tempo forms a symbiosis between reflection and spontaneity – the profound and natural connection with nature and the community, counterfeited in the 'visionary' posture of the Romantics – which is the poetic inspiration of the school and the feeling for existence that it counterposes to bourgeois society. In its purest state, this second movement of the imagination can be found in *Iracema*, where the world evoked is never allowed to remain on the distant horizon of objectivity. In this novel, in every sentence, or at intervals which are not much greater, the images are always passing by, getting closer, disappearing into the distance, making up for another one in space, in time, in the imagination – an 'inspired' changeableness which loosens the rigidity of pure objectivity and brings back the element of vital interest and excitement in memory and perception. The same thing can be seen in *O guarani* [*The Guarani Indian*], and the beautiful introductory description of *O tronco do ipê* [*The Trunk of the Ipe*, a native Brazilian flowering tree] *Mutatis mutandis*, this is the rhythm of the great Romantic meditation in which, by an effort of silence and mental intensity, the complexity of the world is grasped and retained, to be recomposed – in moments of exaltation, plenitude and clarity – in the continuous, unbroken flow of the imagination. Note, however, that however affirmative these visions may be, in Hölderlin or the English poets for example, the world they construct is always unreal – the unstable, tremulous world of a visualization governed by the mind – whose plenitude 'returns' to men the feeling of nature and of life which modern society seems to have taken away from them. That is an important difference: Alencar's nature has a great deal of this in it: it too is saturated with nostalgia, but there are moments when it is just the Brazilian landscape, and nothing more. Where the Romantics, polemically attacking their own time, restored perception and nature back to an imaginarily pristine state, what Alencar is doing is contributing to the glory of his country, singing the beauties of its landscape and teaching his fellow-countrymen to see it. The Romantic spell allows him, thus, to give value to his homeland, instead of rediscovering it, like his European models, in opposition to his less sensitive contemporaries. In this way, the Romantic exaltation of nature lost its negative pull in the Brazilian context, and ended setting up the patriotic model as far as landscape description goes. The prestige of a modern literary movement gave prestige to the country, which others thought uncouth, while the discovery of our country by this same literary movement backed up its claim to truth (see Antonio Candido, *Formação da literatura brasileira*, Vol. 2, p. 9). Very pleased with themselves, and proud of being in tune with progress, our elites got themselves up to date with feelings which told them to despair of civilization. That's what you call being a young country. That's the reason for the very peculiar juxtaposition in *Iracema* of a poetry of distance, which gilds the Indian names and features of the landscape with a Romantic glow, to a purely informative, or propagandistic intention. It's a juxtaposition which opens up a space for indifference, between true literature and mere jingoism, or real nostalgia and postcard conventionalism, a combination picked up later, in a comic – and so, this time, genuine – vein, in the early poetry of the Modernists. In a degraded version, completely deprived of naiveté, the confusion between Brazil, the empirical country, and paradise – the 'genteel fib' that Mário de Andrade spoke of – is today the daily bread of official propaganda.

However that may be, the breeze of Romantic meditation also got as far as the Realist novel, however much it may have been diluted by the prose medium, and hindered by such worldly subject-matter. Instead of being set in untamed nature or in an isolated village, now we have the developed totality of the social world: to give his readers the equivalent of the contemplative plenitude of the poet, the novelist forces himself to blend into his prose the necessary mass of factual knowledge, their analytic and critical amplification, and finally the unimpeded flow of reflection – a synthesis which goes entirely against the tendency of the times, in which these three requisites clashed with one another, as indeed they still clash. Again, Balzac will be the model. His visionary posture, which is rehearsed and not always convincing, pretends to be the 'genius's' capacity to take in the France of the era of capital in a single mental glance; to divine its complex movement from any given suggestive detail; freely to fantasize about it, without this stopping him uttering all kinds of witty, original, extraordinary (etc.) truths. The nature of the subject-matter, however, gets in the way: this reflective tone, in such close intimacy with the bourgeois world, can only be kept up with a struggle – transactions are not landscapes or destinies – which is why we occasionally get the impression that Balzac's visionary power is also an immense urge to gossip. Alencar, who is trying to get the same atmosphere, achieves good results when he is being *retrospective*: leaving the main conflict (where he is less successful), he goes back, to set out, from the beginning, the story of one of its elements, which he does with a sure, interesting, economical - and poetic - skill. Apart from the earlier history of Aurelia, that of Seixas, and Chapter 10, Part I of *O tronco do ipê* are good examples. Brief and informative by definition, such retrospective stories limit any ideological reflections on the part of the narrator or the character (reflections which spoil Alencar's urban, critical novels), and the crazy, complicated plots (which spoil the novels of adventure). It is realist by definition: its method is the clear, suggestive concatenation of the actions, with the aim fixed on the situation which originated the flash-back in the first place. The result is a less tense shaping of the actions, which is interested above all in the description, and not the criticism, of the most important forces affecting the story. It is a narrative style in which mimetic talent, local, Brazilian culture, and Alencar's wider vision of it stand out, while at the same time the clashing effects produced by our ideological life are minimized. Alencar only has occasional recourse to this style in *Senhora*, but it is central in *Til* and *O tronco do ipê*, the novels he sets on plantations. These are books with an abstruse plot, linked to a subliterary conception of destiny and the expiation of guilt - but this very conception lightens their prose, in the way we have seen in the case of the flash-back. Instead of the analytical complexity of the problems dealt with, we have the force of destiny. In either case, we are dealing with rich plantation-owners, who have to pay, comprehensively, for the forgotten ill-deeds of their youth, However, when destiny comes onto the scene and falls on the unfortunate mortals, the weight of their guilt coincides in large measure - to the advantage of the story - with the weight of the past, with the concatenation and the purgation of the objective conflicts of the world of real plantations: illegitimate children, slaves gone mad with fear, embezzled property, hired toughs, murders, arson, superstition, revolts in the slave-quarters, etc. The chapters surrounding the fire in *Til* (Chapters 1-9, Part 4) can be read to get an idea of the strength and the extent of this kind of action. And in fact, it is in the unity and strength of the construction of long, varied sequences like this one, that the romantic, 'subjective' power of the narrator shows itself. It is also there, in the spontaneous manner with which images and words come to him (it is so spontaneous that at times it verges on the nonsensical) that Alencar's diction comes close to that of common, pre-literary speech. The narrative movement, in its turn, fragments into short episodes, compatible with the narrative of popular tradition. For me, considering what might have been, these are his two best books.

21. *Senhora*, p. 1203.

22. *Obra Completa*, Vol. I, p. 650.

23. *Ibid.*, pp. 608, 652.

24. The expression and the problems were suggested to me by Alexandre Eulálio, who sees Alencar's diction as a readjustment of the juridico-political prose of the student coteries of São Paulo [the Law Faculty which Alencar attended, *Ed. note*], which would always mark his fictional prose style.

25. In a note appended to *Senhora*, p. 1213.

26. *Senhora*, pp. 955, 959, 968, 1054.

27. *Diva*, p. 527.

28. *A pata da gazela*, p. 609.

29. Gilberto Freyre takes note of the problem, perceptively as far as its lasting presence in Brazilian life, but blinkered by class as far as its difficulties are concerned - above all, without the least aloofness from it, in spite of the almost hundred years that have passed: 'So we should be aware of this contradiction in Alencar: his antipatriarchal modernity in some respects - he is even in favour of 'a certain emancipation of women' - and his traditionalism in other respects: including his delight in the authentically Brazilian figure of the virginal young

girl of the patriarchal plantation.' 'It is as if Alencar, through this Alice, at the same time so traditional and so modern, had anticipated the attempt at the renewal of Brazilian culture on a modernist and traditionalist base which the Regionalist Movement of Recife [founded by Freyre in 1926: *Ed. note*] represented, alongside the grander Modernism of São Paulo, one wing of which also tried to combine these same conflicting tendencies'. Gilberto Freyre, *José de Alencar*, Cadernos de Cultura, pp. 15, 27-8.

30. With the opposite intention, Paul Bourget makes the same observation: 'Reading his books, one feels a singular respect for this noble spirit who, although given to daring analysis and to dangerous forms of curiosity, managed to keep the cult for everything gentlemanly, for women and for love.' *Pages de Critique et de Doctrine* (Plon, Paris 1912) p. 113. Perhaps affected by the Paris Commune, Dumas fils is more direct: 'The time has passed when one could be witty, charming, libertine, sarcastic, sceptical and fanciful; these are not the times for that. God, nature, work, marriage, love, children are serious matters'. (Preface to *La Femme Claude*, quoted in *Anthologie des Préfaces de Romans Français du XIXe Siècle*, ed. H.S. Gershman and K.B. Whitworth (Julliard, Paris 1964), p. 325.

31. The distinction between conformism and conciliation in Alencar was pointed out to me by Clara Alvim.

32. Antonio Candido, 'Critica e sociologia', in *Literatura e Sociedade*, Ca. Editora Nacional, São Paulo 1965, pp. 6-7.

33. *Senhora*, p. 954.

34. *Ibid.*, pp. 1044, 1028.

35. *Ibid.*, p. 955.

FIVE

Machado de Assis:

A Biographical Sketch

Machado de Assis was born in 1839, in Rio de Janeiro, just before the beginning of the long reign of the Emperor Dom Pedro II (1840–89), which he would later chronicle. These are decades in which the post-colonial character of the country and its capital take on a more definite shape (political independence came in 1822). Since Machado is a writer who was very alert to the contemporary scene, it is as well to remember too that liberal capitalism was reaching its apogee in Europe at this time, and entering into decline.

Little is known of Machado's childhood, apart from the fact that his family were poor. At fifteen, when he published his first poems, he was an apprentice typesetter. Later, he earned his living as a journalist, an occupation in which he made lasting friendships with eminent literary and political figures. However, this career seemed too unsettled and unstable to him, and at the age of twenty-seven he left it for another: he became a government employee, the job he was to hold until his death. At twenty-nine, he completed his establishment as a member of the bourgeoisie, marrying the sister of a Portuguese poet and friend of his. The authorized version transmitted to posterity tells us of unblemished married bliss (even though in his mature novels, excepting the last, the view of marriage is always a tormented and disillusioned one). With time he received considerable promotion, becoming a senior civil servant. He was also the founder and president of the Brazilian Academy of Letters – modelled on the Académie Française. He is possibly the greatest Brazilian writer to have lived, and certainly the one most honoured and celebrated during his own lifetime. He died in Rio de Janeiro in 1908, laden with honours and praised in speech after speech. He left to posterity, as well as his extraordinary literary *oeuvre*, his armchair, his desk and his pince-nez, which, at his wish, the Academy preserves. The *belle époque* came to an end soon afterwards.

Critics usually emphasize the difficulties of this brilliant career: Machado was dark-skinned and was a worker's son – moreover he had a slight stammer, and he was epileptic. More recently, however, the tendency has been to go in the opposite direction. We are reminded that 'some of the most representative figures of our liberal Empire were men of humble origin and mixed blood', and that, in the final analysis, Machado's career was tranquil rather than tempestuous.[1]

This disagreement exemplifies a constant difficulty in the understanding of the Brazilian nineteenth century, and perhaps of the same period in Latin America. For, if we take poverty, the status of the worker and the position of the mulatto in the connotations they now have in modern class society, Machado will seem to us to be a notable example of the self-made man, held back by none of the obstacles in his way. However, in their real contexts, these notions had a very different meaning.

Thus, Machado de Assis's father was a house-painter, but it would be a mistake to equate this situation with that of the European proletarian. His social position was somewhat defined by the labour market, and a great deal more by his links to a family of landowners, on whom he was dependent. Men in this position were numerous, and they were called *agregados* (retainers). The grandson of slaves from a house on the Morro do Livramento,* and the son of freed blacks who lived and served on the same property, Machado de Assis's father had an intermediate position. He tried to live in the city, independently, but he came back to the Morro do Livramento, where he married a white girl, from the Azores, who was also an *agregada*.

In other words, Machado was the son of a worker, but a worker was not what we imagine today. To illustrate the difference, we might consider the fact that the godmother of the future writer was the proprietress of the house in which the Assis family lived. This lady was the widow of the former Inspector of gold in Rio de Janeiro, and her second marriage had been to a senator and minister of the Empire. Thus, the *agregados* were a long way from what is today understood as freedom, but they were very

---

*A hill relatively near to the centre of Rio.

close to the dominant classes, and so to their culture. Another suggestive detail: in the self-same ceremony in which this great lady acted as Machado's godmother, Machado's father acted as a godfather to a slave child on the same property. In three generations, the Assis family had covered a lot of ground, without, however, leaving the confines of the property: they had come from slavery to relative respectability. It should be added that both Machado's mother and father could read and write, which was exceptional.[2]

So, Machado was the great-grandson of slaves and the son of a worker, but he didn't rise from nothing. He was the godson of an illustrious lady, and may have lived in her company to some extent in his childhood; he lived on a large property; his parents could read and write, and had been married by the Church, another sign of respectability in a country in which the family system had not yet reached stability.

I underline these facts, in order to make it plain that the distances to be covered, and the steps on the way, were not the same in Brazil and the countries which give us the sociological and novelistic constructs we have adopted. A poor Brazilian's career had little to do with the individualist or 'Napoleonic' model, rooted in the modern bourgeois order, and which was decisive for the European novel of Julien Sorel, Rastignac and Raskolnikov. If it remains true that the Assis family had come a long way, they had always stayed within the protection of the owner class. Machado naturally broke this subordinating link – one of the facts about his life which he would carefully hide. On the other hand, he recognized the problematic, contemporary dimension of this same clientelism – which has immense importance in Brazilian life – and freed it from the traditional framework in which it had been understood.

Really, however, it is inaccurate to say that Machado was breaking with paternalism. He did escape from the position of the 'agregado', in which dependency can have a brute, humiliating aspect. Placed in a less bad position, the young writer applied himself to the task of civilizing and refining paternalist relationships. He wanted to cleanse them of their authoritarian, destructive aspect, in which the dependant is at the mercy of his or her protector. In such cases – this was his argument in his first novels[*]

---

[*]*Resurreição [Resurrection]* (1872); *A mão e a luva [The Hand and the Glove*, University of Kentucky Press, Lexington 1970] (1874); *Helena [Helena*, University of California Press 1984] (1876); *Iaiá Garcia [Yayá Garcia*, Peter Owen, London 1976/*Iaiá Garcia*, Lexington, University of Kentucky Press 1977] (1878).

– the protector and the country are the losers, for they are deprived of the abilities of their most talented protégés. And in fact, Machado practised the you-scratch-my-back-and-I'll-scratch-yours system of paternalism with insuperable elegance, something that was immediately admired and acknowledged by well-born contemporaries, who never tired of praising his politeness and delicacy. To a degree, they were being educated by their own dependant.

With one exception, the central figures of Machado's early novels are intelligent, strong young women, born in a modest, dependent situation. How can one rectify this 'mistake of birth'?[3] Does the protégé owe obedience to his benefactor? Or perhaps he owes him no obedience whatever, since human beings and love were born free? Does he have the right to covet the wealth of the rich? Might it not be better to escape from them, since access to them depends on favour and so on personal dependency? In the toings and froings of this conflict 'authoritarian' and 'enlightened' paternalism are opposed. It is quite clear that the latter is superior, and benefits both the interested parties: by giving initiative and dignity to the protégés, it spares them the humiliation of subservience, and civilizes and enriches the society of the protectors. Machado in a sense was justifying an alliance between the people of property and their most gifted dependants.

I emphasize these early novels because the problem they deal with, which obviously has connections with Machado's own life, allows one to define Machado's position more closely.[4] The social analysis they develop, intelligent and vigorous as it was, did not aim to transform the order of things, but to perfect it – it was also a way of making oneself accepted and admired. Nowadays, we do not value such points of view: we cannot see mental energy or profundity in conformism.

For contemporaries, this energy was evident, and there was no lack of favourable comments on 'Machadinho''s talent. He distinguished himself everywhere. He practised poetry, literary and theatrical criticism, published 'crônicas' and stories, adapted drama from the French, wrote his own plays, recited celebratory verse, was a member of the Conservatório Dramático,[*] of the Arcádia Fluminense, took part in chess competitions, was on the board of the Beethoven Club, frequented the Teatro Lírico, for which he

---

[*]The Conservatório Dramático was an official organization which acted as a censor in the field of drama. The Arcádia Fluminense was a literary circle founded in the mid-1860s. The Teatro Lírico was the main opera theatre.

composed librettos, was an (unwilling) candidate for a seat in the Chamber of Deputies, wrote and translated novels. In other words, he took part in the nascent cultural life of Rio de Janeiro on a grand scale, at a time when the creation or the existence of such a life no doubt seemed more important to most people than its quality. What today looks like conformism, at the time was more like a patriotic, civilizing struggle: it was necessary for the young country to acquire the institutions and the intellectual disciplines which it still did not have, something which, in its turn, presented the young writer with a way up the social scale.

We can understand, therefore, the curious mixture of personal ambition, patriotic merit and artistic mediocrity which characterizes the first phase of Machado's work, which lasted until he was forty. His predominant preoccupation was the *acquisition* of techniques and forms, in a sense which lies at the polar opposite of what we understand by art today. In place of critical intent, the dedication of the good pupil, looking for applause. However, served by Machado's extraordinary energy, this rather schoolboyish dedication already took him a long way. Though his works never have the wit and charm of artistic freedom, they do represent a wide-ranging, varied and detailed transcription of the current attitudes of the time – within the limits imposed by the edifying intentions. They can be read with profit, though not with pleasure. So, when around his fortieth year the writer came into possession of the disillusioned vision which was to be his trade-mark and which made a great writer of him, he had at his disposal, in intimate detail, a mental universe which he now went on to laugh at.

It would be nice but naive to see the transition from the first to the second phase – from mediocre to excellent literature – as the passage from conformism to criticism. If in his second period Machado is a writer without illusions, capable of terrifying perceptions, it is not because he is a critic, but because he hides nothing. At one moment he is reputed to have said, 'Anything, my friend, anything, rather than live as an eternal dupe!',[5] a phrase which is a good definition of his new commitment to truth. From the social point of view, this evolution is linked to Machado's rise in society, which was now complete. After looking at Brazilian society from the point of view of the poor dependant, who shines by the discernment with which he expresses his esteem for the established order, developing his talent in order to be recognized and co-opted by the ruling élite, the writer would now look at society from the point of view of someone nicely set up within it. The time had come to relativize the experience he had gathered. Instead of the positive vision, he now adopted the disillusioned one, whose aim is not to criticize, but to vouchsafe the splendour and the calm of an unfettered intelligence; it is as if understanding the mechanism of society were a consolation for the lack of meaning of this very mechanism, and for its horrors. Even in this sense, Machado was undertaking the work of civilization, for his pessimism gave dignity and a certain poise to the sense of impasse in which our liberal, slave-owning, and paternalist elites felt themselves caught. In sum, it was a nihilist art, but not *maudit*.

Between 1880 and 1906 Machado wrote five novels and dozens of stories which made a first-rank writer of him. It is an *oeuvre* in which Brazil is portrayed in depth. However, it is a fact that these books are not the direct presentation of any of the great ideological currents that roused people at this time. They are not adepts of determinist philosophy (neither positivist, Darwinist, nor monist, etc.). They are not abolitionist (slavery was abolished in 1888), they are not Republican (the Republic came in 1889), and they do not submit to the literary school of Naturalism, then triumphant. What is worse, they treat of all these matters - some more, some less - always ironically, with a distance which contemporaries noted, either to regret it or disapprove of it, never to approve, something which strangely did not prevent them from recognizing Machado's excellence as a writer. Now that time has passed, this distance looks more like the very expression of his superiority, of Machado's profound affinity with the Brazilian historical process. He may not be the solution for all our ills, but he gives us the indispensable spectacle - perhaps the only one in our literature - of a mind without prejudice, and truly independent (in a man who respected external conventions).

Notes

1. Antonio Candido, 'Esquema [Sketch] de Machado de Assis', *Vários escritos*, Duas Cidades, São Paulo 1970, p. 15.

2. For a detailed biographical account, see Jean-Michel Massa, *A juventude de Machado de Assis*, Civilisação Brasileira, Rio de Janeiro 1971, from which I have taken the facts and many of the comments for this sketch.

3. Machado de Assis, *A mão e a luva, Obra completa*, Aguilar, Rio de Janeiro 1959, Vol. 1, p. 142.

4. The thematic unity and the biographical inspiration of the early Machado novels has been pointed to Lúcia Miguel-Pereira, *Prosa de ficção* [1950], José Olympio, Rio de Janeiro 1973, pp. 65-7.

5. Araripe Júnior, 'Machado de Assis', *Obra crítica*, MEC/Casa de Rui Barbosa, Rio de Janeiro 1960, Vol. 4, p. 282.

SIX

Complex, Modern, National
and Negative

To Sara Hirschman

Machado de Assis was not the first Brazilian novelist, but he certainly was
the first great one. What were the historical conditions, literary and non-
literary, at work in his achievement? How did they lead him out of a
provincial tradition, tangible derivative, to the seriousness of great writing? I
hope to persuade you that the loose form of his novels is part of a vigorous
composition which formalizes and reveals decisive dynamisms of Brazilian
society. Literary quality depends upon contemporary history, although, of
course, in unexpected ways.

Let me begin with a passage from the *Posthumous memoirs of Brás Cubas*,
a novel he published in 1880. Its comedy, as you will notice, depends upon
an unusual arrangement of terms, an arrangement that differs from the one
a European – or a reader of European novels – would expect. After br ; ging
out this difference, I shall consider it from two perspectives: first, in its
relation to an original artistic pattern, and second, in its relation to the
peculiar form of Brazilian society. In sum, I shall offer you an example of
the dialectics of literary form and social process.

To get the passage right, keep in mind that the title is meant to provoke
us, since it is not possible to write memoirs posthumously;[1] that the
dedication, in the form of a tombstone, to the worms in the ground is an
open act of disrespect; that in the prologue, the author devotes his
ingenuity to insulting us; and that in the opening lines of the book, we
encounter foolishness, elevated language, considerations of method, the
buzzwords of the day, and the preposterous comparison of the author's

narrative procedure to that of Moses in the Old Testament. This said, let us turn to the text.

At the end of Chapter I, Brás Cubas remembers the successive stages of his extinction: his body was becoming a plant, a stone, clay, nothing at all.

> I died from pneumonia, but, if I were to tell you, my reader, that it was not really pneumonia that caused my death but a grandiose and pragmatic idea, would you believe me? And yet it is true. Let me briefly present the case to you, so you can decide for yourself.

II *The Plaster*

> As it happened, one morning I was strolling on my estate when an idea got hold of the trapeze that I carried in my brain. Once it grabbed it, it flexed its arms and legs and began to perform the most incredibly daring somersaults. I just stood and watched. Suddenly it made a great leap, spread out its arms and legs into an X and said: Decipher me or I devour you.
>
> This idea was nothing less than the invention of a sublime medicine, an anti-hypochondriac plaster, meant to help our despondent mankind. As I drafted the application for a patent, I called the government's attention to the truly Christian properties of the plaster. Yet, to my friends, I did not hide the pecuniary advantages that would result from the wide distribution of a remedy with such vast and profound effects. Now, however, that I am here on the other side, I can confess it all: what lured me most was the desire to see printed in newspapers and pamphlets, on store signs and street corners and finally on the plaster-boxes themselves these four words: 'The Brás Cubas Plaster'. Why deny it? I had a passion to beat my own drum, billboards and pyrotechnics. Perhaps the meek will condemn me for this defect. Yet I trust that the shrewd will call it a strength. Thus my idea was like a medal: it had two sides, one turned towards the public and the other towards me. On one side, philanthropy and profit; on the other, thirst for reputation. Let us say: – love of glory.

On closer inspection, the order of priorities in these lines is striking:

In his application to the government, Brás Cubas states humanitarian reasons; yet to his friends he confesses his hopes of pecuniary advantage. Thus far, nothing surprising: to uncover egoistic calculations behind a generous façade is a usual move of the realistic novel. A move, in fact, which testifies to the link – a critical link – between the realistic novel and the new individualistic order capitalism had brought about.

Yet, Brás Cubas proceeds to a further explanation, this one final and bizarre, an explanation coming from beyond the grave where there is no reason to hide anything. His true motive – he now states – had been the desire for publicity, the pleasure of having his name in lights. The desire for pecuniary advantage therefore had been nothing but an excuse.

It is the hope for economic advantage then which provides an excuse for the desire for personal recognition, and not the other way round. The search for economic profit is itself a façade and does not differ, in this respect, from the 'truly Christian purpose' stated in the application to the government, for both are there to veil the one true motive, the wish to be recognized.

The same unusual conjunction appears at the end of the paragraph: 'Thus my idea was like a medal: it had two sides, one turned towards the public and the other towards me. On one side, philanthropy and profit; on the other, thirst for reputation. Let us say: - love of glory.' Again, philanthropy and profit are not - as one would expect - on opposite sides of the medal. Quite to the contrary, they go hand in hand and are both on the side turned to the public. On the other side, the true and secret one, is the thirst for reputation. This is the private and effective reality, so unlike what is given to the public, which includes both Christian sentiment and economic ambition.

In short, egoistic calculation - the dark and driving force of modern life, according to the European realistic novel - is looked upon by him as something socially cherished, that should even be advertised. This is original. Original, too, is the idea that economic calculation is not a *real* motive, but a good alibi for another desire, a more secret and less serious one, although the truest of them all. Economics and Christianity are frivolities for display, while hankering for attention, which would seem to be frivolity itself, turns out to be the ultimate and prime mover of reality.

What are we to make of this view of things? We could read it as a whim that later developments in the novel will set straight. Or we could also take it to be the distinctive trait of a silly character. Yet these suppositions will not do, for this view takes a firm grip on plot and characters, narrative rhythm, phrasing, mixture of styles and vocabulary, subject matter, and so on. The novel lives it out with a truly implacable thoroughness, proper only to great works. Should we therefore think of it as a satirical inversion of reality? Or rather as an early attempt at the dissolution of the conventions of the realistic novel? Up to a point, both things are true. As a matter of fact, everything in these memoirs sounds extravagant, and the whimsicalities of the narrator break all the agreements upon which the realistic sense of verisimilitude depends. But still, once you are under the spell of the whole, there is a strongly realistic ring to it, and a very desolate one. Besides, as people familiar with nineteenth-century Brazil will notice, the comedy of motives enacted in the passage bears an undeniable resemblance to the country's ideological climate. Summing up these remarks, we may ask why this outlook – if there is reality to it – should sound so foolish? And if it is foolish, how can it be realistic? And if it is realistic, what kind of world does it describe? Before attempting an answer, let me comment on the novel's form, so you may see that in fact the passage we read is not one-off eccentricity.

The outstanding feature of this and other novels by Machado is the extraordinary volatility of the narrator, who will change his mind, his subject and his mode of speech at almost every sentence, and will not hold to the same course for longer than a short paragraph. There is an aspect of self-gratification to this changing disposition and to the rhetorical virtuosity that goes with it, a sort of kick to be derived from each one of these switches of level, which links up with the desire for recognition we just talked about. It will be decisive for my argument. And since this feature subordinates everything else in the book, we may call it the principle of its form.

To see it at work, let us go back to our passage. In the sentence that precedes it, the dead author mentions the states of matter death had led him through: he had become a plant, a stone, clay and nothing at all. These ontological stages, which presumably are to be the common fate of us all, have a gravity of their own, which, however, in the next sentence is to give way to pneumonia. This term brings in individual death, with its elements of bad luck and medical explanations. These in turn – with an equally mocking contrast – will give way to a loftier *causa mortis*, with positive contradictions in liberal ideology, namely a grandiose and pragmatic idea. As the author puts it, it is for the reader, a man of reliable judgement, to make up his mind among these different aspects of death. Yet the next sentence will conceive of the human mind as a sort of trapeze that ideas grab at and let go in order to go through their somersaults – a circus metaphor which hardly connotes confidence in independent judgement. At each one of these steps there is a disruption of some sort either in idea or in form, which forces the reader to laugh and procures a kind of victory for the narrator. This exacting kind of comicality is a peculiar aspect of Machado de Assis' prose, an aspect one at first takes to be unattractive and a weakness, but which on further reading comes out as a particularly important achievement: it is the conscious enactment of the authoritarian and malignant aspect of volatility. Later on we will see more of this.

Next, the author will pose in quick succession as an inventor, as a man of Christian purpose, a man interested in pecuniary advantages, a man with a passion for publicizing his own name, etc. Since the changes in character, subject and tone will continue at the same pace right up to the last chapter of the book, there is no point in following them up one by one. Yet we may remark that there is more than simple variety to this series. Its terms are chosen so as to convey a high degree of abstraction, of mock-abstraction, that in its way sums up the totality of the world, which thus is submitted as a whole to the narrator's caprices. For example, the author speaks now as a Christian citizen who petitions the government, now in his private capacity, as a friend among friends, and then from beyond the grave, as an absolutely sincere soul, all in the limited space of a few lines. Together, the three points of view make for a complete and definite world, of which they are to be the constituent parts. In the same sense, the 'meek' and the 'shrewd' who will respectively condemn and admire Brás Cubas for his showiness stand for the whole of the public, or even of humanity. The same holds true for the two sides of an idea (public and private), for the set of motives (philanthropy, profit and love of glory), and the stages of decay (from the human to the vegetable to the mineral). They are arrangements that imply an embracing and articulate view of a whole, which in this way is put at the disposal of the imagination. On the other hand, since these abstractions are themselves clearly arbitrary, it is not merely the outside world that falls prey to the narrator's changing ways: the very act of abstraction is taken over as well. In the novels of Machado, the faculties of abstraction and reasoning are peculiarly comical. Impalpable and belonging to the domain of logic, they do not seem to be appropriate subject matter for fiction. And yet, in them can be found the most extreme expression of volatility and arbitrariness. In the same way, well-ordered syntax, with its display of constructions, becomes a comic expression of wilfulness. And finally, to come full circle, the dead man writing his memoirs is a narrative situation which is contrived to deprive fiction and its reader of an easy relation to one another, and this itself becomes an object of constant teasing.

In sum, the whimsicality of the narrator is not modest in scope, for it emphatically reaches out to the world at large and to the artistic medium in depth. By the same token it becomes much more than the expression of a psychology; it is a fully developed literary form, as well as a way of looking at the world. The amount of work that is required for the achievement of this form should be clear by now. Machado worked out a technique that allows for the ever-renewed and never-completed subordination of current bourgeois reality to personal arbitrariness. Such a form is of course a *feat of construction*, and there is little that is spontaneous in it. Yet the result is a striking likeness to nineteenth-century Brazil. Thus the sense of immediacy and resemblance of realism is by no means the effect of surface imitation, but depends upon rigorous modes of construction which have abstractions at their heart.

Having considered the narrator as such, we shall now ground him in the plot, so as to take his full measure.

As a whole, the novel is held together by Brás Cubas' life, intertwining digressions, anecdotes and more or less allusive stories, with a chronicle of Rio de Janeiro of his time, and we may say that it is volatility in slow motion. There is plenty of lively desire and no continuity of purpose whatsoever. So far, it fits a wealthy gentleman with no occupation. This makes for an erratic plot without tension, very original in its way, for it is a plot that is not stretched by conflict, since conflict would require a continuity of some sort. Its complexities are not linked to the unfolding of contradictions – these being attenuated in the mirror of whim – but to the subtleties and rhythms of unconscious change, of boredom and of aimless movement from one station of life to another (a subject matter, by the way, which makes this novel one of the early modern anatomies of time and will). These stations are the ones an elegant son of the Brazilian ruling class might go through: a degree in Law at Coimbra (the Portuguese university), love, poetry, politics, philosophy, journalism, science, philanthropy and death. Conspicuously absent are work and, more generally, every form of sustained effort or ideological commitment. In other words, the spheres we mentioned, which are in one way or another, the acknowledged repository of the values of modern life, appear as objects of mere fancy, which is to say that their own logic will take second place to the hero's need for self-enhancement. Brought into the field of capriciousness, they serve only to provide the mind with a quick satisfaction, a satisfaction spiced, so to say, by their historic claim to grandeur. Worked upon by caprice, they adopt cheapened forms: for science, there is the invention of the plaster, for politics, there is Brás Cubas' fiery intervention in Parliament, in which he advocates a reduction of two inches in the biretta of the National Guard, for poetry, there is the attempt at vocal effects in the reciting of a funeral ode, for philosophy, there are the social thoughts that come to Brás Cubas' mind when looking at two dogs fighting for a bare bone, etc.

A plot with no necessity to its main line, and yet with pressing necessities all along, as its moments are commanded by the imperiousness of the whim of the narrator and the characters that appear: this is a strange combination, for it makes for a life that is at once full of satisfaction and void of meaning. Accordingly, there is comedy in all the novel's moments, yet the sum total is desolate and ends up in nothing, as is explicitly stated in the last chapter of the book, called 'Of Negatives'. Here, Brás Cubas enumerates the things he did not come to be, and concludes that he has come out slightly ahead by virtue of the most extreme of negatives: the well-known 'I didn't have children, and didn't leave to any creature the legacy of our misery'. This impression of desolation is multiplied by the countless comments, shifts, and digressions of the narrator, who at high speed relentlessly enacts the same fusion of intensity and aimlessness that the plot takes more time to reveal.

In spite of this aimlessness, a distinct trajectory can be discerned in Braz Cubas' tale, something like a movement of movements: a rhythm in which the interest of the narrator, of the characters, as well as of the reader, repeatedly rises and falls, within an overall drift from vigour to lassitude and death. This is a rhythm with a truth of its own, a strange one, particularly as it is portrayed as utterly independent of objective and binding purposes. We will see in what sense all this is an appropriate solution to the problems posed to the form of the novel by Brazilian society. (This rhythm was to be repeated by several of the best Brazilian novels of later times especially *Macunaíma,* with its extraordinary final sadness.) Now, however, let us mark its difference from the plot of the European novel, whose tension usually depends upon the ambitions of a resolute young person who suffers in his clash with society and therefore exemplifies the contradictions between these ambitions and the reigning social order. In the end, what is said is that its bourgeois order is contradictory and doesn't deliver on its promises. While Machado's plots tell us that life for wealthy Brazilians was wonderful, but in the words of Oswald de Andrade, 'run on a non-existent track'.

Recapitulating, one might say that the plaster is to medicine as the National Guard's biretta is to politics, as Brás Cubas' thoughts on fighting dogs are to philosophy, and as the aimless plot is to the plot with an energetic hero. One side of each of these pairs is a comic distortion of the other. Yet, as we read the novel, we come to acknowledge that the nation's logic is built upon the unserious side, which therefore, as far as the novel goes, has the weight of reality. How, then, are we to explain our experience of it as an outrageous caricature? Why should the lack of reality not be

---

*See note to 'The Cart, the Tram, and the Modernist Poet' (p. 119).

found on the other side? Indeed, a double standard is at work: from the point of view of objective norms, such as philosophy, medicine, etc., the characters and situations are foolish, yet from the point of view of the novel's action, it is the norms themselves which lack reality and appear foolish, since they contribute nothing. In one case, the norms are authoritative, while in the other, they are instruments of whim. The same double standard determines the changing value of capriciousness, which invades and shapes each and every dimension of life, and yet – according to nineteenth-century bourgeois civilization – is irrelevant and marginal. In the same way, the narrator's malign and comic strokes are achieved at the expense of the system of bourgeois virtues, virtues which he recalls only to deride, yet the authority of these virtues remains. The awareness of being despicable is therefore essential to the narrator's situation. He is like Dostoyevsky's underground man, who, despising Western rationalism, won't go to the doctor for his diseased liver, yet nevertheless despises himself for failing to take care of his health. The same sort of incoherence gives form, though not obviously, to Machado's novel and is the source of its restlessness and its movement towards nothing. And far from being a weakness, this incoherence is a substantial realistic achievement; an explanation of how this can be so will lead us to consider Brazilian national circumstances.

Although well known, the ideological and moral problems of the Brazilian ruling elite, especially of the group close to the Crown, are rarely seen as consequential. These problems are well-described in the remarkable book of Joaquim Nabuco on *Abolitionism* (1883). Forced by their role as international representatives, these liberal rulers of a country with a slave economy had to beg daily, for their fatherland as well as for themselves, the recognition of the 'civilized world', the elementary principles of which, however, they would violate with equal constancy, given the demands of their social reality. In 'Misplaced Ideas', I attempted a sociological reconstruction of this double bind and its effect upon the life of ideas. Here it is enough to point to the resemblance between the oscillation created by this impasse and the volatility we have seen in the memoirs of Braz Cubas. In a gamut that goes from the comic to the obnoxious, this volatility also joins the violation of bourgeois norms to the thirst for bourgeois acceptance, a combination, which, given its countless repetitions, has effrontery as its second nature. This sort of pairing makes up the characteristic and basic unit of the novel's prose. Thus, if our remarks are correct, the principle of Machado's art would be something like the miniaturization and schematic depiction of the ideological to-and-fro of the Brazilian ruling class, in its unavoidable links to the international market and Western progress as well as to local slavery and the forms of social dependence among free men that go with it. A to-and-fro that epitomizes the vexations of a nation, and does something more as well, since it also points to a global history in which Brazil was a real, although morally disapproved of, partner. When seen in these global terms the bourgeois order does not in fact conform to bourgeois norms.

Obviously, there are differences in tone between the ideological discomfort of our elite and Machado's prose. With a malign detachment that fiction permits, the latter renders explicit the grotesque aspects of the former. Still, Machado's impartiality goes further. Although illegitimate by European bourgeois standards, and therefore deemed worthless as a principle of judgment, the world of capriciousness comes to reveal the non-absolute character of the norms themselves. This perspective led him to what turns out to be some of the central concerns of modern literature, which are fundamentally linked to the limits of bourgeois civilization. In sum, the fatherland's inferiority is granted, but the principles by which it is measured are not innocent themselves, although historically dominant. His stance is anti-mythical and involves two negations: there is no regressive patriotic pride in it, and no abdication of the intellect in the face of Europe and progress; it is a rational position with no absolutes which has not aged after one hundred years.

All this may help explain how foolishness – contingent and individual by its very nature – has the ring of inescapable necessity. Commenting on the situation of French writers after 1848, Sartre speaks of an 'objective neurosis':* a pathology imposed by a real state of affairs from which there is no escape. Similarly, the double standard which is at the heart of Machado's achievement may be the literary formalization and exploration of something like an 'objective *ressentiment*', an ideological and moral incongruity imposed by the contemporary world upon the enlightened milieu of Brazilian society. Here, of course, the term 'enlightened' has strong implications of class.

---

*For this notion, see Jean-Paul Sartre, *L'Idiot de la Famille* (Gallimard, Paris 1972), Vol. III, Book 1.

Note

1. It is therefore a pity that the English translation is entitled *Epitaph of a Small Winner* and that it omits the dedication.

SEVEN

The Poor Old Woman and

Her Portraitist

Everything in Machado de Assis's novels is coloured by the *volatility* - used and abused in different degrees - of their narrators. The critics usually look at it from the point of view of literary technique or of the author's humour. There are great advantages in seeing it as the stylization of the behaviour of the Brazilian ruling class.

Instead of seeking disinterestedness, and the confidence provided by impartiality, Machado's narrator shows off his impudence, in a gamut which runs from cheap gibes, to literary exhibitionism, and even to criminal acts. Paradoxically, the result is a social portrait more revealing than that of the Naturalists, his contemporaries, who nevertheless strive to be objective.* And since our topic is the representation of poverty,** we should note that a deliberate bad faith in the treatment of the poor exacerbates the feeling of injustice in the reader perhaps more deeply than the long descriptions which this same Naturalism indulged in. In any case, the recourse to literary effrontery, with the aim of critical revelation, was not unheard of at the time. Baudelaire, for self-styled philanthropic reasons,

---

*Naturalism was popular in Brazil at the time when Machado was writing: the novels of Zola and the Portuguese Eça de Queirós had considerable repercussion, as did those of the Brazilian Aluisio Azevedo (*O mulato* [1881], *O cortiço* [*The Slum*] [1890] etc.), and others.

**This essay was originally part of a collection of over thirty essays on many authors, entitled *Os pobres na literatura brasileira* (*The Poor in Brazilian Literature*) edited by Schwarz (Brasiliense, São Paulo 1983).

recommended that people should beat street-beggars, as the only means of forcing them to rediscover their lost dignity – when they tried to get their own back.[1]

The teacher who gives Brás his first lessons, had taught children 'for twenty-three years, silent, obscure, punctual, ensconced in a little house on the rua do Piolho' [lit. Flea Street: *Ed. note*]. When he dies, nobody – 'not even me', as the narrator says mockingly – mourned him. A life of humble, honest work, which has no recognition at all: that is the kernel of this episode. At another moment, when he finds a childhood friend in rags and begging, the reaction is the reverse: what Brás deplores is that his ex-schoolmate disdains work and has no self-respect. 'I wanted to see a dignified poverty.' To sum it up, the dignity which Brás does not see in real work is something he nevertheless demands of the layabout. In both cases, his aim is to stay on top, or, more exactly, to have no obligations to the poor; I owe nothing to someone who has worked, and someone who has not worked has no right to anything (except to moral disapproval). Convention has it that either the bourgeois norm or contempt for it must be valid. This scandalous duplicity or shift between criteria, set to a lively rhythm, is the essence of the volatility mentioned at the beginning. It has its origins in the historical situation of the Brazilian ruling classes in the nineteenth century, who had one foot in the institution of slavery, and another in European progress, and profited from both.

The situation of the poor is defined in a manner which complements this: what is historical play-time for the rich – with two measures and two criteria at their disposal – for the poor is *lack of security*. With no property, and with slaves responsible for the greater part of economic production, they live on a slippery terrain: if they don't work, they are social outcasts, and if they do work they will be paid or recognized only if they have the great luck to receive favour.

So, according to a complaint common at the time, the existence of slavery deprived free labour of its value. In consequence, though this is nothing to boast of, the work ethic – one of the pillars of the contemporary bourgeois ideology – did not enjoy much credence in Brazil.[2]

In the twentieth century, in conjunction with signs that the ideology of work was in historical terms reaching the point of exhaustion, that scepticism which is the privilege of a 'backward' people was taken up again with a positive connotation, and could be given universal resonance in the meditations on indolence of Mário de Andrade and Raul Bopp, and in Oswald's utopias.[3] Recently, Antonio Candido has shown how much, from the beginning, this scepticism had contributed to the originality and the scope of the Brazilian novel.[4] Possibly more modern than the Modernists, whose euphoric note does not withstand serious reflection, Machado saw the other side of the coin: in the middle of the bourgeois era, work without recognition or pay is an acme of historical frustration. As an example, let us look at the portrait of Dona Plácida, in *The Posthumous Memoirs of Brás Cubas*, which is one of the greatest and the harshest moments in Brazilian literature.

Dona Plácida's life fits into a few lines: it is a succession of backbreaking labour, of misfortunes, illnesses and frustrations. There is in itself nothing remarkable about this, nor is it sufficient to explain the terrible effect of the episode. The poor woman sews, makes sweets to sell, teaches local children, all of this without distinction and without rest, 'so as to eat and not to fall'. 'To fall', here, is a euphemism for contingencies like begging for alms in the street or compromising one's honour, humiliations which, however, will be unavoidable, as the narrator notes, with evident satisfaction. Later, forced by poverty, Dona Plácida ends up giving her services as a go-between, even though she is a sincere devotee of marriage and family respectability. In the same way, although she is untiringly hard-working, there comes the moment when she is obliged to seek the protection of a wealthy family, to whom she attaches herself; but this still doesn't prevent her dying in a state of total indigence. Summing it up, honest and independent existence is not within the grasp of the poor, even when they are stoical. In the eyes of the rich they are presumptuous when they strive for such a thing, and despicable when they give in – this is one of the formulae of the contemptible class humour of Brás Cubas, which Machado exposed and formalized.

But let us return to Dona Plácida's labours. Work indifferent to its proper end (sewing, cooking, teaching) and with no object beyond the payment, belongs to the world of capitalism; while total lack of regard for effort belongs to the world of slavery. In parallel fashion, we can note that the benefits which are the other side of these evils – that is, the bourgeois dignification of work 'in general', and the leisure that slavery can give to non-slaves – are absent. In other words, the worst of two worlds is summed up in Dona Plácida: work in the abstract, but with no right of social recognition. Her efforts, whose material reward is uncertain and minimal, are also uncompensated on the moral plane – which perhaps explains the character's extraordinary sadness. Harshness, when it lacks the redemption of a meaning, is absolute.

From the point of view of Brazilian realism, the character of Dona Plácida is of capital importance, and I have already indicated the general class implications involved in her character, and the way in which she corresponds to the social structure of the country. All the same, a portrait, however accurate it may be, only has literary power when it also provides us with perspectives of a less obvious nature. In this sense, we can see that poverty stripped even of consolation is not only a portrait of destitution, but also a logical and critical consequence, an element of its reasoning which is indispensable to a more advanced conception of society. Deprived of the pre-capitalist feeling for the particular nature of a job, and for the corporative order (both of which are thwarted by the realities of abstract work), and of the value which bourgeois ideology places on that same work (a value which slavery gives the lie to), *what remains is a radically de-ideologized notion of effort*, which is stripped of intrinsic merit. This is a notion which does not lend itself to mystification, and which makes us breathe the rarefied air of great literature. At a different date, an analogous conversion of privation into lucidity gives life to these lines by Carlos Drummond de Andrade: 'Heroes fill the parks of the cities where you shuffle by,/and extol virtue, self-denial, *sang-froid*, and conception'.[5] On another level, we are close to the formula of Marx, who behind the illusions of modern wealth sees the mental and muscular efforts of the workers, and nothing else. To sum it up, a materialist – that is, a disillusioned and enlightened – sense of work, whose relevance transcends the bourgeois order, since contemporary socialism is, in its turn, *productivist*.

But it is not exactly true to say that Dona Plácida's life has no meaning. If the sad lady were to ask why she had come into the world, Brás Cubas imagines that her parents would say the following: 'We have called you to burn your fingers in boiling pans, ruin your eyes with sewing, eating badly, or not eating, going from one place to another, working all the time, getting ill and getting better, just so you can get ill and get better again, now sad, soon desperate, tomorrow resigned, but always with your hands in the pans and your eyes on your sewing, until you finish up one day in the gutter or in the hospital; that was what we called you for, in a moment of mutual attraction.' The mockery of these lines is complex. First of all, it lies in feigning that the unacceptable realities of modern poverty fulfil an aim ('That was what we called you for'). The condemnation cuts both ways: social reality is negative because it has no human meaning, and the urge to find an aim in it at any price is also negative – in this context, the illusions of Divine Providence and its secularized surrogates are exposed to ridicule in a

Voltairean fashion. To sum it up, neither the present order of things nor theological argument can satisfy Reason, which brands both as irrational. But we can also note that poverty is described as a regular, even functional, cycle, and that there is method to its madness. In this sense it does have an end, even though it is a humanely indefensible one, that of reproducing the social order that condemns it. Where does this leave us? The result is something like the mockery of mockery, a kind of crying without tears, to which should be added the enjoyment that so much inferiority provides to the narrator's social superiority. These, then, are justifications which belong to the modern world, which have affinities in the scientific realm – the reproduction of the species, of society and of injustice – and lack a transcendental dimension. Looked at as a whole, it is a dizzyingly compressed reversal of the perspectives of providentialism, of the Enlightenment and of faith in science, all for the convenience of the Brazilian ruling class, which in this way *universalizes* its own incongruities.

The compass of this mélange extends into the modern world: we are far away from the Christian vale of tears, from which, however, the prose borrows its tone when it describes hardship and drudgery. But in this secularized context, the humble conformism of the language sounds like one more sign of spite. This joining of what artistic styles and the logic of concepts tend to separate is a constant and one of Machado's strengths. It can be noted, also, that the explanation of the aim of Dona Plácida's life has the essential brevity of the eighteenth-century *conte philosophique*, but that it takes in the world of terrible calamities described by nineteenth-century Naturalism, without forgetting that its analytic coldness – universalizing and classical in its style – has something at once mocking and crazy about it, which serves as *local Brazilian colour* in its class characterization of Brás Cubas. In its turn, the insouciant ease with which this multiplicity of prestigious registers is manipulated is characteristic of the avant-garde.

In other words, the mirroring of social positions in each other and in the variety of historical styles does not destroy the reality of social classes, as the purists of the popular point of view think. On the contrary, this variety gives substance to the way in which class points of view – in their profound complexity – are reciprocally mediated, something which a more 'common-sense' or alternatively a more doctrinaire notion of mimesis fails to capture. It is this intensified realism which gives the humble figure of Dona Plácida her plethora of connotations, as well as her historical relevance, rescuing her from obscurity and from her apparent limitations. There is a scope and depth here in the understanding of poverty which only a cultivated and refined writer, at ease in a variety of styles, of philosophies and of class experiences could achieve – and offer to others; and this is something which, from a dialectical point of view, is not a paradox.

Notes

1. Cf. Charles Baudelaire, 'Assommons les pauvres!', in *Le Spleen de Paris*, 1869. For a political analysis of this *petit poème en prose*, see Dolf Oelher, *Pariser Bilder (1830–1848)*, Suhrkamp, Frankfurt 1979.

2. To appreciate the contrast between the European and Brazilian situations, with regard to what is obvious and what needs to be proved, see the first paragraphs of the *Critique of the Gotha Programme*, of 1875. There, Marx attacks the high, and mythificatory, value placed on work within the working-class movement itself, reminding his readers that it is an expression of bourgeois interests.

3. The philosophical importance of Mário's interest in sloth was pointed out to me by Gilda de Mello e Souza. [For notes on Mário, Bopp and Oswald, see Chapter 1, n. 4, Chapter 9, note (191), Chapter 1 n. 9 *Ed. note*].

4. Antonio Candido, 'Dialética da malandragem' ['The dialectics of roguery'], *Revista do Instituto de Estudos Brasileiros* (São Paulo), 8 (1972).

5. 'Elegia 1938', in *Sentimento do mundo*. [Carlos Drummond de Andrade (1902–87) is widely regarded as the greatest Brazilian poet of this century. In the 1930s and 1940s, in volumes like *Sentimento do mundo* [*The Feeling of the World*] and *A rosa do povo* [*The People's Rose*] he came closest to a (rather despairing) form of outright social commitment: *Ed. note.*]

EIGHT

'Who can tell me that this character is not Brazil?'

The question in the title was asked by a contemporary of Machado de Assis, and refers to Pedro Rubião de Alvarenga, the central figure of *Quincas Borba*.[*] And it is true that Rubião is naive (though not honest) in his dealings with money, philosophy, love and politics, and a mad vision of grandeur finally destroys his wits – which could be seen as an allegory of Brazil, even if the allegory is not that plain. Other authors, on the contrary, criticized the lack of a national sense and colouring in Machado: according to this point of view, his writings betray too much foreign influence, and a lack of interest in Brazilian problems. This argument has come down to our own time. Just recently it caused a polemic in the Chamber of Deputies, when the patron of Brazilian letters was being chosen. Surely José de Alencar, the celebrated creator of several Indianist novels,[**] must be more Brazilian than Machado de Assis? The opinion of the most refined brand of

---

[*] A novel published by Machado in 1891, translated as *Philosopher or Dog?* (Avon, New York 1982; in Britain, *The Heritage of Quincas Borba* [W.H. Allen, London 1954]. Its central plot concerns Pedro Rubião de Alvarenga, who inherits a huge sum of money (and a pet dog) from the mad Quincas Borba, moves to Rio from the interior, and is there taken up by Palha, an aspiring businessman and financier, and his wife Sofia, to whom Rubião is hopelessly attracted. Encouraged, and milked, by them, he squanders his money and in the end dies mad.

[**] The most celebrated are *O guarani* [*The Guarani Indian*] (1857) and *Iracema* [*Iracema*] (1865). Both are attempts to create a nationalist myth in which Indians and Portuguese are the co-founders of the 'Brazilian' race.

criticism (which to others appears elitist and insufficiently Brazilian) goes in the opposite direction: the author of *Quincas Borba*, on this view, is the most profoundly Brazilian of our writers.

Machado de Assis himself felt the importance of this problem. Writing just after the Indianist vogue, and himself a contemporary of Romantic localism and later of Naturalist descriptivism, he attempted to define his position in a deservedly famous passage:

> There is no doubt that any literature, above all one recently born, should nourish itself on the subjects offered it by its own country; but let us not establish doctrines so absolute as to impoverish it. What should be demanded of the writer above all, is a certain intimate feeling, which should make him into a man of his time and of his country, even when he deals with subjects remote in time and space. A notable French critic, analysing some time ago the work of a Scottish writer, Masson, quite rightly said that, in the same way as you can be a Breton without talking about gorse all the time, so Masson was a good Scot, who never said a word about thistles, and explained what he had said by saying that there was an interior *Scottishness* in him, different and better than if it had merely been superficial.[2]

Machado de Assis's works certainly display a Brazilianness of this interior type, which up to a point has no need of local colour. The trouble is that it is a difficult attribute to define, and even more to explain.

It should be noted that the obvious peculiarities of the country – those in which Brazilians recognize themselves, whether with pride or humour – are not absent from Machado's novels; but they do not set their tone. We could say in resumé that instead of identificatory *elements*, Machado was looking for *relations* and *forms*. The national nature of these latter is profound, but it is not obvious.

Thus, in *Quincas Borba* the reader finds allusions to important moments of Brazilian history, regional peculiarities, observations about the country's natural beauty, popular expressions, and a largish gallery of carioca types. All this however in brief mentions, without the insistence of historical, regionalist or urban novels, or those engaged in the establishment of national myths, which specialized in the exploitation of such things. Machado, who was in competition with them, was not going to be left behind: he gave proof of mastery in each of these areas, but at the same time he relativized them all. He had the modesty to take his compatriots into account, and, behind it, perhaps, the determination to outdo them all.[3] Without ignoring the picturesque, he took it as a stepping-stone – whose unplanned role he underlined – on the way to more significant realms.

Criticism has been aware of just this and so has divided. To some, his irony in the treatment of local colour and of everything which is on the more immediate level seemed like a discourtesy. For them, Machado was lacking in a love of the things which typify us (nature, social questions, nationality).[4] Others saluted in him the first Brazilian writer with universal concerns (which gave them the feeling of soaring above the localistic narrowness of the first group).[5] On the side of this second group, it should be said that universalism is in fact one component of Machado's writing. Among other sources, it found inspiration in the psychology of the French moralists of the seventeenth century, concerned with so-called general human nature, and also in the recent 'clinical' curiosity in mental functioning and its unconscious aspects.*

One for, the other against, both positions take note of the *diminished* place of local allusions in Machado's novels, and so conclude that they only have a minor importance. However, this is certainly a mistaken conclusion. To prove the point, one need only mention that a short while ago a long sociology book was published on the transformations that Brazil went through during the Empire and the Republic, entirely based on the documentary value of these allusions.[6] The incontrovertible evidence is that Machado not only was not inattentive to such things – rather, he was the most attentive of all our writers. However, impressed as he was by the quantity and the precision of the social details that he found, the author of the above-mentioned study took them above all as *information*, leaving the irony which always accompanies them in the background (an irony felt very keenly by those who insisted on the divorce between the writer and his immediate circumstances). As a consequence, the book fully documents the breadth and the fidelity of Machado's work as a chronicler – and, as far as that goes, perhaps puts an end to the polemic – but fails to analyse its character. To sum up, all positions have their validity: observation of local reality is frequent and highly insightful: this doesn't stop it having something intentionally diminished about it, which can be felt above all in the mocking contrast between it and the so-called universal subjects which it serves as material for. *Far from being a defect, we will see that this unequal*

---

*Machado's interest (from about 1875 on) in such contemporaries as Eduard von Hartmann (*The Philosophy of the Unconscious*), Henry Maudsley (*Crime and Madness*), Théodule Ribot (*Les Maladies de la mémoire*) and others is revealed in his newspaper articles and the inventory of (what remains of) his library.

conjunction is one of the secrets of Machado's narrative and of its Brazilian character.

A third current sees Machado as exemplifying a dialectic of the local and the universal. It notes that he has gone further than others in presenting the facts of social life, and in taking critical advantage of preceding Brazilian literature, which paradoxically led him to do without the aid of the picturesque and the exotic, and allowed him to integrate the numerous foreign models he used into his work without being submissive or servile. As a consequence, he is the first Brazilian novelist who can be read without allowances having to be made for the fact that he is our fellow-countryman, though he is no less Brazilian for that. In my view, this is the most interesting point of view, and it is the one that this study draws on.[7]

However, there is also a dialectic between dialectical positions. The conflict between localists and universalists was linked to the cycle of political independence and to the – long-term – liquidation of the colonial complex. It was necessary to differentiate the country from the Portuguese ex-metropolis, and to uphold its status as a cultured nation. As a result, some insisted on the originality of Brazil, others on the Western nature of its civilization. The dialectic between the local and the universal reflects the balance of this opposition, placing the warring terms inside a single movement towards the affirmation of national identity, in which they harmoniously complement one another.[8]

The trouble is that the concert of civilized nations, in which we aspired to take part, and which this dialectic promised to lead us towards, has fallen into discredit. In its place, what has come to the fore is the world history of Capital, of which the colonization of America, the imperialism of one side and the economic, political and cultural dependency of the other, as well as the class struggle, form integral parts. The dialectic between local, national, universal and other such terms has not, however, lost its usefulness. But its terms are redefined, and its promise of harmony disappears. Or, better, the harmony of this system seems to demand and to reproduce inequalities and alienations of all kinds, on an inconceivable scale, so great that it is difficult to imagine the damage being undone. In the light of this situation, which goes back to the 1930s, but which has been brought home to an ever greater number of Brazilians in the years since 1964, and which is certainly not the end of the process either, the past seems darker too: instead of a Brazilian contribution to the diversity of cultures, what comes to the fore is the history of national malformation, as an instance of the grotesque or catastrophic march of capital.[9] (So, with the appropriate mediations, national peculiarities find their place in a wider history, no longer as an original quality to be cultivated, but as aspects of a de facto disadvantaged situation in the international system.) In such circumstances, the definition of the national character of a literature or a writer cannot remain unaffected.

Machado did not share this perspective, since what he determinedly fought for was the creation of a national culture. But he was certainly not a creature of harmony. Carried along by the sense of Brazilian reality that he had, and attuned to the European *fin de siècle*, Machado did not look forward to the future with much enthusiasm. In his work, construction and destruction are intimately associated. A truly impressive quest for and invention of authentic Brazilian forms is accompanied by the ironic (and emphatic) affirmation of their arbitrary nature. Machado's novels are part of the construction of Brazilian literature, and of the destruction of forms to which the avant-garde everywhere was beginning to commit itself, as a part of the general crisis of bourgeois culture which was then beginning to appear. It is a combination which accurately reflects the situation of the country itself, which was trying to set itself up as a cultured nation at the moment when imperialist expansion was opening up a crisis in the idea of nationhood and within bourgeois civilization.

In *Quincas Borba*, the reader will find the 'local' and the 'universal', at every moment, side by side and quite distinct. Machado was not interested in their *synthesis*, but in their *disparity*, which was what seemed characteristic to him. Was this, to use his own words, one of the 'subjects offered to him by his own country'? In this cohabitation without harmony, in which we can see the key to a historical and cultural situation, each term makes the other look ridiculous. And actually, the very fact that these different levels are so emphatically fixed, to the extent that they constitute different historical levels, is already a comic resource, something like a mark of alienation. For example, comadre Angélica shelters a large variety of animals in her garden in Barbacena: birds, dogs, hens and cows – and a peacock.* However, in spite of the picturesqueness of the figure, this is a

---

*A 'comadre' is, literally, a godmother in relation to her godchild's parents: the word has some of the connotations of 'neighbour' and 'gossip' too. In the episode in question, Rubião suddenly realizes that, to be rid of it, he has given her the dog which is the condition of Quincas Borba's vast bequest. Naturally, he is anxious to have it back. Unaware of his panic, she shows him her menagerie:

Rubião went on; the comadre, instead of showing him the way, went with him. There

perfectly classical type of motivation for human conduct, and could be expressed in an abstract psychological theory – we could say that the owner is more interested in her peacock than in the sufferings of her neighbour. The theory is universal, but comadre Angélica is from Barbacena. The chapter's humour lies in the differing levels – and not in the harmony – of the general nature of the theory and the local detail of the character. What sense would there be in saying that the character has been universalized? And if there is no prospect of seeing the comadre as a universal figure, perhaps we can say that the presence of universality in a back garden in Barbacena represents an incongruity, which makes us laugh – but why? To Machado, as he meticulously constructed it, it was the incongruity that seemed meaningful.

Seen one by one, a good part of these incongruities are innocent enough, and all of them are amusing. But the whole is depressing. The profusion of life implied in the variety of social existence described is given no dynamism, for the jump, systematically repeated, to universalist considerations, hinders its movement. Since it is much more abstract – that is the reason for the disparity – reflection can only retain one aspect, and an arbitrary one at that, of the variety of aspects that description had presented us with. The description is thus lowered to the level of a trivial pretext for the reflection, and deprived of the meaning which would be present at its own level, or in its own logical continuation. Or, better, this deprivation is precisely what Machado wanted to denote. On the other side, seen in the light of the mimetic density, and of the vitality of the description, their very arbitrariness removes the authority of the flimsy reflections on universal themes: this removal of authority is something that Machado also wanted to convey. It is reciprocal removal, in fact. Description and reflection are a comedy duo, like the fat man and the thin man in the movies.

The impression of emptiness is powerful and clear-cut. All the same, it is difficult to define the area in which it operates, which is not obviously marked out. Even though it is a formal principle of Machado's novels, the curt transition between the local anecdote and its reflexive reworking on

---

was the dog, inside the enclosure, lying some way away from a bowl of food. Dogs and birds were jumping all around outside; on one side, there was a henhouse, a bit further away some pigs; further away still, there was a cow lying down, sleepily, with two chickens by it, pecking at its belly, grubbing for ticks.

'Look at my peacock!', the comadre was saying.

the universal level, excludes recourse to synthesizing terms. But it is in such terms – more general than the strictly local, less abstract than the universal – that the experience gained in reading should be made into a meaningful whole. We can say that the process is put in motion in literary terms, that it does operate in the course of reading, but it is not denoted, nor is it the object of reflection within the text. It is the reader who has to take the work on.

In other words, our hypothesis is that Machado's Brazilianness does not lie in the extraordinary thoroughness of the local observation that he undertook, though of course it depends on it, nor is it cancelled out by his universalist discourse, which is an important level of his work. These two dimensions, which are palpably present, combine with each other, and with yet other elements, in forms and formulae which relativize them, of which they constitute dissonant parts, and which in their turn do convey the 'intimate feeling of his time and country' that Machado refers to.

We can say that these forms and formulae are the literary transcription of real and decisive, though not obvious, aspects of the Brazilian historical process. As far as their subject goes, Machado's novels are aggressively arbitrary and futile. Their composition, however, fixes and explores rules, movements and opinions, which practical life in Brazil forced people into contact with. *Rules which are not common to the whole of humanity, nor matters of chance, but necessities imposed by Brazil's historical situation, and such as only reflection over many years could gather and give shape to.* On the level of the subject-matter and the surface form, Machado limited himself to the capricious, fragmentary randomness of the weekly newspaper column: on the level of the latent form, however, his novel imitates the structural necessity of the country as a whole. If it is possible to say it in this way, it gives a shape to our *logical* singularity.

Notes

1. Araripe Júnior, 'Sandices do ignaro Rubião' ['Ignorant Rubião's foolishnesses'], *Obra crítica*, MEC/Casa de Rui Barbosa, Rio de Janeiro 1960, vol. 2, p. 309.

2. Machado de Assis, 'Instinto de nacionalidade', *Obra completa*, Aguilar, Rio de Janeiro 1959, vol. 3, p. 817.

3. On this matter, see the definitive words of Antonio Candido in his *Formação da literatura brasileira*, Martins, São Paulo 1959, vol. 2, pp. 117-18.

4. 'Machado de Assis has shown disdain for the Brazilian people in almost all his work' (Silvio Romero, *Machado de Assis*, Laemmert, Rio de Janeiro 1897, p. 80).

5. 'He has a delicately literary quality, something elegant and Attic, which a barbarian is unable to see': Lafayette Rodrigues Pereira defending Machado's free, superior irony against the provincial demands of Silvio Romero (*Vindiciae* [1898], José Olympio, Rio de Janeiro 1954, p. 12). 'As a poet or a prose-writer, he is only concerned with the human soul. Among our writers, all of them with their attention more or less fixed on the picturesque, on the external aspects of things, all of them principally either descriptive or emotional, many indeed with their whole art taken up with description, and so condemned to be secondary, only he goes further and deeper, searching, under the surface of an easy contemplation and an equally easy narration, to discover the very essence of things. This is his other achievement, and perhaps the more important one'. (José Veríssimo, *História da literatura brasileira* [1916], José Olympio, Rio de Janeiro 1954, p. 350). At other moments, Veríssimo's position is different. In fact, at the price of some contradiction, he anticipated a large part of what critics would say in the following hundred years, almost.

6. Raymundo Faoro, *Machado de Assis: a pirâmide e o trapézio*, Nacional, São Paulo 1974.

7. The programmatic statement of this point of view was made by Machado de Assis himself, in the essay quoted above, 'O instinto de nacionalidade'. José Veríssimo takes up these same terms and applies them to their author's work, thus establishing the cliché view, which is true but not specifically defined, of the novelist who was both Brazilian and universal. This position was given greater depth by Lúcia Miguel-Pereira, in *Prosa de ficção* [1950], José Olympio, Rio de Janeiro 1973, and by Antonio Candido at several moments in his work.

8. There is an account of this development in Antonio Candido's *Formação da literatura brasileira*.

9. Cf. Antonio Candido, 'Literatura e subdesenvolvimento' ['Literature and under-development'], *Argumento* 1 (October 1973) Paz e Terra, Rio de Janeiro.

NINE

The Cart, the Tram and the

Modernist Poet

Oswald de Andrade invented an easy and poetically successful formula for looking at Brazil.* In this case the ease was not a defect, since it accorded with an argument put forward at the time, which said that the esoteric aura surrounding matters of the intellect was an obsolete, antidemocratic fog – at bottom, a fraud – which should be dissipated. When Lenin said that the state, once it had been revolutionized, would only need the skills of a good cook to administer it, he manifested a belief of the same kind. He was not underestimating the abilities of the people: rather, he was affirming that the

---

*Oswald de Andrade (1809-1954) was one of the most important leaders of the Brazilian Modernist movement, which began in São Paulo in the early 1920s. Generally regarded as its *enfant terrible*, he published novels, plays and (later) philosophical studies. Of particular relevance in the context of this article, he published two polemical tracts, the 'Manifesto of Brazilwood Poetry' in 1924, which was published as an introduction to the collection *Poesia Pau-Brasil (Brazil-wood Poetry)* from which the poem studied here, and the others quoted, are taken, and the *Manifesto antropófago*, published in 1928. In both, and more aggressively in the second, he argued (under the influence of the European avant-garde) for a poetry of simple vision ('Seeing with free eyes'), and for foreign influences to be 'cannibalized'. His standing was for many years a subject of polemics, but received an enormous boost in the 1960s and 1970s from the concretists, notably Haroldo de Campos. For a very useful and informative discussion, see Randal Johnson, 'Tupy or not Tupy: Cannibalism and Nationalism in Contemporary Brazilian Culture', in John King (ed.), *Modern Latin American Fiction: A Survey*, Faber and Faber, London 1987, pp. 41-59; for Campos' view, see 'The Rule of Anthropophagy: Europe under the Sign of Devoration', *Latin American Research Review* (Jan.-June, 1986), pp. 42-60.

irrationality and the complication of capitalism were becoming super-fluous; soon they would be replaced by a social organization without secrets, which would conform to good sense. The same kind of confidence in the materialist, subversive potential of the obvious (carefully chosen) can be found in Brecht's poetics. He proclaimed his intention of reducing his vocabulary to the everyday level of Basic English,[1] defended the timeliness of unsophisticated thought (*plumpes Denken*), and above all, constructed *artistic prototypes*, easy to imitate and play productive variations on, which, as is well known, have a central role in his theory of didactic theatre. He tried to bring theatre up to date by (a) incorporating into it the standard procedures characteristic of industrial manufacture, of scientific research, and of the class struggle (!!); (b) creating a modern way of giving the more demanding kind of culture a general appeal; and (c) attacking the worship of the *personal imprint* in artistic invention. Without ignoring the political and aesthetic differences between these three men, it is worth pointing to a certain common horizon of thought, dictated at the time by the general crisis of the bourgeois order, and by the radically democratic and antitraditionalist perspectives opened up by industrial progress.

Now that time has passed, neither the cultural landscape - nor the political one for that matter - appear to have become clearer, though both have certainly changed a great deal. At least for the time being, it certainly does not seem as if the historical process has moved in the direction of the libertarian objectives which inspired the political and artistic avant-gardes. So, these objectives, together with the energy they aroused, have ended up functioning as dynamic ingredients within a different kind of tendency: today, then, they can be understood as a kind of ideology, whose meaning should be thought through again. Not that they are simply pure illusion, especially if we think, as Adorno does, that the lies of ideology do not consist in expressing aspirations, but in saying that these same aspirations have been realized.[*] Something similar happened with Brazilian Modernism, which did not emerge unscathed either, and whose present-day success on the grand scale, in the media, has to do with its integration into the discourse of conservative modernization. In part this happened in spite of itself, in part it was the logical consequence of its own internal propensities.

---

[*]See Theodor Adorno, 'Cultural Criticism and Society', in *Prisms* (MIT Press, Cambridge, Mass. 1986), p. 32.

But let us return to Oswald's formula for the production of 'Brazil-wood' poetry. His raw material is obtained by two operations: the juxtaposition of elements characteristic of colonial Brazil with those of bourgeois Brazil, and the raising of the product of this juxtaposition – disjointed *by definition* – to the dignity of an allegory of the country as a whole. This is the basic unit with which he works. Note that this juxtaposition was something that could readily be observed in the day-to-day life of the country, long before it became an artistic effect, which gave a certain realistic foundation to the allegory: it also explains the irresistible force of Oswald's recipe, a real 'Columbus' egg' as Paulo Prado correctly said.[2] Our sociological reality continually set bourgeois and pre-bourgeois features side by side, in innumerable combinations, and it is still impossible to step outside your front door without coming across them. This duality has aroused varied reactions: its dilemmas go back to Independence, and since that moment they have inexorably imposed themselves on cultivated Brazilians; it may be no exaggeration to say that it has inspired the most important part of our literary tradition. A few years ago, Tropicalism gave us its post-64 version.[*] Machado de Assis looked at the question from an analytical angle, without forgetting the moral problems involved, as I hope to show in a work to appear soon.[**] The same subject-matter is present in the Naturalist novel, where the colonial world is joined with the exuberance of the Tropics – this latter seen as an aspect of the physical determinism dear to the movement – so that all hope of a well-ordered bourgeois existence is destroyed.[***] Gilberto Freyre, Sérgio Buarque de Holanda and Caio Prado Júnior also wrote their classic books on the topic[†], and it would be easy to lengthen the list.

---

[*] A movement of the late 1960s, centred on popular music. Its central figures are Caetano Veloso and Gilberto Gil, and their songs (e.g. 'Tropicália', 'Superbacana', 'Alegria, alegria') were aggressively avant-garde in their language and arrangements, juxtaposing ultra-modern and backward Brazil in the space of a couple of lines. They were supported by the concretists, in particular by Haroldo de Campos's brother, Augusto, in *Balanço da bossa e outras bossas* (1974): their initial impact coincided with the reevaluation of Oswald de Andrade by the same group, and with the hardening of the military regime in 1967-8, which gave a contemporary cutting-edge to their satire. See Charles Perrone, *Masters of Contemporary Brazilian Song 1965–1985*, University of Texas Press, Austin 1989, pp. 47–88.

[**] This work was published in 1990: *Um mestre na periferia do capitalismo: Machado de Assis* (Duas Cidades, São Paulo), 227 pp.

[***] On Brazilian Naturalism see note p. 94.

[†] Gilberto Freyre, *Casa-grande e senzala* (1933) [tr. *The Masters and the Slaves* (Knopf, New York 1964)]; Sergio Buarque de Holanda, *Raízes do Brasil* [The Roots of Brazil] (1936); and Caio Prado Júnior, *Formação política do Brasil* (1933).

With Oswald however, this theme, usually associated with our backwardness and failure as a nation, takes on a surprisingly optimistic, even a euphoric air: pre-bourgeois Brazil, almost innocent of puritanism and economic wiles, assimilates the advantages of progress in a judicious and poetic manner *and so prefigures post-bourgeois humanity*, unrepressed and fraternal; aside from this, it provides a positive platform from which to attack contemporary society. A kind of critical jingoism, if that doesn't seem too paradoxical.

Having said this, to define a poet one has to do more than describe his raw material. Apart from noticing the incongruous juxtaposition of things, and giving it the status of an unofficial national glory, or of a mini–maxi-aid to the understanding of the country, the Brazil-wood artist has to hit upon first-rate examples of it, clean them up, rearrange them, refine them, and so on. The focus of the invention is always on exposing the structure of the historical out-of-phaseness, something which can be achieved by the most surprising and unorthodox variety of formal means, all disciplined and highlighted by the simplicity of the elements used, by the search for a maximum brevity, by a certain cultivation of the accidental '*trouvée*', and of clean poetic lines. The freedom and the irreverence that Oswald operates with derive from the European aesthetic avant-garde, and in its turn the combination of anti-traditional style and essentially 'old-fashioned' materials brings into existence, in its way, the synthesis that each poem tries to capture.

Determined to establish the poet's seriousness, and counteract his reputation as a mere jokester, criticism has emphasized the similarity between Oswald's methods and the now classic innovations of the international avant-garde. Thus we have the well-known picture of the front-line modernist, the expert subverter of linguistic conventions, critical and revolutionary to the extent that this is what he does. However, the formal achievements of Brazil-wood poetry can also be analysed in another perspective, by looking at the material it tries to give shape to, a perspective which forces us to rethink it in a more specific historical light.[3] The figure of the artist revealed by such a study will be no less important, though it will be different. To give a correct example, let us look at a poem taken from 'Postes da Light',* a group homogeneously conceived – and very *paulista*, too.

---

*The phrase literally means 'telegraph poles' – the 'light' was a Canadian company which controlled a large part of the distribution of electricity in Brazil.

Pobre alimária	Poor brute
O cavalo e a carroça	The horse and the cart
Estavam atravancados no	Were stuck in the
trilho	tramline
E como o motorneiro	And as the driver
se impacientasse	was getting impatient
Porque levava os advogados	Because he was taking the lawyers
para os escritórios	to their offices
Desatravancaram o veículo	They extricated the vehicle
E o animal disparou	And the animal bolted
Mas o lesto carroceiro	But the light-footed carter
Trepou na boléia	Jumped onto his seat
E castigou o fugitivo atrelado	And punished the harnessed fugitive
Com um grandioso chicote	With a fearsome whip.[4]

The city in the poem is modern, since it has trams, and backward, since there is a horse and cart stuck in the tramlines. Another sign of modernity are the lawyers, though it is only a relative modernity – a tramful of legal men suggests a rather simple society, whose professional gamut remains idyllically, comically small. We shouldn't forget that progress really needs engineers, and that in this sense – as is true even today – the phalanx of solicitors is going the wrong way, pointing in the direction of 'the posh side, the erudite side, the one that quotes the right authorities' ('o lado doutor, o lado citações, o lado autores conhecidos').[5] The progress is undeniable, but its limited nature, which allows it to be placed in the same context as the backwardness in relation to which it can be defined as progress, is no less undeniable.

On the one side, the tram, the lawyers, the tram-driver and the rails; on the other, the horse, the cart and the carter: they are contrasting social classes, times and worlds, placed in opposition to one another. The victory of the tram is inevitable, but since the difference in size between the antagonists is not great, and they are both equally familiar presences, the confrontation has a kind of comic equilibrium. I hope I'm not pushing things too far by imagining that, in the rather reduced space of this sepia-tinted provincial photograph, something of the immobility of the one is transferred to the other.

The driver breaks the deadlock. He is playing on the modern side, and he takes its struggles to heart; but his origins must be on the other side. Under the sign of the imperfect subjunctive, a verb tense reserved for the erudite, his irritation ('E como o motorneiro se *impacientasse*') reflects his identification with those above him on the social scale, against his equals and inferiors. The anonymity that the subject of 'They extricated the vehicle' is relegated to – the 'they' would certainly be ordinary people who happened to be around – is due to the same self-important posture, which doesn't condescend to specify the help of third parties. In the process the cart itself changes category, and is raised to the level of a 'vehicle', a word which reminds one of the 'party' [elemento] of police parlance. In the opposing camp, with a no less fiery imagination, the carter is 'light-footed', in the style of ancient heroes, overshadowing whatever mediocre grandeur the impatience of a harmless flock of lawyers might have. However, the epic dimension fails to avoid a familiar Brazilianism, not correct in good Portuguese ('Trepou na boléia"), which casts an ironic light on this dimension itself, and confines it to the world of wounded sensibilities and imaginary compensations. From the pinnacle of his glory, the lordly carter judges and punishes the 'harnessed fugitive', who in the more compassionate title had appeared as the 'poor brute'. By means of this illuminating stylistic shift, the heroi-comic formula brings together ignorance, erudite echoes, and pretentiousness, all of which completes the analogy with his rival and opponent, whose subjunctive was only on loan anyway. On the one hand, there is a real opposition, since the climactic final whiplash is intended to prove that the carter isn't intimidated by tram-drivers, trams or lawyers – no one can teach *him* anything when it comes to courage. On the other, there is also a hierarchy and a social machine to which they all belong: sustained by the lawyers, the tram-driver takes it out on the carter, and the latter, sustained by an even more noble social principle (though also displaced) takes it out on the horse; and who is to say that the lawyers are not engaged in the same make-believe, pretentiously sustained, in their turn, by certificates, degrees and so on borrowed from more illustrious societies than their own? People, animals, things and places, as well as opposing each other, all in unison yearn for a superior form of society, somewhere less backward, where carts can be vehicles, tram-drivers respectable officials and where lawyers wouldn't have to suffer such contretemps. However, according to the paradox which is central to 'Brazil-wood' poetry, this exile is paradise.

---

*As will be plain here and at other moments in this article, the Brazilian version of Portuguese differs in marked ways from the Portuguese one, which was nevertheless regarded as the norm when Oswald was writing: the Modernists set out to reflect the spoken language in their writing, and to satirize obsession with 'correct' grammar and vocabulary.

Apropos of the difference between Germanic discipline and the easy-going Viennese, the story is told that a German asks for the time of a certain train, only to be shocked rigid when an Austrian replies that it 'is in the habit' of passing at such and such a time. The joke is in the gap between timetable and habit, and it reveals lack of spontaneity on the one hand, lack of adaptation to the modern world on the other. In Oswald's poem, if we examine the reasons which lead to the tracks being cleared, we find a sense of the comic with a similar basis. The reasons why it is done have nothing to do with public service, but lie in the temperament of the tram-driver, and that in its turn is due to the pleasure with which he represents the point of view, not of passengers in general, but of the lawyers and their offices. In other words, the operation of modernity is entirely integrated into the schemata of traditional patterns of authority, which, in their turn, are only too delighted to adopt the façade of new, impersonal ways of functioning. These serve as a way of conferring distinction and eminence on those who use them, rather than as a simple rule of action, something which makes the 'advanced' side of the opposition appear in an old-fashioned light. Symmetrically, the act that the carter puts on is intended partly for his own benefit, partly for the universe in general, but more than that for the lawyers, by whom he wants to be respected, and to whom he wants to give proof of his own worth – all of which hardly adds up to one world in radical opposition to another. The progressive side do not relinquish their backwardness, and the backward side, far from being convincedly retrograde, are no less in favour of a little 'progressive ray of sunshine' [sol-zinho progressista]:[6] all in all, a picture whose organizing features work in an unexpected way – one which we will return to – and which is funny.

The poem is made up of simple elements: the cart, the tramlines, the offices, etc., nouns in a raw state, deprived of the ration of suggestion and of music without which, for the fans of what had existed before this time, there was no such thing as poetry.* The deliberately rudimentary aspect of everything functions on several levels, and reflects the primitivist agenda of the avant-garde. As is well known, the latter asserted that aesthetic tradition had created a tissue of alienations and prejudices which had to be abolished so that reality could shine through. As soon as facts had been freed of the

---

*The state of poetry before the Modernist revolt was extraordinarily conventional and stuffy – the dominant school was still Parnassian, though Symbolism had made some mark. Its social incisiveness can perhaps be summed up best in the phrase 'o sorriso da sociedade' ('The smile on the face of society') used to define its role by Afrânio Peixoto.

crust of nineteenth-century psychological complexity and literary affectation, the reader would find the revitalized poetry of the senses, of intelligence and action: a different kind of poetry, founded on real desires, and opposed to the tormented and decadent subjectivity of the previous period. The less context the fact had, the more naked it was, the more complete the subject's freedom from restraint would be. And it is true, in this respect, that Oswald's poetry does bring to the forefront possibilities which the music of the verse and of subjective lyricism often blunt: he works so to speak at a distance from his object, with an experimental vigour, open to unexpected suggestions and varying his point of view. *The modernity of this attitude strikes one immediately*, none of which gets in the way of the divergent, or even opposing connotations contained within the poem. Thus, in spite of the mobility of the perspective and the compressed composition, both of which push the poem in a constructivist direction, the poet does not abandon his mimetic gift, something which he possessed to an extraordinary degree. Looking at the example we have chosen, the reader will see, I think, that the whole thing suggests an anecdote recounted from experience, whose narrator has the bluff, facetious tone of a *paulista* from the interior of the state* (the ideal avant-garde lyrical subject?) with a word for everything, preferably a familiar one, a bit blunt, the rail [*trilho*] in the singular, the lawyers and their offices in the all-embracing, vaguely deprecatory plural.

On the one hand, we have the down-to-earth register, calling a spade a spade, in which appearances don't deceive; on the other, the equally real, but by no means so abstemious desire to disparage or impress others, or in other words, to inflate appearances and so assert oneself. The cleansing away of all incidentals, signified by the near-absence of adjectives and syntactic links, aimed to free the new poetry of the flabby, redundant matter of everyday chatter, of useless personal details, of the perverse complicity between various twisted, compensatory desires to impress others. But what actually happens is that the concrete, noun-centred tone of the diction is associated with a veritable flood of these same alienations. The very obvious tension between these two things, rather than being a problem, is a real *trouvée*, which is perfectly integrated into Oswald's raw material: the active, liberated subject of avant-garde poetry exists alongside the generalized urge for recognition by our 'superiors', proper to an Ancien

---

*The author has in mind the *caipira*, the 'backwoodsman' or 'yokel' of the Brazilian countryside.

Régime of personal dependency, whose origins lie in the colonial period. Having said this, since by definition it exists in isolation, this same material has an affinity with the 'things-and-words-in-liberty' of modernist taste. But only up to a point, for the classificatory power of its formula – polarized in terms of archaism and progress, and with its aim of finding a definition of Brazilian national identity – is very great, and it frames and labels things which avant-garde procedures aimed to free. Isolated from their habitual connotations, or from their immediate practical context, there is no doubt that words, things and people take on the unhierarchized, almost toytown look that was one of the revelations of modern art. However, in Oswald's hands, this decontextualization only partly has this meaning. The resulting concretion [concreção] works in a paradoxical manner, because it also works in another register, as an *abstract* (!) term, or rather, as a quasi-sociological generality: a rail is a rail and nothing more, as well as being an integral part, easily replaceable of course, of an allegory and a quasi-theory of Brazilian national identity. The gently humorous atmosphere relativizes, but does not, I think, completely eliminate the intellectual precariousness of the status of the image – sensorial and patriotic, literal and allegorical, concrete and abstract. Seen from this angle, the similarity between Oswald's ingenuousness and the first cubist collages, Klee's doodles, Kafka's aimless creatures, in which modern art tried to free itself from any kind of connivance with conventional social values, is only there on the surface.[7] The undated, unlabelled world proposed by the Anthropophagy Manifesto in fact carries dates and labels, as is revealed by its subject-matter laid out according to historical cycles and permeated with national values; the ideological indifference which according to its own theory it possessed, and by means of which the European radicals tried to escape from the pressure of established hierarchies and identities, is transformed into a positive attribute of the Brazilian national character.

Again, more is specified in the poem than appears to be the case. The ostentatious subjunctive, the heroic gesture sabotaged by the uncultured expression, the work without any recognized subject, the pretentious term juxtaposed to the familiar one, the lawyers in their ever-so-slightly sarcastic plural, the rail in the singular: they are minimal deviations from the norm, but they have an internal consistency, very ingenious and unexpected, quite sufficient to raise the image of another existence behind the simplicity of the visible entities. A world of struggling resentments, of value-laden insecurities and ambiguities, of self-respect under tension, entirely opposed to the clean lines advertised in the composition. Extremely characteristic, the details reveal a contradictory society, studied and perceived in movement, in the manner of realist literature. Still, they also allude, by means of the dissonance they also contain, to the dual periodization of the Brazil-wood poetic, and in this case they function conventionally, as allegories of the bourgeois Brazil and its non-bourgeois counterpart. In their turn, the masterly succinctness of Oswald's '*trouvées*' carries with it the connotation of a livelier, sprightlier mode of existence. In miniature, this street scene looks like a summary of a realist novel, with its system of social inequalities and complex, devious feelings: but it still attracts us by its innocence, like one of *douanier* Rousseau's pictures; it works like a cut-out in an album of jingoist imagery.

So, the construction of the poem superimposes incongruous co-ordinates, whose clashes are a direct challenge to historical awareness: avant-garde art versus provincial resentment; cart Brazil versus office Brazil; a rudimentary individualism versus patriotic allegories or the cult of subjectivity. These are oppositions with real weight which, however, because of a strategic effect of the composition, do not carry that much importance, nor do they seem to constitute a problem. We can say, for example, taking up a previous argument once more, that the self-important impulses of the tram-driver and the carter might make us think of a hardened world, one of humiliations, insults and imagined compensations, incompatible in principle with the candid transparency which the poem aspires to, where everything is in the foreground. It so happens however, that, contrary to expectations, these resentments do not disturb the state of innocence of things and people – they are truly integrated into it. That is where the magic trick is: subjectivity is reduced to a minimal mechanism with no secrets, and takes on the aspect of something exterior, so to speak, one object among others, as simple and as palpable as the objects themselves.[8] We have seen that the demand for a grain of fantasy is the common denominator shared by the driver's obstinacy, the furious gesture of the carter, the lawyers' punctuality, the promotion of the 'poor brute' to an epic creature, etc. There's nothing more familiar, more comprehensible, everyday, or comic: *these are our little local foibles* – all we want to do is the right thing: everything else is just fine. 'Would you give me a cigarette / says the grammar / of the teacher and the pupil / and the pushy mulatto / but the good black and the good white / of the Brazilian Nation / say every day / lay off the posh stuff mate / and give us a ciggy'.[9] The element of condescension in this charmed vision of Brazil is huge, and was noticed straight away by Mário de Andrade, who wasn't free of it either.[10] Seen from the other end of the telescope, life looks like one of Tarsila's* drawings, where men, animals and things all move around under an affectionate, tender and diminutive star. This distance, which allows one to pass real conflicts by and envelop the warring sides in the same embrace, is, naturally, itself a point of view.

To characterize it in its social and historical dimension, let us go back, on a more abstract plane, to the terms of the composition itself. Some pages back, we saw that the poem makes fun of a backward version of progress, which, in order to take shape, depends on the presence of another, more advanced kind of progress. This latter makes itself felt within the literary effects themselves, whose formal freedom clashes ironically with the tenuous modernism of the duties of the driver and the lawyers, at the same time as it asserts quite plainly how up-to-date it is, how in keeping with recent European transformations. This dissonance, which is decisive for Oswald's poetry, is primarily the distance between the conservative adoption of a few improvements and the revolutionary radicalism of the twentieth century, which at that time seemed to have no limits. It was natural that in the light of this latter point of view, up-to-date, adventurous, cosmopolitan and above all very *superior*, the parties in the tram and the cart should look a great deal more like equals than enemies. Thus, the emptying out of the antagonism between the colonial and (backward) bourgeois elements, along with the disregard for their subjective content, are caused by a distance which is internal to the poem, and which is, in turn, a transposition of the distance between the local and the universal models for progress. Surprisingly, the result is positive: the suspension of the conflict and its transformation into a picturesque contrast, where none of the terms is negative, goes together with this choice as a symbol of Brazil, a choice which, along with the practice of avant-garde artistic procedures, is among the *prerogatives* of the superiority, of the advanced cast of mind that we are trying to characterize. Therefore, modernity does not consist in breaking with the past or in dissolving it, but in purifying its elements and arranging them within a contemporary – and, of course, a very inventive – perspective. It's as if they were saying, right from up there where they are: 'this is what my country's like.'[11] It is a bright, cheerful lyricism, where everything has a technical solution, at the opposite pole from self-analysis,

---

*Tarsila do Amaral (1886–1973), painter, at one time married to Oswald, and who adopted an innocent primitivism in her painting in the 1920s.

or from any expression or transformation of the subject (whether individual or collective).

In a study of *Macunaíma*,[*] attempting to place the book historically, Carlos Eduardo Berriel links the nationalism of the modernist movement in 1922 to the sector of the coffee oligarchy which, as well as planting, contended with imperialist capital for the control of the marketing of the product, the most profitable part of the business. The argument goes beyond the well-known proximity of the modernists and some of the families of the large plantation-owners:[**] it suggests a certain correspondence between Mário's aesthetic and the accumulated experience of a class which (a) was guided by its own point of view in the area of large international interests (coffee at one stage was the largest item of international commerce *in the whole world*); (b) together with this indisputable cosmopolitan up-to-dateness, was conservative in the domestic sphere, since the persistence of export monoculture, with the labour relations it implied, was the basis for its national pre-eminence, and its ability to participate at an international level; (c) looked on the 'agricultural vocation'[***] of the country as an element of progress and modernity, to which other manifestations of modernity would and ought to be able to subordinate themselves quite harmoniously; and (d) soared far above the defensive, clumsy conservatism of the rest of the wealthy oligarchy of the country.[12] I haven't the historical knowledge to evaluate these hypotheses with any precision (the anything but straightforward relations between coffee cultivation and industrialization have become a matter for specialists), but I think that this outline helps us to understand Brazil-wood poetry, and illuminates the connections we have been dealing with up to now. Before going on, there's no harm in saying that a poet is none the worse or better for giving literary form to the experience of an oligarchy: everything depends on the working out and the elucidatory

---

[*]An (anti-) nationalist novel (actually defined as a 'Rhapsody') published by Mário de Andrade in 1928. In it, Mário created a highly original language, using neologisms and terms from all over Brazil to tell the story of his 'hero without a character', in his vain search for an identity. There is an English translation: *Macunaíma*, Quartet, London 1984/Random House, New York 1984.

[**]Paulo Prado, for instance, who prefaced Oswald's *Poesias reunidas*, was a member of one of the most powerful coffee families: some of the group met in the house of another, Dona Olívia Penteado.

[***]The phrase that Brazil was 'an essentially agricultural country' was a frequently repeated one, often used in the nineteenth century in defence of slavery.

power of his compositions. It is not a matter of reducing art to its social origins, but of making explicit its ability to formalize, explore and carry to revealing limits the possibilities of a practical historical situation; without placing the poem in history, there is no way of reading the history which is condensed and given power within it, and which constitutes its value. We all know today that the hegemony of the coffee growers and exporters had no future and ended with the 1929 crash, but naturally this does not detract from Oswald's poetry, which is still alive.

Oswald himself more than once referred to the 'fertilizing, material causes' of Modernism, 'drawn from the industry of São Paulo, with its class links to the bourgeois golden age of the first boost in coffee prices'.[13] The relationship between the two appears very neatly in 'aperitivo', where 'Happiness is sauntering / on Antônio Prado Square / it's ten o'clock blue / coffee's as high as the skyscraper morning / Tietê cigarettes / automobiles / morning without myths'.[14] The modern (and idealized) plenitude of sensations, free of sin, superstition or conflict, the pleasure in seeing and being seen, so characteristic of the innocence cultivated by Oswald, are riding on the wave of the prosperity brought by coffee. They are a product of power – something which qualifies their ingenuousness, but does not entirely negate it. Economic privilege does not remove poetic power from the insouciance that it provides the space for: the wealth of the saunterer is suggestive, and gives to his contentment something of the fragile feeling of winning the lottery (after all, the price of coffee might go down).[15]

Another of Oswald's peculiarities is the total absence of nostalgia in his delineation of people and objects from the past (the contrast with the Northeasterners, linked to the decadence of the sugar-producing region, is instructive in this regard).* From the technical point of view, this effect is due to an avant-garde, anti-sentimental preference for pure presence, as opposed to temporal depth and other similar relationships. However, what sustains this, in the background, is the future that coffee was thought to have ahead of it, which made the universe of quasi-colonial labour relations that it maintained and recreated appear not as an obstacle in its path, but as a part of life and progress, and moreover, since that was the way things were, of a progress more picturesque and humane than others, since

---

*The most notable novelist who typifies this nostalgic view of the plantation past is José Lins do Rego (1901–57), whose 'Sugar-cane cycle' novels (e.g. *Menino de engenho* [1933] [*Plantation Boy*, 1966]) are highly influenced by the ideas of Gilberto Freyre.

neither side was condemned to disappear. *We could say that Oswald's poetry was chasing the mirage of an innocent progress.*

For the provincial-modern, the totally modern and the archaic to reach an accommodation, they have to meet. The places invented by Oswald for their reconciliation, a kind of public arena, are finds in themselves. It can be the whole country of Brazil, divided down the middle by a train, like an empty space by a meridian;[16] it can be 'atavistic fields', full of 'Elections, tribunals and settlers';[17] or the abstract territory of grammar, where good Brazilian folk, without discrimination between black and white, though with a side-swipe at mulattoes, defeat Lusophile pedantry and put the personal object pronoun in the 'wrong' place – i.e. the right one.[18] In 'bonde', 'Postretutes and famirries are shaken', all mixed up together, quite against their will, jolted about by the verse-form and by the mockery of the cosmopolitan poet.[19] The situation in the poems set in the big city is, in addition, more complex. The modern ingredients are more diversified: tramlines, the Anhangabaú viaduct, the Luz Garden, a pervert in some park, the street photographer, chauffeurs held up by the passage of a procession, the 'berlites' school, Tarsila's studio, football posters, the author's bachelor flat, the Jockey Club, and so on. A wide-ranging album, as one can see, with scenes from every kind of social space. The common denominator is in a certain accommodating progressivism, operating outside normal rules, which is just the element of charm and above all of (national) identity aimed at. It goes a little bit up market when Tarsila is around, a little bit the other way in other contexts. It is interesting that the atmosphere gets denser in the street scenes and in those that take place in public places: there, when members of the lower classes are present, the general unpredictability, the tendency to be law-abiding in spite of everything, and the desire to progress – which in a Jockey Club meeting is just snobbery – make a moving and very interesting combination.[20]

The inventive and distanced use of poetic form seems to place Oswald unambiguously on the critical side of the coin. And it is true that, whenever the target is some kind of official rigidity, the break with convention does have this effect. However, the preference for a certain kind of informality can be ideology too, and can even be a guarantee of national identity, as I have tried to show. With the literary tools most radically opposed to illusion, or, to use Walter Benjamin's term, to 'aura',* Oswald tried to

---

*For this notion, see Benjamin, 'The Work of Art in the Age of Mechanical Reproduction', in *Illuminations* (Schocken, New York 1969), pp. 221–3.

manufacture and 'auratize', so to speak, the myth of the unofficial country, a myth which is no less private property for all that, We all know that Brecht's de-identifying techniques are used on television to make us identify with washing-powders. Just because that is so, it is interesting to see that, already when they were invented, when their corrosive effect would be strongest, these processes on their own were not enough to avoid ambiguities.

Short though it may be, 'poor brute', is a story. About half-way through, the poem has a moment of deliberate awkwardness, on which its effect depends. Up to that point, and from it to the end, the narrative advances by pairs, at the rate of one action every two lines, which demands of each action that it have some kind of importance and extension. The lines in the middle break this norm: in one, the unnamed 'they' 'extricate the vehicle'; and in the next, 'The animal bolted'. To link the two, there is the non-specific conjunction 'and', which accentuates the disparity, as well as a certain equivalence between the subjects – 'they' and the animal – and between their actions. Because it is harnessed – if we can put it that way – the runaway horse throws the unpredictable side of the carter's life into relief. In parallel fashion, we can see how precarious the varnished world of the lawyers is. Notice too that the whip re-establishes order, not because it prevents further traffic obstructions, but because it puts the economy of self-respect back into balance, above a social split which is quite unchanged.

The Brazil-wood programme wanted to take Brazil out of a state of irrelevance. To do this, it attempted to give it an enhanced presence, and an original position, in the history of humanity. That is why there is constant play with cardinal reference points, some very prestigious indeed on the map of world culture, others much less so (which goes to show the difficulty of the undertaking): industry, the jungle, Rui Barbosa, carnival, the blue Cabraline sky, Wagner, vatapá, the exchange rate, Paolo Uccello's perspectives, Maricota reading the paper, etc.* In 'versos baianos', for example, the same waters on which can be seen a balsa-wood fishing-boat [*jangada*] with 'dark-skinned men / with straw hats' were also 'the battlegrounds / of the Renaissance', the 'crowded rendez-vous / of Dutch

---

*Rui Barbosa: a Liberal politician and minister, for satirical purposes the incarnation of oratorical pomposity; Cabraline: of Pedr' Alvares Cabral, the discoverer of Brazil; vatapá: a spicy fish or chicken stew, typical of Bahia; 'Maricota reading the newspaper' appears because the conjunction of the traditional housebound young girl and the paper is itself surprising, a sign of modernity.

of Counts and of Priests' and are now perfect 'for the landings / of the hydroplanes of my century'.[21] This procedure aims at bringing together elements which a colonialist ideology, and above all its interiorization by the victims of colonization, separate into distinct compartments. Oswald is trying to do nothing less than achieve a reciprocity between local experience and the culture of the 'central' countries, as is shown by the demand for a poetry capable of being exported, and which will break the routine of one-sided importation. The critical, transformatory value of this project, and the felicitousness of its ambitious formulations, even now makes the Modernists a most salutary presence. Even so, it's clear to me that the irreverent use of famous names, dates and ideas is no less a kind of inverted reverence for all that. It is a rather precarious way of making up for the lack of density of the object, a lack which reflects, on the cultural plane, the silencing inherent in the one-sidedness of colonial, then later imperialist relations, and inherent too in the system of class domination in the ex-colonies themselves. As is well known, the resultant lack of substance and complexity of their native subject-matter is the torment of artists in such countries, but to keep a sense of proportion it is worth remembering that Machado de Assis had already overcome this disadvantage with paramount skill in the previous century. Changing the angle, we can see how the modernist taste for pure presence pushed the dimension of the relation between people onto a secondary level, suppressing, in a certain sense, their conflictive and negative sides.[22] We have also seen the correspondence between this aesthetic and the conservative progressivism of the cosmo-politan coffee bourgeoisie. Articulated in this way, the *parti pris* of ingenuousness and 'seeing with free eyes'[23] has something in it of a decision not to see, or rather, to forget what any reader of a naturalist novel knew perfectly well. That is why the *trouvées* of Oswald's innocent mode pay for their fullness – of itself a very remarkable thing – with a certain admixture of unreality and childishness. But since Oswald is a great and a very astute artist, he got hold of counterweights to his decision to place our provincialism and our dreadful rural oppression into the 'present of the universe'[24] – and all this, under an aggressively positive star!: he gave everything a certain air of jokiness. It is in this latter quality, once the complex situation to which it responds is taken into account, that the real truth about Brazil-wood poetry, one of the really important moments in Brazilian literature, can be found.

Notes

1. The comparison between the laconic, objective manners of Oswald and Brecht was noticed by Haroldo de Campos: cf. 'Uma poética da radicalidade', introduction to Oswald de Andrade, *Poesias reunidas*, Civilização Brasileira, Rio de Janeiro 1974, p. 21.

2. Paulo Prado, 'Poesia pau-brasil', also in Oswald de Andrade, *Poesias reunidas*, p. 67.

3. '... we all know of the role that primitive art, folklore, and ethnography had in the defining of modern aesthetics, which paid a great deal of attention to archaic and popular elements repressed by academic conventions. Well, in Brazil primitive cultures are present in everyday life, or are living memories of a recent past. The daring shocks administered by Picasso, Brancusi, Max Jacob or Tristan Tzara at bottom fitted our cultural heritage better than theirs.' Antonio Candido, 'Literatura e cultura de 1900 a 1945', Nacional, São Paulo 1965, pp. 144-5.

4. Oswald de Andrade, *Poesias reunidas*, p. 120.

5. Oswald de Andrade, 'Manifesto da poesia pau-brasil', *Do pau-brasil à antropofagia e às utopias*, Civilização Brasileira, Rio de Janeiro 1978, p. 5.

6. 'escala', *Poesias reunidas*, p. 148.

7. For the affinity between Kafka's prose, Klee's scrawls and Webern's music, see Theodor Adorno, 'Anton von Webern', *Klangfiguren*, Suhrkamp, Frankfurt 1959, pp. 178-9.

8. Another aspect of this objectivism can be seen in the astonishing 'capacity for photographing stupidity' that Mário acknowledged in Oswald. Cf. Mário de Andrade, 'Osvaldo de Andrade' (1924), in Maria Rosseti Batista, Telê Porto Ancona Lopez, Yone Soares de Lima (org.), *Brasil: 1° Tempo Modernista*, IEB, São Paulo 1972, pp. 222-3.

9. 'pronominais', *Poesias reunidas*, p. 125.

10. 'Pau-brasil is a condescending, vague label meaning illuminatingly for us the necessity for national identity', Mário de Andrade, 'Oswald de Andrade: Pau-Brasil', *Brasil: 1° Tempo modernista*, p. 231.

11. 'Let us now again be, to carry out our ethnic and protective mission, jacobinistically Brazilian', Paulo Prado, 'Poesia pau-brasil', *Poesias reunidas*, p. 69.

12. Carlos Eduardo Berriel, *Dimensões de Macunaíma: filosofia, gênero e época*, MA thesis, UNICAMP, 1987, pp. 28-35. I have adapted the argument a little for my purposes. When he analyses the policy of pushing up the price of coffee, carried out by the ruling elite of the period, Celso Furtado points out its 'exceptional daring' as well as its long-term impracticality. *Formação econômica do Brasil*, Fondo de Cultura, Rio de Janeiro 1959, p. 213.

13. Oswald de Andrade, 'O caminho percorrido ['The journey so far'], *Ponta de lança*, Civilização Brasileira, Rio de Janeiro 1972, p. 95.

14. 'aperitivo', *Poesias reunidas*, p. 126.

15. On the 'bourgeois' impression made by the São Paulo modernists on the rest of Brazil, see Drummond's article on Mário in *Confissões de Minas*: Carlos Drummond de Andrade, 'Suas cartas' ['His letters'], *Poesia e prosa*, Aguilar, Rio de Janeiro 1979, p. 930. On the mixture of *paulista* modernism, European avant-garde and haute bourgeoisie, see the numerous observations of Alexandre Eulálio, 'A aventura brasileira de Blaise Cendrars', in the book of the same title, Quiron, São Paulo 1978.

16. 'noturno', *Poesias reunidas*, p. 98.

17. 'prosperidade', *ibid.*, p. 98.

18. 'pronominais' ['Uses of the pronoun'], *ibid.*, p. 125.

19. 'bonde' ['Tram'], *ibid.*, p. 106.

20. The class alliances which took place in the literature of the modernist period were new, and it would be worthwhile to compare the different authors in this regard. Studying

the elements which went to form the characteristic tone of Manuel Bandeira, Davi Arrigucci Jr calls attention to the importance of the poor lodgings and areas of the city inhabited by the poet, which were transformed into imaginary spaces where illness, solitude, European symbolist poetry and the process of coming down in the world socially are blended with the life style of the lower classes of Rio. Davi Arrigucci Jr, 'O humilde cotidiano de Manuel Bandeira', in *Enigma e comentário*, Companhia das Letras, São Paulo 1987, pp. 9–28.

21. *Poesias reunidas*, p. 148.

22. Commenting on the relationship between the human figure and the background in the *nationalist* painting of Tarsila, Gilda de Mello e Souza writes: 'the simplification imposed on the secondary elements, so that they fit in to the stylization of the whole, did not essentially alter the nature of the fruits, the birds, the boats; but the same technique applied to a black lad removed dignity from him, and made the whole thing look decorative in the manner of a poster advertisement'. See 'Vanguarda e nacionalismo na década de vinte', *Exercícios de leitura*, Duas Cidades, São Paulo 1980, pp. 268–9.

23. 'Manifesto da poesia pau-brasil', p. 9.

24. 'It's well known that a group of young Brazilians has tried to shake Brazil out of the artistic apathy it lived in, bringing the national consciousness right up to date with what is going on in the universe', Mário de Andrade, 'Osvaldo de Andrade', p. 223.

TEN

Culture and Politics in Brazil,

1964-1969

NOTE (1978): *The following pages were written between 1969 and 1970. It will be readily observed that their prognosis was incorrect, which hardly argues in their favour. Nevertheless, I believe that there is something to be gained from reading the rest of the material, until someone convinces me otherwise. Of course, one is always tempted to rewrite the passages that have been proved false by time and events. But why should one replace the errors of the past with the opinions of the present day when the latter are just as likely to be as mistaken as the former? Given the choice, the mistakes made by a contemporary observer are always more interesting. Especially so in my case, since the social analysis that was being made was not intended as a scientific study as such, but as an attempt to capture and explain the collective experience of a generation with reference to a given historical moment. Rather, I was attempting to give a literary account of a contemporary situation, in as much as I was capable of doing so at the time. So when I say now, the observations, mistakes and judgements of the period in question must be allowed to speak for themselves. The reader will see that things have changed, but not that much.*

In 1964 the military seized power in Brazil in order to protect capital and the continent of Latin America from the threat of socialism. Goulart's populist government, despite the huge mobilization of left-wing forces it had undertaken, was fearful of the class struggle and backed down at the prospect of civil war. As a result, the triumph of right-wing elements was able to take the usual route of an agreement amongst generals. This time the people, mobilized but unarmed and unorganized, could only look on passively as the change of government took place. It soon felt the consequences: interference and terrorization in the unions; terror in rural areas; a general reduction in wages; purges, especially in the lower ranks of the Armed Forces; a military investigation in the universities; churches were broken into; student organizations were dissolved; censorship prevailed; *habeas corpus* was suspended, etc.

However, to everyone's surprise, the cultural presence of the left was not suppressed during this period, rather it has continued to flourish and grow to this day. The works produced by the left dominate the cultural scene, and in certain areas their quality is outstanding. *Despite the existence of a right-wing dictatorship, the cultural hegemony of the left is virtually complete.* This can be seen in the bookshops of São Paulo and Rio, which are full of Marxist literature; in incredibly festive and feverish theatrical premières, threatened by the occasional police raid; in the activities of the student movement or the declarations of progressive priests. In other words, at the very altars of bourgeois culture, it is the left which dictates the tone. This anomaly – which is now being threatened by the extremely severe penalties that the dictatorship has decreed against those involved in socialist propaganda – is the most obvious characteristic of the Brazilian cultural scene between 1964 and 1969. As well as an indication of class struggle, it is evidence of a commitment.

Before looking at its effects, it is essential that the nature and context of this hegemony be determined. The dominance of the left appears to be concentrated in the groups which are directly involved in ideological production, such as students, artists, journalists, some sociologists and economists, the rational sectors of the clergy, architects, etc. – but it does not extend beyond these groups, nor can it, because of the police. Brazilian intellectuals are left-wing, but the materials they prepare for government commissions and for the representatives of capital on the one hand, and for national newspapers and radio and television stations on the other, are not. The only truly radical material produced by this group is for its own consumption – which is in itself a substantial market. This situation became crystallized in 1964, when, in general, socialist intellectuals were spared the imprisonment, unemployment and exile they had been expecting. The only ones who were tortured and given long prison sentences were those who had organized meetings with workers, farm-labourers, seamen and soldiers. Having broken the links between the cultural movement and the masses, the Castelo Branco government made no attempt to prevent the circulation

of doctrinal or artistic left-wing material, which flourished to an extraordinary extent, albeit within a restricted area. With its ups and downs,
this ingenious solution lasted until 1968, when a new group, capable
of supplementing their ideology with practical strength, emerged: the
students, who were organized in a semi-clandestine manner. During the
previous four years, at the same time as they frequently complained about
their confinement and their impotence, left-wing intellectuals had been
studying, teaching, publishing, filming, discussing, etc., and without
realizing it had contributed towards the creation, within the petit-
bourgeoisie, of a massively anti-capitalist generation. The social importance
of this radical band of the population, and its readiness to become involved
in the class struggle, could be seen in, among other things, the actions of the
groups who took up arms in the cause of revolution. The regime's response,
in December 1968, was one of severe suppression. In 1964 it had been
possible for the right to 'preserve' cultural expression, since it had only been
necessary to eliminate all contacts with the working masses in cities and
rural areas; in 1968, when students and those who enjoyed the best films,
the best theatre, the best music and the best books had become a politically
dangerous group, it would become necessary for teachers, producers,
authors, musicians, books, publishers to be replaced or censored – in other
words, the active culture of the moment would have to be eliminated. The
government has already taken several steps in this direction, and who
knows how many more they will take. As far as the destruction of
universities is concerned, it can already boast significant achievements:
Brasília, São Paulo and Rio, the three largest in the country.

In order to understand the nature, the implantation and the ambiguities
of this hegemony, one needs to go back to its origins. Before 1964, the
socialism which had spread throughout Brazil was strong in its anti-
imperialism but weak in the propaganda and organization of the class
struggle. This was due, in part at least, to the strategy of the Communist
Party, which argued in favour of an alliance with the national bourgeoisie.
As a result, a toothless, parliamentary version of patriotic Marxism
emerged, an ideological complex which spoke of both combat and
conciliation. Such an approach fitted in well with the nationalist populism
that was dominant at the time, whose original labourist ideology was losing
ground. Conciliation prevailed within the workers' movement, with the
Communist Party exercising its influence among the unions in order to
keep the struggle limited to the question of wage claims. Combat was
reserved for the struggle against foreign capital, for foreign policy and

agrarian reform. The whole package was tailor-made for the populist bourgeoisie, who were looking for socialist terminology in order to intimidate right-wing landowners, and for nationalist feeling, authenticated by the left, so they could implant noble sentiments in the workers. One ought not, of course, to conclude that populism was created by the Communist Party; rather it was populism which had consolidated a tendency whose huge practical success within the Party would render it invulnerable to the left, as we shall see. Once this union was consummated, the division of the spoils immediately became problematic. Nowadays all of this seems obvious. Nevertheless, it was a complex which occupied first place in the minds of Brazilian theorists, whether in the face of psycho-sociological theories on the 'national character', which were already anachronistic at the time; or of the simplistic nationalism of modernization, unaware of its own contradictions; or of Christian imitations of Marxism, which interpreted imperialism and capital in terms of personal autonomy and alienation; or, finally, in the face of rival Marxisms, banging tirelessly away to the tune of classical Leninism, content to voice their habitual abstract refusal of a populist commitment.

The strong point of this stance, which would eventually reach the masses and deepen their political awareness of patriotism, lay in demonstrating that imperialist domination and internal reaction were linked, that one could not be changed without the other. Given the political climate of the period, the repercussions of such a hypothesis were enormous. Anti-imperialist literature was translated on a huge scale and newspaper columns were filled with feverish articles. This was the age of Brasilino, a character who, throughout an entire booklet, could not lift a finger without encountering some aspect of imperialism. When he switched on the light in the morning, the power was provided by Light & Power Inc. As he travelled to work on a General Motors bus, he would be using Esso petrol. The sausages he ate at lunch were courtesy of Swift & Armour, etc. For the price of one cruzeiro, *Os Cadernos do Povo* [*The People's Notebooks*], for their part, would report at length on the manoeuvring that went on in the petroleum market, on the relationship between *latifundios* and endemic diseases, on questions of agrarian reform, besides discussing who should be regarded as 'the people' in Brazil, etc. The country was in a state of excitement, and its options in the face of world history were the daily bread of those who read the main newspapers. It was a period in which both the vocabulary and the political logic of the left became acclimatized to everyday speech, which was itself losing its provincial aspect. This gave rise to a certain degree of abstraction and a specific rapidity in modern films and the theatre, in which world options arise every 20 seconds and for the slightest of reasons. The results are sometimes disastrous and sometimes extremely funny, but always there is the desire to consider particular questions in the light of their historical consequence, or a caricature of the same. When the lover in one theatrical work[1] can say to his girlfriend, who is proving to be insufficiently Marxist in the face of their family complications: 'generalize, dammit!' – evidently, these are times in which popular enlightenment occupies the podium.

But let's get back to the main point. If the Communist Party could be commended for increasing people's awareness of the link between imperialism and internal reaction, the way in which this connexion was particularized was the major failing of their strategy and would lead to the disastrous events of 1964. The Party was far more anti-imperialist than it was anti-capitalist and, within the ruling classes, distinguished between a retrograde, pro-American agrarian sector and a national and progressive industrial sector, allying itself with the latter against the former. Undoubtedly, this opposition did exist, but not to the extent that was claimed, and it would never be as great as the opposition between the land-owning class, en bloque, and the danger of communism. And while the Communist Party believed in its alliances, transforming them into a vast ideological and doctrinal movement, they were never believed in by the bourgeoisie. Consequently, on the eve of civil war it was ill-prepared for the conflict. *This mistake has been at the centre of Brazilian cultural life since 1950*, and has enjoyed a lasting success in practical terms. Herein lies the difficulty. And no left-wing critic has been able to destroy the myth, since the past appeared to speak in its favour. Goulart was predictably establishing closer and closer links with the Communist Party, whose influence and popularity were on the increase. But the only thing that could not have been anticipated in any practical way, since any precautions taken in this area would have upset the 'favourable' disposition of the president, was the military *dénouement*. In the circumstances, it was entirely logical that the Communist Party should have reached the threshold of revolution trusting in the military intentions of the President of the Republic. In other words, its mistake was founded on some very convincing appearances.

At the time, the expression and application of this mistaken view of things constituted the raw material of left-wing criticism and apologetics. In brief, the argument was as follows: the main ally of imperialism, and therefore the major enemy of the left, were the archaic aspects of Brazilian society. These consisted basically of the *latifundio* system, against which the people, i.e. all those interested in the progress of the country, should rebel. On an economic and political level, therefore, an explosive but fundamentally bourgeois problematic arose concerning modernization and democratization. To be more precise, it had to do with the expansion of the internal market by means of agrarian reform, within the framework of an independent foreign policy. On an ideological level, we were introduced to an apologetic and sentimentalizable notion of 'the people', which embraced (and without distinction) the working masses, the lumpenproletariat, the intelligentsia, the financial barons and the army. The metaphor of this salad can be seen in the huge parties of the time, recorded by Glauber Rocha in *Terra em Transe*, [*Land in Anguish*] where the wives of capitalists, samba, capitalists themselves, diplomats of socialist countries, army progressives, left-wing Catholics and priests, Party intellectuals, torrential poets and other patriotic folk would rub shoulders, some in formal dress, others in blue jeans. In other words, having laid to one side all thought of the class struggle and the confiscation of capital, Marxism was left with no more than a rosy hue which worked in the interest of some sectors (the industrial bourgeoisie? the state bureaucracy?) of the ruling classes. And indeed, it was in this form that it became part, to a greater or lesser degree, of the ideological arsenal of Vargas, Kubitschek, Quadros and Goulart. Thus, the populist deformation of Marxism in Brazil was inextricably linked with power (particularly so during the Goulart administration, when it became the confessed ideology of important government figures), multiplying the *quid pro quos* and establishing itself to the extent where it became the very ideological atmosphere of the nation. Its problems were reflected in various ways by sociologists, theologians, historians, in the cinema, theatre, in popular music and architecture, etc. However, this implantation also had its commercial aspect – an important feature when one considers its subsequent survival – since the material produced by the left became big business and in a very few years transformed the face of publishing and the arts in Brazil.

However, although during this phase socialist ideology was actually helping to resolve the problems of capitalism, each moment of impasse brought about a gradual turning of the tide. The masses would riot in order to exert pressure on the landowning members of Congress who, fearfully, would react by approving measures for bourgeois modernization, with particular emphasis on agrarian reform. But Congress as a whole would not correspond, and the right, unlike the extremely moderate populists of the left, raised the spectre of socialization. Gradually, then, due to the very scale of official popular campaigns, and to their failure, there arose the growing conviction that it would not be possible to implement the necessary reforms in Brazil within the confines of capitalism and, therefore, of populism. Though somewhat diluted, this conclusion had the same vast ambit as government propaganda itself. It was adopted by government committees, teams of experts, students and the *avant-garde* of the working class, who immediately, in the face of the military coup of 1964, questioned not so much Marxism itself as the application that had been made of it by the Communist Party.

This scenario also helps explain something of the character and social position of a part of Brazilian Marxism. In a country which is dependent but committed to its own development, where capitalization is weak and the government is entrepreneurial, all ambitious initiatives are made via some kind of contact with the State. This mediation provides the vanguard of the various sectors of initiative with a national (and paternalistic) perspective, and their theoreticians would discover that their relationship with the state already contained fundamental difficulties, in the form of limits imposed upon it by imperialist pressure and, soon, by the framework of capitalism itself. This applies to cultural activity as a whole (education included) which lacks resources; it applies to public administration as well as to key areas in the private sector; and, to be a little more specific, it even applied to individual Brazilian capitalists and to army officers. Thus, the main feature of Marxist criticism was a nationalism that was, then, anti-imperialist and anti-capitalist minus the contact with the problems of the masses that one might have expected. It was a Marxism which specialized in discussing the invalidity of capitalism, but which took no steps towards revolution. However, as intellectuals did not control their own resources, the theory could not fully be translated into their professional activity, no matter how crucial or influential it was to the shaping of their critical consciousness. As a result, small groups of indispensable and dissatisfied professionals emerged, linked in their professional capacity to capital or the government, but politically sensitive to the approaching revolution – this was due to technical reasons, having to do with difficulties in the growth of production; reasons, in other words, whose translation into political terms is not immediate, or is a matter of chance, and thus not easy to grasp in its movements. In short, a new nationalist league had been formed, consisting entirely of youthful, militant and up-to-date elements – barons and generals were now excluded – who would constitute the public in the early years of the dictatorship. This was the soil in which the criticism of the compromises of the past would yield its fruit. And its vitality was such that – even with the sight of government tanks trundling periodically along the streets – there was no shortage of complaints against the cultural terrorism of the left.[2]

This, in brief outline, was the mechanism by which a dubious socialist programme was able to dominate the scene. However, since an ideology can never be completely autonomous, its aims and cultural results ought not to be considered as identical in all aspects to its function. Contact with new international tendencies and with the radicalization of populism, resulting finally in several months of pre-revolutionary activity, would engender new outlooks and definitions which could not be traced back to the original ideological movement, and were, indeed, incompatible with it. Given our earlier analysis, this is a useful observation: it was only to the extent to which it broke with the system of compromise in which it had become enmeshed, and which was nevertheless a source of impetus, that the work produced by the left could be regarded as anything more than pure ideology. This occurred in several ways. For example, the demagogic emotions of an 'independent foreign policy' (Jânio Quadros giving a decoration to Che Guevara) or of Goulart's campaigns led to an interest in the study of Marx and imperialism in the universities. Thus it was from university teachers – those ancient dinosaurs – that the earliest, most convincing and most comprehensive accounts of the unfeasibility of reformism, and of its deceptive nature, could be heard. Another indirect consequence was that academic study paradoxically breathed back into the writings of Marx and Lenin the life that had been denied them by the Communist Party's monopoly; so much so that on leaving their lecture-halls, student militants would defend the strict principles of Marxism in the face of the compromises of the leadership. To be brief, just as *os grupos de 11* and peasant leagues managed to escape the populist machinery, though they belonged to the environment for which the latter had been created, there were times when culture, in the form of isolated works or even collective experiments, was able to scatter the Communist Party's theoretical fog, despite the fact that the Party also provided the climate which gave it a ready-made audience and immediate acclaim. Finally, for a more complex example of the disparity between reformist practice and its cultural results, we will consider the Movement for Popular Culture in Pernambuco (beautifully evoked in Antonio Callado's 1967 novel, *Quarup*). The Movement began in 1959, when Miguel Arraes was prefect and was running for the governorship of the State. His immediate aim was an electoral one: to educate the masses, who would surely vote for him if they could (in Brazil, those who cannot read or write, i.e. 50 per cent of the population, are not allowed to vote). He also tried to encourage the setting up of all kinds of community groups for people to take an interest in real matters such as their city, district and even their local folklore, which would compensate for the misery and marginality of the masses; it would be a means of protecting them from the ravages of electoral demagogues. Inspired by the tenets of Christianity and reformism, the central idea behind the programme was the 'improvement of mankind'. However, in its effects on culture and its established forms, the Movement for Popular Culture was of much greater significance.

Let us begin by looking at the Paulo Freire method for teaching adults to read and write, which was developed at this juncture. This extremely successful method does not conceive of reading as an abstract technique, but as a force in the game of social domination. Consequently, it attempts to couple the peasant's access to the written word with an awareness of his/her political situation. The teachers, who were students, would go to rural communities and, using the living experience of the inhabitants as a starting-point, would emphasize certain topics and key-words – 'generating words', in Freire's terminology – which would be used both for discussion and to encourage literacy. Instead of undergoing the humiliation of having to learn, at thirty years of age, that the cat sat on the mat, rural workers were able to make a simultaneous entry into the world of letters and that of trades unions, the constitution, agrarian reform, i.e. of their own historical interests. In such a situation, the teacher is no longer a bourgeois professional who merely passes on what he has learnt; nor is reading a procedure which merely enables one to get a new job; nor are words, much less the pupils, merely words and pupils. Each of these elements is transformed in the method – within which one can feel the momentum of a contemporary revolution: it conceives the notion that poverty and its foundation, illiteracy, are neither accidental nor residual, but rather play an integral part in the routine movements of capital's domination. In this way, the political triumph of learning to write broke free of the original framework of study, transfer of knowledge and consolidation of the prevailing order for which it had been designed. The same is true of the theatre. On one occasion, the Arraes government decided to extend farming credit, so that in two months the number of small farmers who were able to benefit jumped from only 1,000 to 40,000. Theatrical groups would first of all approach the peasants for information and then attempt to dramatize the problems of innovation. In such cases, who was the author? Who the student? Does artistic beauty still adorn the ruling classes? Where does it come from? The themes, materials, possibilities and the very structure of cultural production were changing, together with its audience.

During this brief period, in which the police and the legal system did not act merely in the interests of property (and particularly so in Pernambuco), discussions on how to produce culture that was truly democratic sprang up at every turn, living in a state of happy incompatibility with the forms and prestige of bourgeois culture. It is difficult to determine with any precision the complex complicity and complementarity that often exists between police repression and the accepted forms of art and culture. These were times of splendid irreverence. In Rio de Janeiro the CPCs (Centres for Popular Culture) would improvise political theatre at factory gates and in trades and student union meetings; and in the slums they were beginning to make films and records. The pre-revolutionary winds were decompart-mentalizing the national consciousness and filling the newspapers with talk of agrarian reform, rural disturbances, the workers' movement, the nationalization of American firms, etc. The country had become un-recognizably intelligent. Political journalism, hand in hand with satirical humour, was making great strides in the big cities. There were even a number of parliamentary deputies who made some interesting speeches. In short, intellectual production was beginning to reorient its relationship with the masses. Then came the coup, and with it the repression and silence of the first few weeks. The generals' artistic tastes were somewhat more traditional. In São Paulo, for example, at an admittedly later date, the Commander of the Second Army – who became famous for the statement that he would eat up the left for lunch before they could have him for dinner – hosted a much talked about literary evening, in which he recited sonnets penned by his father and, giving in to the insistence of those present, eventually read out some of his own work. The Movement for Popular Culture in Recife was immediately brought to an end, and its headquarters transformed into the inevitable Social Security Office. The liveliest and most interesting period of modern Brazilian history had become a thing of the past.

In the wake of the repression of 1964, another geological stratum began to dominate the Brazilian scene. 'Ancient hearts, hidden corners in the hinterland, who would have thought ...?' Even before the coup, the right, by making good use of capital and of advertising techniques, had managed to activate politically the archaic sentiments of the petty-bourgeoisie. Beautiful examples of rural and urban stupidity could be seen on the streets in the shape of 'Family Marches with God and for Freedom', with petitions being organized against divorce, agrarian reform and the communization of the clergy; alternatively, those who stayed at home could pray their 'Family Beads', a sort of warlike rosary designed to encourage the generals. God could not help but take note of such public and private appeals and duly descended upon the Communists like a ton of bricks. Immediately after the coup, public support for the military increased while the workers' and peasant movements were silenced by repression. The investigations made by the police and the army into subversive activities prompted the re-emergence of such curious old phrases as: Does the philosophy teacher believe in God? Do you know all the words to the national anthem? How can we be sure our University girls are all virgins? What if they are practising free love? What if my name is on the list of those who are going to be next against the wall? As an ardent ex-liberal neatly put it: 'The General Commission of Investigation has a noble task ahead of itself.' In those provinces which could provide further education, a mixture of local rivalry and personal interest caused secondary school teachers and local lawyers to covet the well-paid University posts which normally went to graduates from the capital. In São Paulo, radio and television presenters took it upon themselves to broadcast political terrorism. The State Governor, an incarnation of Ubu, would repeatedly invoke the name of the Virgin at the microphone, referring to her as an 'adorable creature'. The Minister for Education was the same man who, only a few years previously, had purged Paraná University library as its Rector; on that occasion he had ordered the immoral pages in the novels of Eça de Queiroz to be torn out.* In the Faculty of Medicine, an entire group of lecturers were expelled and replaced by another, less competent, set who had taken advantage of the wave of police activities to settle old scores.

In short: when its side-effects are seen as a whole the coup appears as the massive return of everything that modernization had left behind; it was the revenge of the provinces, of small proprietors, of sexual and religious prudery, of small-time lawyers, etc. To grasp the extent of this regression, remember that in Goulart's time, public debate had been focused on

---

*The great Portuguese nineteenth-century realist novelist, author of *O primo Basílio* (*Cousin Basílio*) (1878). *O crime do Padre Amaro* (1880), etc.

agrarian reform, imperialism, the minimum wage or votes for illiterates, and so had more or less corresponded, not to the experience of the average citizen, but to the *organized* experience of the unions, industrial and rural, of bosses' and student associations, of the mobilized petty bourgeoisie, etc. However confused and muddled it was, it concerned real issues, and it proceeded according to terms which the development of the nation as a whole prompted as time went on, to the principal contenders. After 1964, it's a different picture. The old, ritual formulae which preceded populism and with which the most antiquated and marginalized sectors of the bourgeoisie disguise their lack of contact with what's going on in the world come back: the nucleus of the nation is the family, Brazil is a proud country, our Christian traditions, phrases which no longer reflect any reality whatever, although they are a kind of password for people of kindred feelings, and are, for those who use them, a guarantee of their politico-ideological 'correctness'. In its way, the counter-revolution repeated what a good part of the most highly regarded Brazilian poetry of this century had done: it breathed life back into the funeral cortège of those that capitalism had passed by. Poor poets, who saw their beloved elders in processions, brandishing cudgels and dripping with obscurantism! However, although it was victorious, this alliance of the defeated was unable to impose itself, and was put on one side straight away by the necessities of the times and by the technocratic policies of the new government. (It did, however, have its moment of artistic glory, as a subject of mirth.) Its unique style of reasoning has been immortalized in the three volumes of the *Febeapá* – the abbreviation for Festival of Asininity that's Devastating the Country [*Festival de Besteira que Assola o País*] – an anthology compiled by Stanislaw Ponte-Preta.* And in an indirect way, the spectacle of such social anachronism, of the daily phantasmagoria that it presented, provided the material for the *tropicalist* movement – a complex Brazilian variant of pop, with which a growing number of avant-garde musicians, writers, theatre and film directors, and painters identify themselves. Later, I shall try to describe it. This alliance had its second chance just now, in 1969, this time in the wake of the military régime's struggles (backed by repressive force) to construct an ideology with which to oppose incipient revolutionary war.

However, let's return to 1964. The government which had just carried out the coup, unlike the petty bourgeoisie and the rural middle class, which

*Pseudonym of Sérgio Porto (1923–68).

137

it had mobilized but which it was not going to represent, was not backward. It was pro-American and anti-popular, but modern. It was carrying out military and economic integration with the United States, and a concentration and rationalization of capital. In this sense, the clock had not been turned back, and the apologists of rural and suburban private property were not in power. What interest can a technocrat, by definition a cosmopolitan, have in the feelings which fuel the outback? It's much more interesting for him to see what his fellows in London, New York and Paris are seeing – *Hair, Marat-Sade*, Albee and even Brecht. In just the same way, while they were marching in the streets against communism, dressed in skirts and blouses and without their high-heels, society ladies had no intention of forgoing their more elaborate ensembles. The bourgeoisie had handed over the Presidency of the Republic and lucrative posts in the administration to the military, but had kept international standards of taste. At this time, however, the cultural avant-garde of the West has only one topic, the social rottenness of capitalism. In their turn, the military hardly brought their ideological endeavours into the public domain – something which will be much more decisive in the stage which is beginning now – for, since they had brute force at their command they could do without popular support. In this vacuum, it was natural that the market together with the authority of the experts, would win out, and they returned the initiative to those who had had it in the previous government. Cultural life got moving again, with the same people as before, in a different national situation. Through campaigns against torture, American greed, military investigations and the stupidity of the censors, the Brazilian intelligentsia came together and triumphed morally and intellectually over the government, with great effect in terms of propaganda.

Only at the end of 1968 did the situation change again, when the existence of a state of revolutionary war in Brazil was officially recognized. To stop it spreading to the masses, police repression became really tough, denunciation of acquaintances was encouraged and protected from reprisals, torture took on terrifying proportions, and the press was silenced. As a result, the importance of ideology increased, all of which meant a proliferation of Brazilian flags, of propaganda leaflets, and the setting up of courses in gymnastics and civic values for university students. The phraseology of law-and-order patriotism, suddenly back in favour, could be found everywhere. What chance did the government have of forging a real national ideology? If it needs it, it is only because it has to confront subversion. In the previous situation, it preferred to do without it, since in

essence it is a government associated with imperialism, with demobiliza-
tion of the people and with technological solutions, to whom any verifiable
ideological commitment will always seem like a limitation. Aside from that,
there is also the massive, and well-established penetration of US culture,
which does not sort well with God, family and country, at least, not in the
Latin-American sense of those words. So, resistance to the spread of a
fascist type of ideology is inherent in the situation. On the other hand, such
a resistance will hardly find much support in the liberal conscience, which
had moments of courage after 1964, but now seems to be almost dead. In
1967, when the student movement was very active, the dock police were
brought to São Paulo. Their sinister brutality, routinely applied to the
workers, was for a moment turned against the children of the bourgeoisie,
causing shock and revulsion. Such violence was unknown in the city and
nobody had thought that the defence of the regime needed such specialists.
That is the way things still are. Shamefaced, the bourgeoisie accepts the
cultural programme laid out for it by the military.

Simplifying a little, what is being repeated in these comings and goings is
the combination, in moments of crisis, of the new and the old: more
exactly, of the most advanced manifestations of international imperialist
integration, and of the most ancient – and obsolete – bourgeois ideology,
centred on the individual, on the indivisibility of the family and on its
traditions. Superficially, this combination only represents the coexistence
of symptoms linked to different phases of the same system. (For the
purposes of this argument, we are not interested in the celebrated cultural
variety of Brazil in which it is true that one finds African religions,
indigenous tribes, workers sometimes sold as slaves, share-cropping and
industrial complexes.) The important thing is the systematic character of
this co-existence, and its meaning, which can vary. While in the Goulart
phase modernization involved relations of power and property, and
ideology, which would have to give way in the face of the pressure of the
masses and of the necessities of national development, the 1964 coup – one
of the crucial moments in the Cold War – was founded on the defeat of this
movement, through the mobilization and confirmation, among other
things, of traditional and localistic forms of power. Thus, imperialist
integration, which immediately modernized the economy of the country
for its own ends, is reviving that part of ideological and political obsoles-
cence which it needs to preserve its own stability. From being an obstacle
and a residue, this archaic world becomes an intentional instrument of a

very modern oppression, just as modernization itself, from being libertarian and nationalist, becomes a form of oppression.

In such conditions, in 1964, simple homespun thinking suddenly rose to historical pre-eminence – a crushing experience for the intellectuals, who had become unaccustomed to such things. This experience, with its own logic, provided the raw material for an important artistic style, that of *tropicalism*, which reflects on it in various ways, exploring and defining a new artistic, intellectual and class situation. With no pretence to having the final word, I am now going to attempt a sketch of its main outlines. Venturing a little, perhaps one can say that the basic effect of tropicalism depends precisely on its subjection of such anachronisms, at first sight grotesque, but on second thoughts inevitable, to the white light of ultra-modernity, so that the result is transformed into an allegory of Brazil. The stock of images and emotions belonging to the patriarchal country, rural and urban, is exposed to the most advanced or fashionable forms and techniques in the world – electronic music, Eisensteinian montage, the colours and the montage of pop art, the prose of *Finnegans Wake*, theatre which is at one and the same time raw and allegorical, with physical attacks on the audience. It's in this internal contrast that the peculiar attraction, the trade mark of the tropicalist image lies.³ The result of the combination is strident, like a family secret dragged out into the middle of the street, like treachery to one's own class. It is literally an absurdity – this is the first impression it gives – however, the misfit reveals to the onlooker a real historical abyss, a junction of different stages of capitalist development.

There are many ambiguities and tensions in this construction. The vehicle is modern and the content archaic, but the past is noble and the present commercial; on the other hand, the past is atrocious and the present authentic, etc. Politics and a kind of collective social exhibitionism were combined: its artistic power derives from quoting, without sympathy or collusion, as if they came from Mars, the civic values that have come out on the streets – but intimately, for Mars is actually back home; it also derives from a kind of affectionate treachery, which shows family and class secrets off to the profane eyes of a less restricted public. Virginal brides, senatorial countenances, phrases of the most impeccable dignity, cheap tango passions – unprotected by social distance and their prestige-laden context, recorded in some plastic-metallic-phosphorescent, electronic material, these figures take on a strange glow, and it becomes unclear whether they are forsaken and abandoned, or malign, ripe for some kind of fascism. Again, this background of traditional images is often represented by its debased copies in radio soap-operas, operettas, club repertoire, and so on, which produces one of tropicalism's best effects: the old and authentic was as hungry for fame as are the commercial excesses of our own day, with the single difference that it is out of fashion; it is as if a top-hatted gentleman, who insisted on his superior morality, were told that nobody wears hats any more. To express this in a more systematic way: the crest of the wave, which is where the tropicalists are now, is at one moment measured by its critical aim; at another it is measured against the success of what is most up-to-date in the great capitals of the world. This indifference, this absolute value of what is new, allows the historical distance between theme and technique given definition in the typical tropicalist image, just as it may express an attack on reaction, to express also the triumph of the city-dwelling grandchildren over their provincial grandparents – the undeniable achievement of having been born later and of reading foreign magazines. Against the ambiguous background of modernization, the line between sensibility and opportunism, or between criticism and social integration is blurred. An analogous ambiguity appears in the combination of violent social criticism and bare-faced commercialism, whose results can easily turn out to be conformist, but can also, when they cast an ironic light on its doubtful side, capture the hardest and most difficult contradictions of present intellectual production. In fact, to judge by the indignation of the right (which isn't everything), the irreverent, scandalous and commercial side seems to have carried more political weight than the deliberately political side.

What is the social position of tropicalism? To judge it, one needs to have a certain familiarity with international fashion – something which is commoner in some arts than it is in others. This familiarity, without which one loses that sense of distance, of *lèse-majesté* towards the patriarchal heritage, is the monopoly of university students and the like, who, by means of it, can speak a language exclusive to themselves. As we have already seen, tropicalism submits one system of private, prestigious notions to the language of another milieu and another time, an operation from which it gets its demythifying, leftist energy. However, this second language is also private, though it belongs to a different group. We're not going from the particular to the universal, but from one sphere to another, admittedly a much more politically advanced one, which finds a form of identification within it. More or less, then, we know whom this style is talking to: but we still don't know what it is saying. Faced by a tropicalist image, faced by the apparently surrealist nonsense which is the result of the combination we have been describing, the up-to-date spectator will resort to fashionable words, he'll say Brazil is incredible, it's the end, it's the pits, it's groovy. By means of these expressions, in which enthusiasm and disgust are indistinguishable, he associates himself with the group who have the 'sense' of national character. But on the other hand, this climate, this imponderable essence of Brazil is very simple to construct, easy to recognize and reproduce. It is a linguistic trick, a formula for sophisticated vision, within many people's grasp. What is the content of this snobbery for the masses? What feelings does the tropicalist sensibility recognize itself and distinguish itself by? (By the way, just because it is simple it is not necessarily bad. As we will see later, the tropicalist effect has a profound and interesting historical foundation; but this too is indicative of a class position, as we will see in a moment.)

Coming back to the subject: for example, in the Paulo Freire method the archaic nature of rural consciousness and the specialized theory of the teacher of literacy are also combined; however, in spite of this conjunction, there is nothing less tropicalist than this method. Why? Because the opposition between its terms can be resolved – people can be made literate. For the tropicalist image, on the contrary, it is essential that the juxtaposition between old and new – either between content and technique, or within the content itself – should make something *absurd*, should be an aberration, which is the basic point of reference of the melancholy and the humour of this style.

In other words, to obtain its artistic and critical effect tropicalism works with the weird combination of the archaic and the modern, which the counter-revolution has given shape to, or to put it another way, with the *results* of the previous, failed attempt at national modernization. There was a moment, a little before or a little after the coup, in which, at least in the cinema, the order of the day could be summed up in a phrase of Glauber Rocha (who seems to be evolving in a direction far removed from it): 'for an aesthetics of hunger'. Some of the best Brazilian films, in particular *Barren Lives*, *Black God*, *White Devil*, and *The Guns*,* are linked to this idea. Simplifying brutally, one can say that the impulse of this aesthetic is revolutionary. The artist would look for his strength and modernity in the present stage of national life, and would keep as much independence as

---

*See 'Cinema and *The Guns*', Chapter 11, this volume.

possible in the face of the technological and economic machine, which is always in the last analysis controlled by the enemy. Tropicalism goes in the other direction: from the point of view of the international avant-garde and of fashion, it records the backwardness of the country as something aberrant. In the former case, technique is given a political dimension. In the latter, the stage it has reached at the international level is accepted as the parameter of our national misfortune: we, the up-to-date, the ones who are plugged in to the movement of capital, recognize now that the attempt at social modernization from above has failed, that what is absurd is our own soul and that of our country. The notion of a 'Brazilian poverty', which victimizes rich and poor equally, which is typical of tropicalism, is the result of a generalization of this kind. Some Indians in a bleak, poverty-struck landscape, filmed in deliberately humorous technicolor, a china cabinet in the middle of an asphalted motorway, a high society party which after all is said and done is just a provincial knees-up – according to this point of view, everything is in the same state of privation. Obviously, the poor don't have this notion of poverty – for them, lack of food and lack of style can hardly be of the same order of inconvenience.

However, let's move on to another question: what is the historical foundation of the tropicalist allegory? By finding a satisfactory reply to this question, we would also be explaining the really remarkable interest that these images have, which stands out even more surprisingly if they are part of a mediocre work of art. The coexistence of the old and the new is a general (and always suggestive) feature of all capitalist societies and of many others too. However, for the countries which were once colonized and have now become underdeveloped, it is central, and carries the power of an emblem. This is because these countries were incorporated into the world market – to the modern world – in an economically and socially backward role, that of suppliers of raw materials and cheap labour. Their link to what is new is made *by means of*, structurally by means of, their social backwardness, which reproduces itself, instead of cancelling itself out.[4] In the insoluble but functional combination of these two terms, then, the plan of a national destiny is laid out, there from the beginning. What is more, by cultivating 'latinoamericanidad' – in which there is a faint echo of the continent-wide dimension of the revolution – which in Portuguese-speaking Brazil is extremely uncommon, the tropicalists show that they are aware of the implications of their style. And it is true that, once this way of looking at things has been assimilated, the whole of Latin America does turn out to be tropicalist. On the other hand, the generality of this blueprint is such that it embraces all the countries of the continent, at every stage in their history - which might seem to be a defect. What can a formula say about Brazil in 1964 which is equally applicable, say, to nineteenth-century Argentina? However, because tropicalism is *allegorical*, this lack of specificness is not fatal to it (as it would be, in a symbolic style). Schematically, where in the symbol form and content are indissoluble, and the symbol is the 'visible', so to speak the natural form of the idea, in an allegory the relationship between the idea and the images which have the task of expressing it is external, and belongs to the domain of convention. Since they signify an abstract idea with which they have nothing to do, the elements of an allegory are not artistically transfigured: they persist in their material form, functioning as documenters of the truth. They are like the reefs of the real history which constitutes its depths.[5] Thus, it is precisely in the effort to find suggestive and *dated* materials - with which they allegorize their atemporal idea of Brazil - that the tropicalists get their best results. That is why their films, plays and songs look like and sound like inventories, presenting as much material as possible, so that it can undergo a process of allegorical activation. Once this anachronistic conjunction has been produced, along with the conventional idea that this is Brazil, the 'readymade' images of the patriarchal world and of imbecilic consumerism start signifying on their own, in a shameless, unaestheticized fashion, over and over again suggesting their stifled, frustrated lives, which we will never get to know. The tropicalist image encloses the past in the form of images that are active, or that might come back to life, and suggests that they are our destiny, which is the reason why we can't stop looking at them. I think this structure is at work even when the image is at first sight comic.[6]

Commenting on some houses built after 1964, planned by avant-garde architects, one critic has pointed out that they were no good for living in, because their materials, principally bare concrete, were very rough, and because the space was excessively divided up and rationalized, out of proportion with the aims of a private house. However, according to him, it was precisely in this lack of proportion, that their witness to history, their cultural honesty was to be found.

During the developmentalist years, linked to the building of Brasília and to the hopes of socialism, the consciousness of a collectivist meaning for architectural production had matured. So that, for anyone who had thought of rational, cheap construction, on a large scale, as part of a movement of national democratization, for anyone who had thought his way through the labyrinth of the economic and political connections between technology and imperialism, a project for a bourgeois house is inevitably an anti-climax.[7] When the political perspectives for architecture were cut off, what was left however was the intellectual education it had given to the architects, who would torture space, overloading with aims and experiments the houses commissioned from them from time to time by newly-married friends with a bit of money. Outside its proper context, carried out in a restricted sphere and in the form of merchandise, architectural rationalism turns into a mere show of good taste – quite incompatible with its deeper aims – or into a moralistic, uncomfortable symbol of the revolution which didn't happen. This outline, though with a thousand variations, can be generalized for the whole period. The cultural process, which was breaking down the frontiers of class and purely commercial criteria, was dammed up in 1964. Once the contact with the exploited, which was their real aim, was checked, formal solutions were used in a situation and for a public for which they were not destined, and changed meaning. From being revolutionary, they changed to being the saleable symbol of the revolution. They were welcomed triumphantly by the students and by the artistic public in general. Political forms, which had been the most abundant, the liveliest and most instructive attitude they took, full of the materialistic obviousness that previously had been in bad taste, became the *moral* symbol of politics, and this was their most forceful content. The gesture towards instruction or education, even though at times it was naive and taught its cultivated audience nothing that was not obvious – that imperialism exists, that justice is a matter of which class you belong to – had its effect as an *example*, it gave value to what was not permitted in a culture that was hemmed in: political contact with the people.

Thus there came into being a kind of ambiguous exchange, which on the one hand sold indulgences of political emotion to the middle class, but on the other hand, consolidated the ideological atmosphere I spoke of at the beginning. The infinite repetition of arguments well known to all – nothing could be more redundant, at first sight, than the theatre which came immediately after the coup – was not, in fact, redundant: it showed that people were still there, and had not changed their opinion, that a lot could be said if you were ingenious enough, that it was possible to run risks. In these shows, in which not even the shadow of a worker appeared, the intelligentsia identified itself with the oppressed, and reaffirmed their debt to them, inasmuch as they represented our hope for the future. They unleashed exciting, imaginary battles against inequality, the dictatorship and the United States. They established the conviction that what is poetic and alive, today, is the struggle against capitalism and imperialism. That was the reason for the importance of public genres, of theatre, advertisements, popular music, cinema and journalism, which transformed this climate into something like a demonstration or a party, while literature proper left the centre of the stage. The poets themselves felt this way. In a recent public debate, one accused another of not having a single line capable of landing him in jail. This search for the revolutionary which culture imposed on itself and kept up for some time naturally could not proceed without contradictions. Some of them can be seen in the evolution of the theatre during this time.

Theatre's first reply to the coup was musical, which was a find in itself. In Rio de Janeiro, Augusto Boal - the director of the Teatro de Arena in São Paulo, the group which reformulated its aims in the quickest and most methodical way - put on the show *Opinião*. The singers, two from humble backgrounds and a female student from Copacabana, mixed the story of their lives with any songs that might fit in. In this plot, the music acted principally as the authentic summary of a social experience, as the *opinion* that every citizen has the right to formulate and sing about, even if the dictatorship doesn't approve. Thus, popular music (along with football, the cultural expression closest to the Brazilian heart) and democracy, the people and authenticity were identified with one another, and in opposition to the military regime. It was a resounding success. In a less inventive way, the same liberal plan - resistance to the dictatorship - worked for another great success, *Liberdade, liberdade*, in which there was presented an anthology of Western libertarian texts, from the sixth century BC to the twentieth AD. In spite of the tone almost of civic affirmation of these two shows, one of communal protest and mutual encouragement, it was inevitable that one should feel aesthetic and political unease in the face of the total agreement between the stage and the audience which they produced. The real drama was not what was going on on stage. No elements of the critique of populism had been absorbed. Mutual confirmation and enthusiasm might have been important then, but it was also true that the left had just been defeated, which gave a rather inappropriate air of complacency to the wild applause. If the people are intelligent and courageous, why were they defeated? And if it had been defeated, why so much congratulation? As we will see, the lack of a political reply to this question would become the aesthetic limit of the Teatro de Arena.

Redundant in this respect, *Opinião* was new in others. Its audience had many more students in than was usual, perhaps because of the music, and so was more politicized and intelligent. From then on, thanks also to systematic contact with student organizations, this became the usual composition of the avant-garde theatre. As a consequence, the stock of culture common to stage and spectators grew, which allowed an allusiveness and agility, especially in political matters, which had been unknown before. If in the middle of the disgusting tirade of a villain there suddenly poked out phrases from the latest presidential speech, the delight brought the house down. This complicity has, it is true, an easy tautological side; but it does create a theatrical space – which in Brazil the commercial theatre had never had – for live argument, free of false literary values. As a general rule in fact, the most important content of this movement will turn out to have been a formal transformation, a change in the social role of theatre. Continuing the theatre of social and political agitation of the Goulart phase, theatre and with it language and culture were stripped of their 'essential' eminence, whose ideological role, that of being an ornament to the dominant classes, was completely exposed. Suddenly, good theatre, which for years had discussed adultery, freedom or *angst* in well-behaved Portuguese seemed to belong to another age. A kind of Brechtian revolution had taken place, which activists of the right, intent on restoring dignity to the arts, replied to by destroying sets and equipment, and beating up actresses and actors. Without a ritual space, but with imagination – and also without a strong tradition of training in the profession, and without older actors – the theatre was close to the students: there was no gap of age, life-style, or education. In its turn, the student movement was living through its golden age, in which it became the country's political vanguard. This accord between a less 'stuck-up' stage and an activist public produced some extraordinary moments of theatre, and put didactic matters back into the forefront, as the issue of the moment. Instead of offering the students the fathomless depths of a beautiful play or a great actor, the theatre offered them a collection of well-thought-through arguments and actions, to be imitated, criticized or rejected. The distance between the specialist and the layman had been much reduced. Digressing for a moment, it is an example of the fact that democratization, in art, does not involve any kind of cheapening, nor does it depend on the masses being educated at drama school; what it really involves are social transformations and changes in criteria, which necessarily change the terms in which the problem had initially presented itself. Coming back: somewhere Brecht recommends that actors should collect and analyse the best gestures they can observe, to perfect them and give them back to the people, from whom they originally came. The premise of this argument, in which life and art are harmonized, is that the gesture should exist on the stage *just as it does outside it*, that the reason for its appropriateness should not merely lie in the theatrical form that sustains it. What is good in life gives life to the stage, and vice versa. So, then, if the artistic form stops being the restricted centre of the whole, it is because it accepts the effects of the social structure (or of a social movement) – to which it is no longer in essence opposed – as equivalent to its own effects. As a consequence, there is a relaxation at the level of the form, and the work enters into an agreement with its public; it may be able to amuse it and educate it, instead of contradicting it all the time. These speculations, which derive from the idyll that Brecht had imagined for socialist theatre in the GDR, give an idea of what was happening in the Teatro de Arena – where this conciliation was made possible by the rising student movement. The search for what might be attractive, vigorous and funny, or despicable, for a new generation, gave an extraordinary attractiveness to the shows put on by Arena in this phase.

Zumbi, a musical which tells the story of slave escape and rebellion, is a good example. Since they were neither singers nor dancers, the actors had to develop dance and song which would be within the layman's compass, but which would also be graceful and interesting. At the same time, they worked to prevent the solutions they found sticking only to the junction of one actor and character: each character was played by many actors, and each actor did many characters, besides which the principal character was the group. Thus, the characterizations were entirely objectified, so that they could be taken up again, so that the actor could be at one moment a character, at another one of the mass: that is, they were socialized, *imitable*. Gestures could be taken on and off like hats, and so could be acquired. The play was a real investigation into, and presentation of the most seductive ways of rolling around or rolling over on the floor, of lifting your arm, of getting up quickly, of calling out, of showing decisiveness, but also of the most everyday ways that the dominant classes have of lying, or ordering their employees around, or of underlining their own social importance, by a particular movement of the bum. However, at the centre of its relationship with the public – something which only made it the more successful – *Zumbi* repeated the tautology of *Opinião*; the defeated left triumphed on the stage with no criticism, and in front of a full house, as if the defeat had not been a fault.

Opinião had produced unanimity in the audience by means of the symbolic alliance of music and the people, against the regime. *Zumbi* had an analogous, though a more complex structure. The opposition between Portuguese masters and slaves, played out on stage, was paralleled by another, constantly alluded to, between the Brazilian people and the pro-imperialist dictatorship. This trick, which has its own appeal, since it allows one to allude to prohibited things in public, combined an opposition which today is merely moral – the slave question – to a political one, and, on behalf of the latter, capitalized on the relaxed enthusiasm which the former attracts. But the problem is that there was movement in both directions, and of unequal weight. At one moment, slave revolt was blamed on the dictatorship: at another, the dictatorship was re-encountered in the repression of this same revolt. In one case, the plot is an artifice so that we can talk about our own times. The necessarily oblique language has the value of its own cunning, which is a political value. Its lack of fit is simply a sensible way of replying to the reality of police repression. And the relaxed manner of the treatment of the historical material – there are huge numbers of anachronisms – is an aesthetic virtue, since it quite cheerfully points up the procedure adopted and the real topic of the drama. In the second, the struggle between slaves and Portuguese masters is, *already*, the struggle between the people and imperialism. As a consequence historical distinctions – which had no importance if the slave was an artifice, but do have it now, if he is an origin – are blurred, and the inevitable banality of the commonplace takes over: the rights of the oppressed, the cruelty of the oppressors; after 1964, just as in Zumbi's time (the seventeenth century), people are still searching for liberty. The vagueness of this perspective weighs on the means of expression, theatrical and linguistic, which turn out to lack political energy, orientated as they are by the immediate, humanitarian – and so non-political – reaction to suffering. Where Boal plays hide-and-seek, there is politics, where he plays politics, there is preaching. The artistic result of the first of these tendencies is good, of the second bad.

This duality found its most finished artistic expression in Arena's next work, *Tiradentes*. Theorizing about it, Boal said that the theatre should not only create enthusiasm, it should also criticize. As a consequence, he uses the concepts of distancing and identification, in the manner of Brecht and Stanislavski. The opposition between the two, which in Brechtian polemic had had a historical significance and marked the frontier between ideology and valid theatre, is reduced to a question of the suitability of two styles.[8] In fact, in *Tiradentes*, the principal character – the martyr of Brazilian independence, a man of humble origins – is shown in a kind of larger-than-life naturalism, as a mythical incarnation of national liberation. In contrast, the other characters, both his companions in the conspiracy, well-situated and indecisive, and his enemies, are presented in a humorously distanced way, in the Brechtian manner. The intention is to produce a critical view of the dominant classes, and another, more enthusiastic, of the man who gives his life for the cause. However, the result is doubtful: the rich make political calculations, have a notion of their material interests, an ability to make a wealth of pithy statements, and so create good theatre: however, the martyr runs madly in pursuit of liberty, is disinterested, a real, boring idealist, whose theatrical results are much less positive. The Brechtian method, in which intelligence plays a large role, is applied to the revolutionary's enemy; it is the revolutionary who gets the less intelligent method, the enthusiastic one. Politically, this formal impasse seems to me to correspond to an as yet incomplete stage in the critique of populism. What is the composition, in social terms and in terms of interests, of the popular movement? This is a question which populism is not good at answering. Because the composition of the masses is not homogeneous, it prefers to unite them by enthusiasm rather than separate them by a critical analysis of their interests. However, it is only if such a critique were carried through that the real themes of political theatre would emerge: the alliances and problems of organization, which remove notions like sincerity and enthusiasm from the field of bourgeois universalism. On the other hand, this is not to say that theatre will get better just by being able to deal with such matters. It may not even be possible to put them on stage. It is also true that Arena's best moments were linked to its ideological limitations, to its unconditional fellow-feeling with its young public, whose sense of justice, and impatience, which certainly do have political value, improperly took the place of revolutionary interests, pure and simple. After all, it is a common failing in the arts: social experience pushes the artist towards more radical and just solutions, which become so to speak necessary, but good quality does not necessarily follow from it, just as merit does not always get the honour it deserves.[9] However, not searching for such solutions leads inevitably to banality.

Also on the left, but at the opposite pole from Arena, and ambiguous to the tips of its fingers, there developed the *Teatro Oficina*, directed by José Celso Martinez Corrêa. If Arena had inherited from the Goulart period its formal impulse, its interest in the class struggle, in revolution, and certain populist limitations, Oficina arose as a consequence of the bourgeois split in 1964. On its stage, this split is ritually repeated, in the form of an insult. Its productions marked an epoch, and had enormous success and scandalous effect in São Paulo and Rio, where they were the most memorable of recent years. They affected their public by means of brutalization, and not, like Arena, by fellow-feeling: their principal resource is the outrageous offence, and not didacticism. The opposition within committed theatre could not be more complete. Putting it in a nutshell, José Celso would argue in the following way: if in 1964 the petty bourgeoisie sided with the right and gave in, while the upper classes allied themselves with imperialism, any consensus between stage and audience is an aesthetic and ideological mistake.[10] We have to attack the audience. It, for its part, likes being attacked or seeing others attacked, and thus assures Oficina a really remarkable commercial success. That is the problem of this form of theatre. To understand it, it should be remembered that at that same period, the question of the attitude of the student movement was much discussed: was it determined by its petty bourgeois social origin, or did it represent a particular social function – one that was in crisis – with more radical interests? The Arena adopts this second reply, and founds its positive, political relationship with its audience on it; as a result its problems are new, for they anticipate a theatre for a revolutionary society; but they also have the mark of the pious wish, for the real prop for this experiment are the consumers, in the theatre, paying and laughing, right in the middle of the dictatorship. The Oficina, which in practice adopted the first reply, slaps its audience in the face, collectively, with no distinctions made. Paradoxically, its success among the students, especially among those who were irritated by the populist remnants in Arena, was very great: they identified, not with the audience, but with the aggressor. In fact, Oficina's hostility was a radical answer, more radical than the other, to the defeat of 1964, but it was not a political answer. In consequence, in spite of the aggressivity, its theatre is a step backward; it is moral, and operates within the bourgeoisie, it has connections with the pre-Brechtian tradition, whose dramatic realm is the moral conscience of the dominant classes. Within this retreat, however – just because there is, historically, no such thing as repetition – there was a kind of evolution – the crisis within the bourgeoisie, after the prolonged immersion in Marxism which the intelligentsia had gone through, was no longer taken seriously, and is repeated like a kind of contemptible ritual, destined to stop their public enjoying life. The moral meaning that withdrawal to bourgeois horizons would have (for that part of the bourgeoisie touched by socialism) took concrete form. Just by the way, this crisis has already reached a kind of stability, and has a considerable number of people quite comfortably installed within it. To return, however: with unheard-of violence – but accredited by world theatrical fashion, by the cachet of the so-called collapse of European culture, which, in the theatre, exemplifies the contradictions of imperialism – Oficina attacked the normal ideas and images of the middle class, its instincts, and its very person. The spectator in the front row was grabbed and shaken by the actors, who insist that he should 'buy!'. In the theatre aisle, a few inches from the public's nose, the actresses fight over, tear apart and eat a piece of raw liver, which symbolizes the heart of a millionaire TV singer, who has just died. The singer's virginal fiancée, having prostituted herself, is crowned queen of radio and television; and she is dressed like the Virgin, with a cloak and crown. Etc. Supported by the lighting effects, there is an air of revelation about these scenes, and the silence in the auditorium is complete. On the other hand, the elaborate bad taste, plainly intentional, and with affinities with crude caricature, of these 'terrible' creations is plain. Terrible or 'terrible'? Moral indignation or malign imitation? Imitation and indignation, taken to extremes, turn into each other, a twist which has great theatrical effect, in which a political position is summed up and exposed to view with great artistic power. The audience, for its part, is shocked three, four or five times by this manoeuvre, and then is simply bedazzled, for it had not expected so much virtuosity where it had thought there was a crisis.

This game, in which the last word always belongs to the stage, this running around inside a circle of indefensible positions, is perhaps the most important experience which Oficina has given us. In various ways, it has been repeated, and it ought to be analysed. In the examples I have given, two elements of different artistic logic and scope are combined. Thematically, they are images of a deliberately shocking naturalism, satirical and moralistic: all there is in the world is money and sex, that's that. They are however linked to a form of direct action on the public. This second element is not simply to be identified with the explicit aim it was used for, however, that of breaking the audience's shell so that criticisms can get at it more effectively. Its cultural target is much wider, and, for the time being, difficult to measure. When they touch the audience, the actors are not only failing to respect the line between stage and audience, but also the physical distance which is usual between strangers, and without which our notion of individuality cannot be sustained. The colossal excitement and unease which grip the audience come, in this case, from the risk of generalization:

what would happen if everyone touched one another? In the two other examples, taboos are violated also. By its own logic, which is being developed, it seems, by the Living Theater, these experiments would be *liberating* and are part of a new movement, in which imagination and practice, artistic initiative and the reaction of the public take on a new relation to each other. In the Oficina, however, they are used as *insults*. The spectator is touched so that he can show his fear, not his desire. He is shown up in his weakness, not in his more positive impulses. If by chance he fails to be intimidated and himself touches an actress, he messes up the proceedings, which are not prepared for anything of the kind. As far as I could see, what happens is as follows: part of the audience identifies with the aggressor, at the expense of the victim. If someone, having been grabbed, leaves the theatre, the satisfaction of those that stay is enormous. The lack of solidarity in the face of the massacre, the disloyalty created within the audience itself are absolute, and are a repetition of the action on stage. It starts a kind of competition, a spiral of toughness in the face of endlessly repeated shocks, in which any political and liberating intention that the shocks may have had is lost or turned upside down. The situations do not have intrinsic worth of their own, but work as part of a general trial of strength, whose ideal lies in an indefinite capacity to de-identify oneself and identify with the collective aggressor. This is perhaps what is really happening, rather than the overcoming of prejudices. By its content, this action is extremely demoralizing; but since we are in the theatre, it is also an image, and that is where its critical power derives from.

What is presented, criticized and played out here is the cynicism of bourgeois culture faced with its own image. Its formal basis, here, is the systematization of shock, which is no longer a device and has become a principle of construction in its own right. But, in spite of and because of its predatory intent, systematized shock has essential links with the established order in the public's mind, and that is precisely its paradox as a form of art. It has no language of its own, it has to borrow it from its victim, whose stupidity is the explosive charge it operates with. As a form, in this case, shock responds to the desperate necessity for action, for direct action on the public; it is a kind of cultural gunshot. As a consequence, its problems lie in the realm of psychological manipulation - just as in advertising, communication is sought for by tickling our unconscious motives - and these are problems which are not *in essence* artistic. If you want to shock, you don't speak to the passing breeze - yet every artist has to speak to that breeze to some little extent. And if you want to act politically, you don't want to shock ... To sum it up, the barriers between the stage and the audience have come down, but the resultant traffic is only one-way. This inequality, which is a betrayal that has more or less been consented to, no longer corresponds to any absolute theatrical or cultural values, nor, on the other hand, to a political relationship, properly so-called. Encamped in the wasteland of present-day bourgeois ideology, the Oficina invents and explores games which suit the terrain itself, making the nihilistic, post-1964 space inhabitable, disgusting and funny. How can one say then that this theatre carries any weight on the left? The 'hooray-pessimism' of the Weimar Republic, 'Jucheepessimismus', which, while it was burying liberalism, was probably the forerunner of fascism and laid the ground for it is well known. Nowadays, given the world context, perhaps the situation is inverted. At least amongst intellectuals, the blackened earth of liberalism seems to produce either nothing at all or leftist vegetation. The Oficina was certainly part of this scorched-earth policy.

Taken as a whole, the cultural movement of these years is a kind of late flowering, the fruit of two decades of democratization, which has come to maturity now, right in the middle of a dictatorship, when the social conditions for it no longer exist, and now coinciding with the first attempts at an armed struggle in the country. The right has taken on the inglorious task of cutting its head off: its best singers and composers have been imprisoned and are now in exile, Brazilian directors are now filming in Europe and Africa, university teachers and scientists are leaving, if not going to jail. But on the left the situation is complicated too, because although it may be in the nature of culture to contest the use of power, it has no means of taking power itself. What use is ideological hegemony, if it not translated into immediate physical force? – even more so now, when the repression which has hit the militants is so extremely violent. If we add the very widespread dissemination of the ideology of decisive, warlike action, which began with the guerrilla warfare in Bolivia, one can understand that the status of those who sit at their desks should be on the low side. Subjected to pressure from right and left, the intelligentsia is entering a moment of acute crisis. The favourite theme of the political films and novels of the period is, precisely, the conversion of the intellectual to militancy.[11] If his own activity, as it has been defined historically in Brazil, is no longer possible, what is left to him but to go over to directly political struggle?

In the months that have passed between the writing of the first lines of this panorama and its conclusion, the purges have continued in the universities, and prior censorship of books has been brought in, to prevent pornography. The first publication to fit in with this definition was the last one in which, even though in a selective, doubtful way, the critical spirit in the country could show itself in public: the weekly *Pasquim*.[12] In other words, culture's nationwide, political diffusion, which is a great part of its importance, must give way to other objects and aims. As a consequence you can hear it said that the Universities are finished, cinema and theatre too, that teachers have resigned en masse, etc. These expressions, which are a witness of the personal dignity of those who use them, nevertheless contain a factual error: the said institutions continue, though in a very controlled state. What is more, it is not very probable that the government will manage substantially to transform them. What has happened every time the police pressure has been relaxed, from 1964 to now, has been a fantastic wave of popular dissatisfaction; silenced by force, the country is the same, where Goulart left it, more susceptible to agitation than ever. The same endurance is also perhaps true in the realm of culture, where it is difficult to change basic motives. In the short term, police repression can do nothing but paralyse, for there is no hope of fabricating a new past from one day to the next.

What chance do the military have of making their position ideologically active? The pro-American group, who are in power, none;* subordination does not inspire one to song, and even if they are managing to produce a temporary solution in the economy, it is at the price of not transforming the country socially; in these conditions, of widespread, visible poverty, the ideology of consumerism will always be a mocking insult. The unknown lies with the nationalist military, who to stand up to the United States would have to carry out some reform which would give them popular support, as in Peru. That's the way the Communist Party is placing its bets. But on the other hand, the Peruvian military don't seem too keen on mass movements ... However, there is a simpler cultural presence, which has a more immediate ideological effect – physical presence itself. It is perhaps an important social fact that the military are entering civilian life en masse, occupying posts in public and private administration. In the provinces they are also beginning to enter university teaching, in technical disciplines. This diffuse presence of the representatives of order alters the ordinary climate

---

*The group, with General Emilio Garrastazu Médici as their presidential candidate, who took power at the end of 1968.

of thinking. Where before the intellectual conversed and thought for years, without ever having to confront authority, which only very rarely made him responsible for his opinions, and only then because of any effects they might have had, now it is probable that one of his colleagues may be a soldier. In the long term, this situation is bound to carry the problems of social life inside the Armed Forces. In the immediate present, however, it brings their authority into everyday affairs. In these circumstances, a fraction of the intelligentsia opposed to dictatorship, to imperialism and to capitalism is going to dedicate itself to revolution, and the rest, without changing their views, will keep their mouths shut, work and fight in a restricted area for better days. Naturally there are defections, as in April 1964, when the theoretical thrust of the coup made a large number of theoretical Marxists convert to structuralism.

An interesting case of an artistic commitment to the dictatorship is that of Nelson Rodrigues, a dramatist with a high reputation. Since the middle of 1968 this writer has been publishing a daily column in two important newspapers in São Paulo and Rio, in which he attacks the advanced section of the clergy, the student movement and the left-wing intelligentsia. It's worth mentioning him, for, since he can write well and has a certain moral daring, he pays fully and explicitly – abjectly – the price which capitalism demands these days of its lackeys. When he began the series, it is true that it produced a certain expectation in town: what disgusting rubbish would Nelson Rodrigues have invented this afternoon? Mainly, he resorts to a stylized form of calumny. For example, he goes at midnight to a plot of waste ground, there to meet a goat and a leftist priest, who there reveals the true, shameful reasons for his participation in politics; and he tells him too that Dom Helder can hardly bear to put up with the unattainable authority of Christ.* In another article, he says that a well-known Catholic opponent of the dictatorship can't take his shoe off. Why? because his cloven hoof would show. Etc. The vulgarly offensive aim of the story is not hidden: on the contrary, that's where the comedy of this expedient lies. However, if it is turned into a method and always turned against the same adversaries – whom the police are also attacking – these openly malevolent and lying fantasies stop being a joke, and carry through a kind of liquidation,

---

*Dom Helder Câmara, the well-known left-wing Archbishop of Recife, who was one of the few people within Brazil who openly protested against the regime after the 'coup within a coup' of 1968.

or suicide of literature: since no one believes in the reasoning of the right, even when they are on its side, there's no need to argue and convince. There is a certain formal fitness, even a sociological truth in this misuse of literary talent: it represents, in a somewhat lively fashion, the atmosphere of 'anything goes' into which bourgeois order in Brazil has entered.

All through this chapter, we have been speaking of Brazilian culture. However, this culture only reaches less than fifty thousand people with any regularity and in any breadth, in a country of ninety million. Certainly, it cannot be blamed for imperialism and the class society. Still, since it is an exclusive language, it is also true that, at least from this point of view, it does contribute to the consolidation of privilege. For historical reasons, which we have tried to sketch out, it got to the stage of reflecting the situation of those it excludes, and took their side. It became an abscess within the dominant classes. Of course, its audacity was founded on its impunity. However, that audacity did exist, which, converging with populist movements at one moment, and with popular resistance to the dictatorship at another, formed a new conception of the country. Now, when the bourgeois state – which has not even managed to reduce illiteracy, has never organized minimally decent schools, has not made general access to culture possible, and has prevented contact between different sectors of the population – when this state abolishes the very civil liberties which are the vital element in its culture, this culture sees its hope in the forces which are trying to destroy the state. As a result, cultural production undergoes exposure to the infra-red rays of the class struggle, with results that are by no means flattering. Culture is the natural ally of revolution, but this revolution will not be made for its sake, much less for that of the intellectuals. It is carried through, primarily, to expropriate the means of production and guarantee work and a decent means of survival for the millions and millions of people who live in acute poverty. What interest could the revolution have in left-wing intellectuals, who were elite anti-capitalists much more than they were socialists proper? They will have to transform themselves, reformulate their arguments, which however had made them allies of the revolution. History is not a benevolent old lady. A traditional figure in Brazilian literature in this century has been the '*fazendeiro do ar*' [farmer of the air]:[13] the man who comes from the rural propertied classes to the city, where, in prose and verse, he remembers, analyses and criticizes the contact with the earth, with the family, with tradition and with the people which the plantation had allowed him to have. It is a literature of rural decadence. In *Quarup*, the recent novel which is most ideologically representative for the intellectual left, the road points in the other direction: an intellectual, in this case a priest, travels round the country in a geographical and social sense, rejects his profession and social position, in the search for the people, whose struggle he will join – a certain literary wisdom comes in here – in a chapter after the last one in the book.

Notes

1. *Animalia*, by G. Guarnieri.

2. For a historical summary of the origins of the 1964 crisis, see R.M. Marini, 'Contradições no Brasil contemporâneo', in *Revista Teoria e Prática*, No. 3 (São Paulo 1968). On the limitations of the national bourgeoisie and on the limitations of the power of populism, see, respectively, articles by Fernando Henrique Cardoso and Francisco Weffort in *Les Temps Modernes*, October 1967.

3. In cases in which the 'antiquated' element is extremely recent and international – the neo-fossil habits of the so-called consumer society – tropicalism simply coincides with forms of pop.

4. For a wide-ranging exposition of these ideas, see André Gunder Frank, *On Capitalist Development* (Oxford University Press, Bombay 1975) and *Latin America: Underdevelopment or Immediate Enemy* (Monthly Review Press, New York 1969).

5. The idea and the vocabulary here are taken from Walter Benjamin's study of German baroque drama, *The Origin of German Tragic Drama* (Verso, London 1977), in which he sets out a theory concerning allegory.

6. Some of the representatives of this line are, in music, Gilberto Gil and Caetano Veloso; in theatre, José Celso Martinez Correia, with *O rei da vela* and *Roda viva*; in the cinema there are elements of tropicalism in *Macunaíma*, by Joaquim Pedro de Andrade, *Os herdeiros* [*The Heirs*], by Carlos Diegues, *Brasil ano 2000* [*Brazil year 2000*], and *Terra em transe* [*Land in Anguish*] and *Antônio das Mortes* [lit. *Antônio of the Deaths*], by Glauber Rocha.

7. Sérgio Ferro Pereira, 'Arquitetura nova', in *Revista Teoria e Prática*, No. 1 (São Paulo 1967).

8. Preface to *Tiradentes*. The play is by Gianfrancesco Guarnieri and Augusto Boal. For a discussion of this theory see Anatol Rosenfeld, 'Heróis e Coringas' [*Heroes and Jokers*], in *Teoria e Prática*, No. 2.

9. This argument is developed by Adorno, in his essay on the values of modern music, when he compares Schönberg and Webern in *Klangfiguren*, Suhrkamp Verlag.

10. In an interview translated in *Partisans*, No. 47 (Paris, Maspero), José Celso explains: 'In the end, it is a relation of conflict, a conflict between the actors and the public. . . . The play attacks him [the spectator] intellectually, formally, sexually, politically. That is, it calls the spectator a cretin, it accuses him of being repressed and reactionary. And we ourselves are in the same soup' (p. 75). 'If we take this public as a whole, the only way of forcing it to undergo a real political process lies in the destruction of its defence mechanisms, all its Manichean and historicist self-justifications (even when they are based on Gramsci, Lukács, and others). We have to put him in his place, to reduce him to zero. The public represents a more or less privileged sector of this country, the sector which benefits, albeit in a mediocre way, from all the lack of history and all the stagnation of this sleeping giant that is Brazil. Today, the theatre needs to demystify, to put this public into its original state, face to face with its enormous

poverty, the poverty of a small privilege obtained in exchange for so many concessions, so much opportunism, so many castrations, so many repressions, in exchange for the real poverty of a vast number of people. What matters is to place this public in a position of total nakedness, defenceless, and to incite it to take the initiative, to the creation of a new, untried way forward, having nothing to do with all the familiar, opportunistic ways (whether they are called Marxist or not). The political efficacy which can be expected of the theatre with regard to this sector (the petty-bourgeoisie) can only lie in its ability to help people to understand the need for individual initiative, the initiative which will lead everyone to throw his own stone at the absurdity which is Brazil'. 'As far as this public, *which is not going to take action as a class* is concerned, the political efficacy of a play is measured less by any given sociological criteria *than by its level of aggression. In Brazil, nothing is accomplished by freedom, and the blame for this is not only to be laid at the door of censorship.'*

11. *Pessach: a travessia* [*Pessach: the crossing*], a novel by Carlos Heitor Cony (Civilização Brasileira: Rio de Janeiro); *Quarup* [*Quarup*] a novel by Antônio Callado (Civilização Brasileira: Rio de Janeiro); *Terra em Transe*, a film by Glauber Rocha; *O desafio* [*The Challenge*], a film by Paulo César Sarraceni. It is interesting to note that the conversion plot turns out to be more politically and artistically convincing when its centre is not the intellectual, but the soldier and the peasant, as in *Os fuzis* [*The Guns*], by Rui Guerra, *Deus e o diabo na terra do sol* [*Black God, White Devil*] by Glauber Rocha or *Vidas secas* [*Barren Lives*] by Nelson Pereira dos Santos. In these latter cases, the illusory, disproportionate nature of the moral crises is either objectified or disappears, which prevents the plot getting caught up in less essential matters.

12. *Pasquim* was not closed down. The mistake is left uncorrected, as a homage to the numerous false alarms which threatened daily life at this time.

13. The title of a book of poems by Carlos Drummond de Andrade.

ELEVEN

Cinema and *The Guns*

Just as the cinema can take us to the savannah to see lions it can also take us to the Northeast to see drought victims. In both cases, proximity is a product, a technical construction. The film industry, with the world and its image at hand, can bring the savannah and the drought to our neighbourhood screens. Since it guarantees a real distance, however, the constructed proximity is proof of its power: it offers intimacy without risks; I see the lion, but it does not see me. The lion may seem close and convincing, but still more impressive is the miraculous technical power of our civilization. The real situation, however, is not one of confrontation between man and beast. The spectator is a protected member of industrial civilization and the lion, composed of light, was in the eye of the camera. It could just as well have been in the sight of a rifle. With films about wild animals our privileged situation becomes clear. Without it, we would not stay in the theatre. Through this prism, however obvious, there emerges a true notion of our power; the fate of animals becomes our responsibility. In other cases, however, the evidence is less clear.

Proximity mystifies, establishing a psychological continuum where there is no real continuum: the suffering and thirst of the northeastern peasant, seen in close-up and from a privileged angle, become ours as well. But human sympathy impedes our comprehension because it cancels out the political nature of the problem. Through identification the true relationship is obscured, the nexus between the Northeast and the chair in which I am sitting disappears. Provoked by the image, I feel thirst, I hate injustice, but I do not really feel responsible. I witness suffering, but I am not guilty. I do not leave the theatre as the beneficiary, which I am, of a constellation of forces, an exploitative undertaking. Even important films with serious intentions, such as *Black God, White Devil* and *Barren Lives** fail at this point, leaving a feeling of malaise. Aesthetically and politically compassion is an anachronistic response. Cameras, laboratories, and financing do not commiserate, they transform. We have to find feelings adequate to the cinema, to the technical stage in our history it represents.

Rui Guerra's masterpiece, *The Guns*, does not try to *comprehend* poverty. On the contrary he films as if it were an aberration, and this distance deprives it of its emotional impact. At first glance, it is as if two incompatible films were alternating: a documentary of drought and poverty and a fiction film. The difference is clear. Following the sacred ox with its devout followers, the speech of the blind man and the mystic chants, the entrance of the soldiers, motorized and talkative, comes as a rupture in style. The documentary sequences reveal the misery of the local population. In the fiction sequences the work is done by actors; these characters are from a world not of hunger, but of rifles and trucks. In the facial mobility of the actors, who are not starving, one encounters desire, fear, boredom, individual will, and a freedom inexistent in the opaque faces of the drought victims. When the focus passes from one sphere to the other the very reach of the image is altered: expressive faces are followed by those that express nothing; the brutish peasants are to be looked at, but plot, psychology and humanity can be read only on the mobile faces of the soldiers. Some faces are there to be looked at, others are to be understood. This rupture and the theme of the film converge. The actors are to the non-actors as the city dwellers with their technical civilization are to the evacuees, as possibility is to pre-determined misery, as plot is to inertia. The visual effectiveness of *The Guns* derives from this codification.

The eye of the cinema is cold, a technical operation. It produces a sort of ethnocentricity of reason, in the face of which, as with contact with modern technology, that which is different cannot be tolerated. The violent effectiveness of capitalist colonization, in which reason and superiority are combined, is transformed into an aesthetic model: it permeates our

---

Deus e o diabo na terra do sol, by Glauber Rocha, and *Vidas secas* by Nelson Pereira dos Santos. Like *Os fuzis* [*The Guns*], these two films appeared in 1963. For discussion of them and other Brazilian films of the time, see John King, *Magical Reels: A History of Cinema in Latin America* (Verso, London 1990), Ch. 5.

sensibilities, which become equally implacable for good and ill – unless it slackens, losing contact with reality. 'Everything that is fixed and callous is dissolved, but the retinue of traditions and archaic conceptions ... profanes that which is sacred, and men are forced, finally, to see with sober eyes their positions and relationships.'[1]

From the beginning of *The Guns* misery and technological civilization confront each other. The former is slow, excessive, an aggregate of defenceless people, discredited through the spiritual and real mobility – the trucks – of the latter. Although the misery seems pervasive and strong, its causes do not matter; it is one side of a relationship, carrying a negative sign. By showing it frontally and from the outside, the film refuses to see more than anachronism and inadequacy. This distance is the opposite of philanthropy: short of transformation there is no possible humanity; or, from the perspective of plot, short of transformation there is no difference that matters. The mass of miserable evacuees ferments but does not explode. What the camera shows in the abstruse faces, or better said, what makes them abstruse, is the absence of explosion, the action that has not been taken. There is therefore no plot, but merely the weight of their presence, remotely threatening. The political structure has been translated into an artistic structure.

The soldiers, in contrast, look as if they could do anything. In the city they are ordinary men of a lower class. In the small town, however, uniformed and godless, they saunter through the streets as if they were gods – the men that came by jeep from the outside. They talk about women, laugh, and do not depend on a sacred ox; it suffices that they are a new element. These are marvellous sequences, in which their haughtiness recovers, for us, the privilege of being *modern*; to be from the city is to be admirable. The same holds for the warehouse owner and the truckdriver. Their actions matter; they are on the level of history, whose local levers – the warehouse, rifles, transportation – they control. Even their unfulfilled intentions are important: their ambivalence concerning their own role, for example, suggests that the final outcome of the conflict might have been very different. In other words, where there is transformation of individual destinies, everything matters: there is plot. A space of freedom has been opened, we feel at home. The nature of the image has been transformed. Psychology colours every face, evoking a sense of justice and injustice, individual and understandable destinies. The soldiers are like us. Moreover, they are our emissaries at the locale, and, whether we like it or not, their practice carries out our implicit politics. It is with them that we identify, much more than with the suffering and superstitious drought victims.

From a narrative perspective the solution is perfect; it precludes emotional reactions and favours responsible reflection. Concentrating on the soldiers, called from the city to defend a food warehouse, the plot forces antipathetic identification and self-awareness: we feel compassion for the drought victims, but we are like the police. The displacement of the dramatic centre from the victims to authority renders the film's material more intelligible and better articulated. For the peasants the world is a homogeneous and diffuse calamity in which the sun, the boss, politics, and Satan have equal roles. The soldiers, meanwhile, participate in a precise but transformable situation. The distance between the drought victims and private property is guaranteed by the guns, which, however, could cross over to the other side. The image, as Brecht would have it, is of a changeable world: rather than stress the moral injustice, the film focuses on its concrete mechanism and human guarantors. Our feelings go far beyond mere sympathy. While we identify, we also despise; so that compassion comes only through the destruction of our emissaries and, by extension, of the existing order of things.

The soldiers strut arrogantly through the small town, but from the perspective of the city from which they come they are quite modest. They are simultaneously the guardians of private property and mere salaried workers. Soldiers by circumstance, they might have been involved in other forms of work; the truckdriver too had been a soldier. They give orders, but they themselves must obey. Seen from below they represent authority, but from above they are 'the people'. This system of contradictions forms the boundaries of the plot. The logic of this conflict appears for the first time in what is perhaps the most powerful scene in the film: a soldier, in front of his companions, explains to the townsmen the functioning and efficiency of a rifle. The reach of the shot is X; it will penetrate so many metres of pine, so many sacks of sand, six human bodies. The information is intended to threaten. By naming each part, he wants to stupefy. The technical vocabulary, impersonal and precise by nature, is passionately enjoyed as a sign of personal and even racial superiority: we are of another species, a species it is wise to obey. Contrary to its supposed vocation of universality, knowledge merely exploits and consolidates difference. The contradictions of this situation, a microcosm of imperialism, involve bad faith. Insisting on technical language, inaccessible to the townsmen, the soldier provokes the animosity of his companions. The specialized vocabulary, mystifying for some, is commonplace for others; to exalt himself successfully the soldier requires the complicity of his companions, who in turn need his humiliation to regain their freedom. His insistence becomes ridiculous and soon traps him: the ignorance of others no longer proves his own superiority, but he must insist and trample the townsmen even more, in order to retain, through their common condition as oppressors, the fugitive solidarity of his irritated companions.

The soldiers see in each other the mechanisms of the oppression of which they are agents. Because they are not merely soldiers, their complicity, necessary to the superior race, has limits; and because they are soldiers they do not reach a radical unmasking. Their position vacillates, as a result, between haughtiness and vileness. They confront two permanent temptations: the arbitrary destruction of the drought victims and their own violent disintegration. Later conflicts repeat this pattern: the murder of the villager, the fight between the soldiers, and the love scene, close to rape in its brutality.

This series of events culminates in the violent persecution and death of the truckdriver. The food is to be transported out of the town, far from the drought victims, who look on impassively. The soldiers stand guard, terrified by the masses of starving people, but also exasperated by their passivity. The truckdriver, an ex-soldier who himself is hungry, does what the soldiers could have done as he tries to stop the transport of the food. Hunted by the whole detachment he is finally caught and riddled with bullets. The frenetic excess of shots, as well as the sinister joy of the chase, makes the exorcism clear: in the ex-soldier the soldiers kill their own freedom, their anxiety about passing to the other side.

Refracted in the group of soldiers the real problem, that of private property, ultimately reduces to a psychological conflict. The collision of consciences, with its own movement, is outlined and incited gradually until the final gun battle. A partial dialectic erupts, one that is merely moral, based on fear, shame, and fury, restricted to the soldiers, even though caused by the presence of the drought victims. It is therefore an *innocuous dialectic*, bloody as the struggle may be, since it does not involve the starving masses that should be its true subject. It is as if, in view of the central conflict, the dramatic development were off centre.[2] The climax does not really resolve the conflicts of the film; even though the gun battle represents the culmination of one conflict, it does not govern the sequence of episodes, which always alternates and separates the world of the plot and the world of inertia. At first glance this decentred construction is a defect: of what value is the crisis if it is a dislocated and distorted version of the primary antagonism? If the crisis is moral and the antagonism political, of what use is their approximation? It serves, in *The Guns*, to mark the discontinuity between the two worlds. It serves as a critique of moralism since it accentuates both moral responsibility and its insufficiency. The important link, in this case, is in the very absence of a direct link.

Even in the final scenes, which parallel the soldiers and the drought victims, the hiatus between the two is carefully preserved. The slaying of the sacred ox does not result from the death of the truckdriver. It is an echo, a degraded response. The persecution and the gun battle, although they may have a political substratum, do not transmit awareness or organization to the drought victims; but they do transmit excitement and movement, a vague impatience. The bearded prophet threatens his sacred ox: 'If it does not rain soon, you will no longer be sacred, you will no longer be an ox.' A continuous act, the edible holiness, which had been preserved, is transformed, as Joyce would say, into Christeak. The victims, inert up to this point, in this final moment are like piranhas. The group of peasants is explosive, and the moral position of the soldiers is untenable. The moral crisis, however, does not feed the hungry, nor can it be resolved by what they have done. The relationship between the two forms of violence is not one of continuity or proportion, but neither is it of indifference; it is aleatory and highly flammable. In the fictional sequences, which represent our world, we witness oppression and its moral cost; the close-up is in bad faith. In the sequences about misery we witness the conflagration and its affinity with lucidity. The close-up is obscure, and if it weren't it would be frightening. In the supposed *defect* of this construction, whose elements do not mix, there is caught and defined a historical fatality: our western civilization glimpses with fear, and horror of itself, the possible access of the plundered to justice.

Notes

1. Source of quote not specified by author.

2. My argument and vocabulary are taken from a study by Althusser, 'Notes sur un Théâtre Matérialiste', in which he describes and discusses a structure of this type, 'assymetrical and decentered'. Cf. *Esprit*, December 1962.

TWELVE

On *A Man Marked Out To Die*

As with all remarkable things, the interest of *Cabra marcado para morrer** is difficult to classify. The film is a triumph of political faith, and for that reason is very moving.

The initial project, which pre-dates 1964, was to film the assassination of a peasant leader from Paraíba named João Pedro, which had happened not long before. The actors were to be his comrades in work and in the struggle, among them his wife, and the setting was to be that of the crime itself. The military coup interrupted the filming and broke up the team, while the reels with the part of the film that had already been made disappeared in the chaos of the escape from the authorities.

However, the director did not forget the project, nor did he give it up. As soon as he could – that's to say, many years later – he went in search of the material that had disappeared. When he had got it, he looked for the actors, who had been scattered by repression and almost two decades of change. He showed the old reels, in which they had taken part, and filmed their present reactions, which in one way or another bring to light the effects of the dictatorship and the continuity of the life of the people. The whole, with documentary material and explanations added, and with a hiatus of twenty years embedded in it, was to constitute the film. The

---

*The title of the film literally means 'A man |*cabra* is in fact a pejorative word for a worker, common in the Northeast in particular| marked out to die'. It was released in 1984.

director, Eduardo Coutinho, was taking up his work and his class alliances again, transforming the time that had passed into a source of artistic strength and into matter for reflection.

In this, the director is like his main figure, the central actress, the peasant militant who was able to disappear, survive the repression, and reappear. In fact, the emotion springs from this parallel: the interrupted film, completed against terrible odds, in a certain way is coterminous with the courageous woman who, after years of suffering, finds her family again, takes on her real name, and reaffirms her convictions. Constancy triumphs over oppression and oblivion. Metaphorically, the heroine who has at last been recognized and the film at last completed re-establish the continuity with the popular movement before 1964, and give the lie to the eternal dictatorship, which will not after all be the last chapter. Or to put it another way, committed cinema and the popular struggle come back into the open together.

Certainly, nothing is more moving than retying a broken thread, completing an aborted project, regaining a lost identity, resisting terror and surviving it. These are basic desires of the imagination, and paradigms exploited by sentimental fiction. If *Cabra marcado* were no more than this, it would be a melodrama. Without undervaluing the political worth of keeping the faith, which of course exists, and to which the film owes its extraordinary appeal, as well as its very being, we should recognize that its qualities are more complex.

For the faithful, when they meet again after the trials they have been through, are not what they were at the beginning. This change, plainly engraved on the documentary material of the film, gives it its density and its power as historical witness. Because of it, its images demand to be seen over and over again, as inexhaustible as reality itself. Beneath what appears to be a re-encounter, what is there are the enigmas of the new situation, and those of the old one, which are asking to be thought through again.

The idea of the first film emerged during a journey of the 'flying' UNE to the Northeast, in 1962, in the context of the CPCs and the MPCs,* and it has the richness of that extraordinary moment. In an atmosphere of cultural renewal, an alliance was born between the open-ended enthusiasm of the students and the most dramatic forms of class warfare, which in

---

*UNE = União Nacional de Estudantes, the main left-wing student organization of the period before and for some after the coup. For CPCs and MPCs, see pp. 1 and 126 ('Nationalism by Elimination' and 'Culture and Politics').

Brazil, because of the inheritance of slavery, usually took place – and still do – in areas which public opinion cannot reach. Given the characteristics of the populism of Jango's time,* the alliance had vague official backing, and seemed to be swimming with the tide.

Its implicit meaning, unless I am mistaken, is more or less as follows: justice and the simple nature of the people's demand for rights gave relevance to student life and to culture, which in their turn would guarantee to the struggle of the poor both nationwide repercussion, and the admiration and recognition of the 'civilized' sector of the country. These aspirations complemented one another in an objective way, and great moments resulted from it, which can be seen in the part of the film made in 1962: the extraordinary dignity of the peasants, the tragic simplicity of the presentation of class conflict, the recognition of non-bourgeois kinds of beauty, etc. These are moments, also, which demonstrate how stupid, aesthetically, the present doctrine of opposition to commitment is.

Today it seems obvious that this alliance had no political future, and that revolution fomented from above could only come to a bad end. At the same time, it did channel real hopes, which the film does tell us about, and in which we get some sense of other, possible, future forms of society. The relation between subject, actors, local situation and cinema people is obviously not of a commercial nature, and points towards new cultural models. Nor can it be said that the director wanted to express himself as an individual: his art tries to discover the beauty of collective meanings. Does it make sense, in such a case, to speak of an author? The film is not a documentary, since it has actors, but such is the degree to which it takes their destiny as its subject, that one cannot say that it is fiction either. For an intellectual audience, on the other hand, the fiction has a documentary interest: in the seriousness and the intelligence of the actors, whose world however is completely distinct from ours, it allows a glimpse of an art with a different social basis from our own. Finally, the film shows how much the oppressed can give to intellectuals, and vice versa (I am not forgetting the objections that can be made to this point of view).

These are perspectives which have come into existence and which have found material cultural expression, even when we take into account the large measure of illusion that they contained. But if today they seem so

---

*Nickname of João Goulart, President of Brazil from 1961 until the military coup of March 1964.

remote, this is not just because of their naiveté. The commercialization of labour relations in general, and of cultural production in particular have advanced a great deal in these last twenty years. Other forms of social organization have become, in our circumstances, almost unimaginable. This may not be a good thing: but in any case, it shows how much the reality of capitalism has deepened and consolidated itself in the intervening period.

Seventeen years later, in 1981, the director goes to the North-east in search of his comrades and characters. He takes the old film and a camera. Behind him, there is no longer the student movement or government help, nor is there any enthusiasm in the country as a whole. Instead of social ferment and its very socialized types of invention, there is a more or less solitary individual, impelled by his fidelity to certain people and to a project, and with only his own meagre resources to rely on. Obviously, he is no longer the same person. The aim of his work will have changed too: though the social intention is still there, it will now take on a commercial form, as is inevitable (this is not a criticism, on the contrary, for the importance of the film lies in its revelation of the transformation that has taken place in the conditioning context of Brazilian life). Finally, not even the peasants are the same. The scenes in which they enjoy and comment on their own earlier performances – a privileged position, which makes one feel something of what Walter Benjamin called the right of the worker to his own image* – are splendid. But they also show the changes imposed by fear and new expediencies, not to mention by time itself. The re-encounter is warm and generous, but the circumstances are different.

The interviews with Elisabete, the militant who disappeared and whose whereabouts the director inquires into and discovers, are the centre of the film. The peasant leader's companion had fled to another state, changed her name and cut herself off from her previous connections, 'so as not to be exterminated' as she explains. She is obviously an exceptional person, in her energy, her vivacity, her prudence, and also in her dignity. The pleasure – half-modest, half-vain – with which she leaves clandestinity behind and reveals her identity in the village where she had lived for so long with a false name, teaching children and washing clothes and dishes, is, within the limits of the possible, the happy ending of an authentic popular heroine.

---

*See 'The Work of Art in the Age of Mechanical Reproduction', *Illuminations* (New York, Schocken 1969), p. 241.

The director's influence on her life is therefore very great. How can we understand it? The first time, in 1962, it was a matter of the meeting of two movements, the students and the peasants, by means of the cinema, in a moment of general political radicalization. It was the future of the country that was involved, and individuals were concerned only as means within this larger context. Now, it is the obstinacy and solidarity of an individual, armed with a camera, who in the context of a political thaw allows another person to return to legal existence, which on top of this allows him to finish the old film. What is at stake now is the redeeming of existences and projects which, unless I'm mistaken, are of an individual nature – or rather, not as individual as that, since the redemption takes place in the context of the cinema, which introduces another aspect of power, one of great significance. Where in 1962 we had a redefinition of the cinema and, by extension, of cultural production itself in the framework of a realignment of the class alliances in the country, now we have the social power of film-making ('Are you from Rede Globo?'') coming into people's private lives to change them – in this case for the better.

This question stands out most acutely in the interviews with Elisabete's children, scattered all round Brazil, almost without any news or memory of their mother, and whom the director has found. After showing them photographs or playing back a tape with her voice on it, there come the questions at point-blank range, with the camera focused on their emotions. We know that the good doctor is judged not by his sympathy with the patient, but by his ability to cure. To some extent this is a valid rule for the cinema of the left, which wants to know about and to reveal what is real, above all in moments of confrontation. What is the meaning of the tears and the confused explanations of a bar owner in the Baixada Fluminense,'' whom the spectator recognizes as the serious and dignified young girl, in one of Elisabete's family photographs? Of course, the context of all this is the misfortunes which have been showered down upon the family (persecution, terror, children shot at in the street, suicide, dispersal), just as they have teemed down on other families, of workers just as enlightened and courageous. However, if this vision of things is not imposed with some

---

'A phrase from the film. Rede Globo is the most powerful and all-pervasive of Brazilian media organizations.

''The heavily populated and generally impoverished hinterland of the city of Rio, notorious for its violence and gang-warfare.

determination, so that it becomes an implicit plot which there is no necessity to make explicit – at the moment, this is an open historical question – the close-ups of the suffering of the poor woman may function as simple exploitation of the emotions of others. Nothing gets away unscathed, not even the simplicity and the integrity which led the director not to give up, and then, to film his characters and scene with a complete lack of facile rhetoric. The attentive, documentary camera – Coutinho's homage to the obvious justice of the popular struggle, which needs no explanation – when it is faced by people who have been forced into an inferior position, and to whom History has refused the opportunity to articulate their case, has the effect of voyeurism. Is it a friendly coldness, or a consolation for the loss of reality characteristic of sentimentality, or is it the indiscreet curiosity of the camera? Of course, we cannot speculate on the subjective intentions of the director (rather question those of the critic): the film gives the conclusive proof of his real solidarity. The ambiguity is not his, it is inherent in the situation. The drama, for anyone who wants to understand their own position, lies in watching the shifts within reality itself and the redefinition of problems that those shifts cause.

The visit to Elisabete's children shows at the same time the reverse of the film and its historical truth. In the foreground is the extraordinary woman, who in spite of everything has the good fortune to retie the broken ends of the thread of her life, and the director, who manages to complete his project. That is what the film *tells*, that is its narrative interest. The visit to the children and to the other members of the original team, who have emigrated to the South, is what the film *shows*, what it records, counter-balancing the happy end in the foreground. They have been thrown around, spread around the whole of Brazil, without any knowledge of one another, without decent work, revealing the extent of the dismemberment and of the retreat in human terms which the evolution of capitalism has meant for the workers of the North-east. Only one, who went to study in Cuba, where he earns his living as a doctor, has ended up well. His few words on his father's martyrdom are in a naive, schoolbook, official language, which adds an important reference-point, in spite of its brevity. The picture we are given is all the more bitter in that the old photographs show a family who was obviously quite exceptional, judging by the intelligent, dignified, fine figure that all without exception make: something which leaves a strong impression. These are fragments of a coherent existence, belonging to the people, which has grown up in the North-east, and which the general development of the country crushes over and over again.

When she speaks about the violence of plantation life, Elisabete turns down the corners of her mouth, in a gesture of surprise, as it were, from which personal misfortunes, fear and even hatred are absent. It's like a kind of objectivity, a necessary taking into account of the amount of destruction and evil that it can do. It is as if it were a huge beast, or some other kind of vast calamity, which has to be dealt with, and whose dimensions it's as well to recognize. It is an unspoken knowledge, that of someone who has seen the face of the monster, and which is expressed without propaganda or dogma: it gives a rare example of the class struggle, free of the officialdom of the left. Many years ago, seeing a photograph of Neruda's funeral, just after the fall of Allende, I thought I could see something similar on the despondent faces of those present.

In spite of what has been said, *Cabra marcado* gives an impression of vitality and hope. How can we explain this? Some reasons have already been expounded: the continuity of the life of the people, the feeling that the period of dictatorship is coming to an end, the attractiveness and the intelligence of the North-easterners, and finally the demonstration of courage given in the making of the film itself. The fact that the ruling classes are absent also helps, perhaps. When one thinks about it, and things being what they are, would such a serious and dignified atmosphere be conceivable in today's Brazil if members of the dominant classes were present? Far be it from me to suppose that members of one class are intrinsically morally superior to those of another – I'm not crazy. However, if we think about the film's world, in which only intellectuals and members of the popular classes are present, I think we will recognize that this make-up is the basis of its extraordinary atmosphere. It is as if at the very moment when the best, most acceptable part of the Brazilian bourgeoisie is taking the reins of power – a moment to be saluted!* – the best film of the last few years were saying, through its very aesthetic nature and without any conscious desire to make the point, that in a serious world this class has no place. But of course life does not always imitate art.

---

*This essay was written in 1985, during the movement for direct elections, and the process in which the military's (civilian) candidate for the Presidency was defeated by the opposition figure Tancredo Neves (who died before taking office).

THIRTEEN

Is There a Third World

Aesthetic?

Unless I'm mistaken, the status of 'Third Worldism' was linked to enthusiastic support for struggles for national liberation, and to reservations about the Soviet Union. And in fact, nothing could be more welcome than a historical movement in which anti-imperialism and anti-Stalinism were joined together. But, however well-founded these sentiments might have been, did they open up a a new way forward for humanity? Headed by such national leaders as Nehru, Nasser or Castro, who deliberately resisted classification, Third Worldism gave many people the impression that it was a new road, better than capitalism or communism. That's what explains the climate of prophetic power and of a genuine avant-garde which communicated itself to a whole group of artists, and gave breadth and aesthetic and political excitement to their work. This is not to deny their naiveté and demagogy, which will also come down to posterity, though only as a document of that time. To our Brazilian public, provincial in the very nature of things, these artists presented the vital spectacle of an intellectual making his mark right in the heart of the modern world. And to First World intellectuals, paralysed by the upsurge of capitalism at the time, and by successive revelations about Soviet life, they presented the pleasing spectacle of a society in movement, where audacity, improvisation and above all the intellectual himself could do something. But now, when the cycle of decolonization is more or less over and the idea of a painless industrialization has been rejected as an illusion by the Third World leaders themselves, what is left of the prestige the idea once had?

The Third World mystique covers up class conflict and gives a naive, though violent view of conflicts between nations, and above all of their interdependence. The aesthetics it inspires does exist, and inherits retrograde aspects of nationalism. It is a relative question, however - it should be pointed out that there is no such thing as *the* aesthetic of the Third World. As for the socialist countries, the existence of an official aesthetic is undeniable: what is doubtful is whether it benefits the arts. Thus, if even in countries where reality is much more tolerable, the work of art owes its strength to *negativity*, I can't see why we should give a positive meaning, one of national identity, to relations of oppression, exploitation and restriction. These things are the reality of the Third World, but they do not constitute superiority. Or better, since reality is to a degree common to exploiters and exploited, it is understandable that these relations should be a motive for satisfaction, as well as embarrassment, to the former.

In aesthetics as in politics, the Third World is an organic part of the contemporary scene. Its presence is the living proof of the iniquitous nature of the organization of the world, both in terms of production and of life itself. And any charm that 'backwardness' may have for someone who doesn't suffer from it is another proof of dissatisfaction with the forms that progress has taken - forms, however, to which the Third World aspires and for which no one can see alternatives. Summing up - a difficult state of affairs, which cannot be understood or resolved with myths.

FOURTEEN

Anatol Rosenfeld,

a Foreign Intellectual

This man is every bit as Brazilian as I am.
Mário de Andrade[*]

When Brazil found its future again, in 1964, Rosenfeld went out round the Jewish community, asking those who were delighted to explain to him what they meant by Fascism. The reply was what he expected: they defined Fascism by anti-Semitism. I remember his excitement as he commented on this – it seemed to confirm him in some deep feeling as to the impossibility of people ever learning anything on this planet. Another time, in a group where conversation was starting to enter the realms of strange coincidences, of the kind that cannot be natural, he didn't hesitate, and came out with the most unlikely story of all. That was the green light: if the philosopher himself, a recognized doubter, could tell stories which can only be explained by reference to the world of spirits, there was no need to restrain oneself. Everybody told their own. When they had all committed themselves enough, Rosenfeld told the assembled company that that was all very nice, but his story had been made up. He told me afterwards that he had tried this experiment out in several places, and it always worked.

---

[*]See note (p. 79) to 'National by Elimination'. Mário is quoted here because he was a passionate (though non-exclusive) Brazilian nationalist.

I recall these episodes because they reveal the sceptical intellectual, the fan of truth, even when he irritates everybody and is of no use to anyone, quite different from the attentive, always constructive teacher that the Brazilian public has become familiar with. In fact, I think that Rosenfeld changed a great deal depending on whether he was in Brazilian or immigrant company, perhaps even depending on what language he was speaking. I have never known anyone more patient and Socratic, when he was speaking Portuguese. In German, though, his sarcasm was near the surface, and he liked to adopt a polemical attitude. Of course, this was because only in Brazil did he completely espouse that full and methodical obligingness which would be his trade-mark as a teacher; while German had been the language of his youth. Also, he spoke German to those of his generation, or older than him, immigrants like himself, whose exertions to make money he didn't approve of, and with whose opinions, on Brazil, on Judaism, on Israel, and on everything else, he disapproved of. And in fact, in the foreign community, there were many people who didn't like him. On the other hand, among his Brazilian friends there was no lack of rich young men and women, whose demeanour, as time went on, can't have been agreeable to him. But he didn't criticize these latter. There were two weights, two systems of measurement. Or, better, two situations: speaking German, amongst immigrants, Rosenfeld was a an ordinary, quarrelsome citizen whereas Portuguese was the language of an intellectual with an immigrant's identity card.

These are things to be thought about without preconceptions. Of course, the immigrant intellectual has to be prudent, since he hasn't the control over the situations he encounters, or the language. But it is not just a question of familiarity: beyond prudence is the fear of being insulted, and, at bottom, fear – however hospitable the people and the state may be. Fear, in the last instance, of being thrown out of the country, and, on a more day-to-day level, fear of being caught up in some touchy question of patriotism, or in some local custom. I remember my own surprise and disagreement when, even before 1964, Rosenfeld preferred not to take up a position on very 'national' questions. I thought this was overdoing it – we were soon to see that it was not. A little later Otto Maria Carpeaux, the author of the *History of Western Literature*, would be accused of spreading foreign ideas in Brazil ... all because he was a teacher of Comparative Literature. Apart from which it would be simplistic to assume that the experience of Nazism would not have cooled any enthusiasm for identification with the nation that an intelligent man might feel. It took me a while to understand this reluctance, even though I had the elements for that understanding: here and there, I too had been called a Jew, a kraut, etc. and had had occasion to experience the subtle feelings that such abuse inspires in one. It's not enough to imagine the disgust such things arouse – the misery of the intellectual faced by the brutishness of a crass myth – one should also remember that at any moment the new country has a plentiful supply of such cold showers ready for the foreigner: all you have to do is press the wrong button. In reply, our reflexes condition us not to provoke, and to give things a wide berth.

Thirty years after his arrival, Rosenfeld still kept the ceremonious behaviour of a visitor. He listened carefully, contributed with his own knowledge, but modestly, just offering information, and hardly ever asserted anything. It was the role that suited him, by its adaptive, defensive aspect, and by the ritual of politeness that it gave rise to. For Rosenfeld, this was part of the life of a philosopher. He hardly spoke of himself, asked questions politely and discreetly, and was so attentive that this social virtue, always worthy of esteem, changed its very nature to become a step on the path to knowledge. A different kind of politeness, free of presumption and pretence, which enchanted at the first meeting (though to others it seemed 'square'). The temporary suspension of his own presuppositions, which he practised as a method, was certainly a kind of concealment; but it was accompanied by a clearly receptive and 'off-guard' posture, methodical as well, which invited his partner to reflect. It was as if the philosopher put himself in parenthesis, so that the customer opposite could become a phenomenologist. And perhaps the perfectly real pleasure of explaining himself and communicating with strangers – like the educated Germans in glasses in the stories of Guimarães Rosa* – helped too. After all, contrary to what is said, formal methods can be useful for getting to the real matter: Rosenfeld's manner brought about love at first sight, and quite often awoke an unexpected intensity in people, and for that matter in unexpected people. It would happen, for example, that in his presence the most solid, compact donkeys would begin to reason, while the rest of the company

---

*João Guimarães Rosa (1908–67), one of the foremost writers of fiction in twentieth-century Brazil, and its most daring experimenter in prose. Although his stories and novels are usually set in the Brazilian backlands, itinerant foreigners frequently appear in them. An example, from his greatest novel, *Grande sertão: veredas* (*The Devil to Pay in the Backlands*) (1956) is 'seu' Emilio Wusp.

would exchange embarrassed looks. On such occasions Rosenfeld would display a perfect, almost unreal courtesy. He never betrayed his inter-locutor for a second, however stupid or slow he might be, and closed himself off from the others' complicity. Though he was sociable and free of arrogance, it was unthinkable for Rosenfeld to become one of a gang, even among his friends.

Of course, these reserved attitudes cannot just be explained by the anxieties of a foreigner. They were in harmony with his ideas about the philosophical life, and, what is just about the same thing, with the repugnance he felt for institutional life. In this, as in other questions – matters of attitude rather than philosophy – he felt in accord with Sartre. When the latter explained that he was refusing the Nobel prize because – political reasons apart – he didn't want to see himself become an institution, *le tout* São Paulo protested against such presumption. Unless my memory deceives me, on that occasion Rosenfeld defended him keenly. Like him, he kept his liberty, and refused to give his ideas any other guarantee than the evidence. And like him, he shocked other people by the simplicity with which he put his convictions into practice. So, in the institutional sense of the word, Rosenfeld was nobody. Aside from not being naturalized, he didn't marry, didn't set up house, was not a university teacher, was not employed by the state, had no stable profession or job. He didn't want to get buried in any of these specialisms, even if this meant living from hand to mouth – he gave private lessons and wrote articles – without the consolation of piling up property, without the security of a salary, pension, social security and other such advantages. Only the tie and the general correctness of manner hid the eccentricity of this behaviour. We could talk about a philosophical sublimation of social ambitions: since he didn't cheat others or act aggressively to them, he had an extraordinary appetite for the exchange of ideas. Like Brecht's heroes, he enjoyed thinking. By the same token, all his abnegations had nothing to do with unhappiness: he lived economically, but with no trace of asceticism – he even had a sybaritic side to him. There was a kind of elementary rationality about this, which was one of the strongest philosophical effects of his personality. On the other hand, he did not talk ill of the institutions he had avoided. As he avoided them in practice, so he did not enter them in theory – whether out of prudence, so as not to underline the affront, or out of courtesy – since his friends were inevitably either married, university teachers or were trying to make money – or because he didn't think they were the stuff of philosophy. Here, perhaps, he paid an indirect tribute to the social order, losing in critical verve what he gained in personal accessibility. The separation between philosophy and the critique of society, which someone who refuses the career of university philosopher appears to escape, returned through the back door. After all, the institutional system is, in the first place, the materialization of the (more or less horrible) interests of a reproduction of society, and not just a graveyard for personal whims. There were also Rosenfeld's anti-psychologist convictions, linked to German Expressionism and to Phenomenology, which made the mention of the empirical conditions of the subject seem indecent. His manner of guiding the conversation was characteristic: reduced to the external person, the thinker was no longer a specialist, a husband, a wage-earner, a candidate for a chair, or any other given, defined person. As if nothing else existed in the world, the issues were taken up and limited right at the level of experience and conversation, as they presented themselves, as long as - paradoxically - the subjective circumstances of the reflection were abstracted. However, these are also objective, and part of the real process, as well as being responsible for the contingencies of the configuration of the object itself. For good or ill, in its relative lack of real interests, the philosophical reasoning had something of an analytical exercise about it. I'm not trying to say that the thought of a teacher or a functionary would be preferable, but that it's unlikely that the advantages will be obvious and measurable. It is as if pure attention defined a focus, in which, as in a microcosm, things spoke for themselves, 'objectively'. That's why Rosenfeld had little affinity with the theoretical style of psychoanalysis and Marxism, which try to interpret any given phenomenon in continuity with processes and interests which it, the given, *manifests* but does not simply represent.

Rosenfeld was one of the first intellectuals to live as a freelance in São Paulo. As well as writing, he gave courses on literature and philosophy. He had got used to these articles and classes, as they happened to come along, and which preserved him from the tedium inherent in specialization. He valued versatility, and a good-humoured expository manner, and grafted them onto the solidity of his systematic knowledge. The result was convincing and strange, something like a centaur. To some extent, his mastery in exposition took advantage of this disparity. And he, who never boasted of the knowledge he possessed, had all the pride of a champion in the little jokes with which he brightened up his lectures and his writings. It is, of course, true that Rosenfeld had no desire to be compared with his university colleagues, and would be revolted by any such thing. However, for the students who frequented his classes, and those of the Rua Maria

Antônia*, the comparison was a natural one. If you put the good courses in the Philosophy Department and his side by side, it was true that in his there was a certain dilettantism – a dilettantism which belonged not to him, for his grounding was nothing if not solid, but to the situation itself. They were courses given in one person or another's house, and followed by cake and tea. There would meet, for instance, future doctors, psychologists, biologists, sociologists, lawyers, and relatives and friends, to learn the rudiments of epistemology. The simple fact of having met was a sign of dissatisfaction and the desire for critical distance, above all in relation to the profession. In the University, the corresponding course would be more difficult and based on recent bibliography, since that was what the students were there for. But it would come within a general context of specialization and professional competition, and philosophy, as we know, can be a way of earning a living, with grades and stages like any other. Which is the reason why it is so difficult for a philosophy teacher to live a life even passably aired by reflection. And if it is true in principle that technical training and philosophy are not mutually exclusive, and even presuppose one another, in reality they are hardly ever to be found together. In Rosenfeld's courses, which had no diploma to be gained at the end, it was easy for the matter to be taught to be combined with random inventions, so that it soon entered the atmosphere of real interest, which doesn't adjust itself easily to the academic compartmentalization of the disciplines. There was an extra-ordinary readiness to allow oneself to be interrupted and to accompany confusions and digressions, without the general direction of the seminar being lost to view. Less because of the material itself – the same, in the end, as that of all introductory courses – than because of the variety and the patience of this movement, his classes gave a truly appreciable idea of what Philosophy is, open, and as free of humbug as possible.

At the end of his 'Reflections on the Modern Novel',** a piece which represents one of his phases well, Rosenfeld warns the reader of the 'possibly vicious circle' of his argument. And in fact, the opposition he makes between the modern novel and nineteenth-century realism, parallel to the opposition between abstract and figurative painting, does move in a circle: a circle which belongs to our own time. Realism is either objectivity itself, in which case the modern novel looks as if it constitutes a loss of perspective,

---

*The original site of the University of São Paulo.

**Published in *Texto/Contexto* (Perspectivas, São Paulo 1969).

or it is an illusion tied to the era of individualism, and in this case the modern novel, in which we see the dissolution of the subject, is the truth. Is the nineteenth century naive when seen in the light of the twentieth? Or is the twentieth a disaster in relation to the nineteenth? These points of view coexist in the essay, which aims to be as 'fluctuating as a Calder mobile'. From this stems an effect typical of Rosenfeld's writings, above those which interpret modern culture: they are very tightly constructed, but not with the aim of being conclusive. His position is not in the theses they expound, always taking their distance, as if they were quoting themselves, but in the real and at times contradictory experience which asks that they be suspended, each one depending on the others. Thus, the liveliest part of his thought comes in the silences, in the numerous mental reservations which Rosenfeld animates his texts with – and doesn't reach the stage of positive affirmation. The result, very influenced by Thomas Mann, is something like the permanent ironizing of ideas, equally distant from intellectualism and irrationalism. As in Mann, the raw material of this style of argument is taken from the arsenal of German Philosophy of History and Culture, whose constructions formulate, in the language of *Zeitgeist* and the clouds, the great themes of bourgeois civilization: work, alienation, leisure, skill, division of labour and the life of the artist, sincerity, hypocrisy and truth, discipline, chaos and emancipation, community v. society, etc. These are parameters with a very peculiar status today, for, while they are abstruse, by the very simplicity of their dialectic they are also relevant and critical, because they are still in contact with everyday experience, and they seem, because of their kinship with Marx and Freud, to carry allusive power, as well as having pedagogical value, since they force us to think of social life as a totality. Of course, Rosenfeld didn't *believe*, with Schiller, that aesthetic education was the solution for the discords of modern humanity, or that we stand in relation to the Greeks as a divided consciousness stands in relation to simplicity. If he expounded ideas of this kind, he did not take his standpoint within their universe. He knew all about psychoanalysis, capitalism, the class struggle, empirical research, and they were the real climate he inhabited; aside from which, he belonged to the left. The superposition of these different horizons of thought, materialized in the more or less humorous combination of philosophical construction and scraps of information, sceptical observations and close reading, lies at the foundations of his writings, and I think it is the historical position of his thought.

However, the really interesting question is this: why did Rosenfeld not go over entirely to the Freudian and Marxist camp, so near and so plausible, and which, after all, had provided a materialist continuation to the concerns of the Philosophy of Culture? Why did he adopt a discourse which he didn't believe in? Why did he prefer to hold to the eclectic variety of his sources?

As we know, Marxism and psychoanalysis are not child's play. First of all, because in their authentic versions they call exploitation and authority by their names, which carries a certain price. Then, because they are discourses which aim to be both scientific and normative, which ups their voltage yet further. In practice, they have grouped vast interests around themselves, have become official, and in spite of many schisms have held on to a very strong notion of a monopoly of truth. This is the reason for the dogmatic form of their judgements, variable as they may be. As far as his vision of the world was concerned, Rosenfeld obviously owed a great deal to Marx and Freud. But he disagreed with the emphatic tone that their discourses had taken on in their followers. He remained unconvinced by the exclusive claim to scientific truth advanced by both Marxist and psychoanalytic discourses. When they were adapted to the literary or philosophical fields, they seemed to him reductionist. In *Texto/Contexto* there is a long study on the tautological application of psychoanalysis to art criticism. He never wrote, but he thought the same of Marxist criticism, for example that of Lukács, whose way of analysing culture in terms of reaction and progress seemed forced to him. More surprising and interesting is the fact that he didn't like Adorno and Benjamin, whose Marxism did not suffer from the impositions of a discipline. To him, they seemed objectionable in their very originality, in the careful, extended manner they had of moving backwards and forwards between formal analysis and the construction of social tendencies. Objectionable, too, seemed Karl Kraus, who, without being a sociologist or a Marxist had considerably refined the social knowledge of literature. He reacted to all three with irritation, as if to an aberration – above all to the very tight way in which they linked artistic details to the global process. He, Rosenfeld, had always asserted the link between culture and material interests. But he preferred to keep it as something to think about, not as a programme for literary criticism. The attempt to show social necessity, with all its grandeur, in such fragile, accidental things as a detail or a poem, was perhaps allowable to him in theory; in practice, he suspected in it the desire for destruction, to bring the pressure of the most violent social conflicts to bear on an area of relative subjective freedom. Others will say that the said freedom is ideological, but in fact there is something disproportionate and anti-poetic – as well as sterile and despotic – in invoking the Oedipus complex and the class society to explain the charm of a book. That confidence in experience of the average citizen, that moment of freedom of choice without which art and self-knowledge, in the modern sense, cannot exist, are removed. In this sense Rosenfeld suspected all dialectics, including that of Hegel, of being a dogmatic *passe-partout*. The other side of the coin is that his critique left itself without terms to define the moment of present validity in its object. He showed their complexity, their place in the artistic tradition, but he could not explain why they were interesting.

I describe these aspects of the man, for they help us to understand that a man opposed to capitalism may not be a Marxist, that a materialist may use idealist methods of thought, that someone convinced of the historicity, and of the 'newness' of the industrial world, may adopt the ahistorical terms of philosophical anthropology. These are the contingencies of progressivism in an upside-down world. The constructions of the philosophy of culture gave to Rosenfeld the social wholeness, discord and teleology necessary to his sense of present-day existence and to the movement of his analyses. With them, he was on the side of dialectics, against positivist sterility, and, paradoxically, also on the side of common sense, against dialectical dogmatism, since it was a merely formal construction, deprived of any likely claim to truth by the real course of History. Naturally, Rosenfeld didn't share their optimism: social reality *is* teleological, but we have yet to see where it is going – something which corresponds to the fluctuating evaluation of modern art that we looked at earlier. A clear, suggestive discourse, with only a relative claim to truth, was what pleased Rosenfeld. It allowed him ironic interruptions, the consideration of conflicting points of view, the exercise of doubt, a Brechtian distance from arguments, things which for him were the key aspects of materialism – aspects which the Marxist tradition still has to absorb.

Rosenfeld was a great expert in, and admirer of Thomas Mann, on whom he had for years been preparing a book. Like him, he refused to throw out the 'dangerous' tradition of German irrationalism (the Romantics, Schopenhauer and Nietzsche), in whom he saw a great deal that was true; and, also like him, he refused to identify himself with this tradition, thinking it reactionary. He wanted an 'enlightened' and ingenious harmonization, in which the interdependence between things of the spirit and vital necessities would be recognized, and co-ordinated in a less unfortunate manner than they are now. The progressive irony of the Master

– that is, of his democratic phase, after the First World War – was one of his ideals in life, and one of his literary models. The other strong influence on him was Nicolai Hartmann, whose pupil he had been in Berlin. It should be said in passing that Hartmann is the only modern philosopher to whom Lukács, in his final phase, gave any value. In his ontology, if it can be summed up in so few words, the world is conceived as a series of superimposed levels, in which the more elementary sustain the more complex, but do not explain them. And the latter, even though not reducible to the former, obey their laws. Thus, the organic sphere does not disobey the laws of inert matter, which underpins it, but it cannot be explained by them. Analogously, the spiritual sphere depends on the organic and inorganic spheres, but mechanical or biological causality is not enough to explain its movement, etc. In its polemical context, this position was as opposed to idealism as it was to Marxist or biological reductionism. Ideological life, for example, is not a pure emanation of the economy or of instincts, but neither can it do without them; to exist it needs them to function. The materialist and enlightened pedigree of these arguments, like that of Mann's irony, is obvious. The determining position of material and vital interests is affirmed, and they are not the negative to culture's positive. Culture must provide the framework inside which they can realize themselves.

Now that the ideology of capitalism is no longer ascetic, these are arguments which have lost a lot of their impact. To understand Rosenfeld's later development, however, it is necessary to note that there is no means of going from an ontological argument, however materialist it may be, to a historical object. At some moments, this discontinuity will have seemed like a guarantee against dogmatism, since it allows one to maintain the precedence of material interests without obliging one to have a particular conception of that precedence. In the 1960s, however, for reasons outside the bounds of philosophy, the other side of this discontinuity came to the fore: to put it in the language of jargon, we now had a materialism which did not lead to the concrete analysis of concrete situations. After all, it didn't take many words for Freud and Marx to tell us that the worlds of representations and of interests are interdependent. Then, however, they spent thousands of pages to analyse the many forms of this inter-dependence, and it is these forms which are their real subject. Since then, analyses of this non-philosophical nature have come to seem necessary to the integrity of the process of reflection. Especially in these last few years, when the general thesis of material interests is no longer critical in itself, since materialism has been taken on by the right too.

After the Manicheistic years of the Second World War, and the frozen years of the Cold War, the sixties shook people up. Cuban echoes, the rise and repression of the popular movement in Brazil, the extraordinary evolution of the war in Vietnam, in which either side, each in its own way, went further than seemed possible, the Russo–Chinese split, youth movements all over the place, Brecht's worldwide fame: the mental climate had changed. In Brazil the most alert students had radicalized and converted to a vague Marxism. To study a question was to look for its social roots. Rosenfeld, who had always been on the left, felt himself a little intellectually out of tune. They were years of a good deal of humour and liveliness, but their characteristic rhythm had little room for irony, as he enjoyed it, linked always to tolerance and patience in the light of the many facets possessed by so many things. One night we went out with H.M. Enzensberger, the German poet and critic, who was passing through. We took him to the Teatro da Arena, to see *Zumbi.** On our way there, Enzensberger was explaining that Thomas Mann had nothing to say to our time, and that the really contemporary authors were Brecht, Karl Kraus, and Benjamin. This hurt Rosenfeld. However, by force of circumstance he had made the same journey. In the last few years his central author had become Brecht, whose theory and whose theatre he had widely promoted, in lectures and good articles in the Literary Supplement of the *Estado de São Paulo.* Involvement and biting humour began to replace his irony. The phase characterized by Thomas Mann, by Hartmann's ontology, and by the philosophy of culture, was followed by another, centred on Brecht, on political theatre and social criticism. Without being optimistic in relation to socialism, the Vietnam War had persuaded Rosenfeld that Imperialism is the worst thing of all. I suppose that then, feeling himself cornered, he looked for a discourse of explanation and of combat. So – I haven't seen him for five years – I found out through a friend we have in common that Rosenfeld now called himself a Marxist. Aside from that, the heterodox Marxism of Brecht, nourished above all on doubt, on observations on oppression, on desire and on discipline, and always opposed to deductive chains of arguments, tuned in well with his old manner. In this period he wrote his admirable *Epic Theatre,* a manual of really exceptional quality. Little by little, also because he taught in the School of Dramatic Art, he

---

*For a description of this play, see 'Culture and Politics, 1964-69' (pp. 148-9).

came to specialize in these matters. Through them, he was linked to the theatrical movement in São Paulo, which seemed to him original and remarkable, and in which he participated with dedication, brilliance and pleasure. This, too, was the field in which he found himself inclined to quarrel, and he fought against the wave of irrationalism, which had been breaking over everything since 1968. As a consequence, he was called a Fascist, by some adept of anti-authoritarian thought – which has its funny side. The process of his naturalization was being completed.

FIFTEEN

A Historic Landmark

'Póstudo' is the deliberately provocative title of this poem by Augusto de Campos, published in the *Folhetim* (the arts section of the *Folha de São Paulo*) on 27 January 1985.* The poem is conceived as a landmark: it is intended to denote a historical turning-point (in the life of its author? in Brazilian literature? in Western culture?), and to give a physical presence to this landmark: to place it in the public arena so to speak. The role of

----

*A literal translation of the poem runs as follows:

		I wanted
to change		everything
I changed		everything
now	post	everything
		exeverything
I change		

Two important aspects of the poem are necessarily excluded from this translation: first, two puns – *extudo* is phonetically identical with *estudo*, 'I study'; and *mudo* can also mean dumb, silent. Secondly, as will be obvious, it is impossible to translate some single words by

187

conveying these latter intentions is given to the large, carefully chosen letters, which cause the words to be seen as well as read, so that they take their place in communal, exterior space, as opposed to the interior space of individual reading and normal-size type. Economy of means and a clear architectural structure also contribute to this effect, which would not be done justice to even in the dimensions of a poster, let alone in cheap newsprint. The poem aspires to monumentality, to inscription on stone. On the other hand, the title is ironic and brings in a subjective dissonance, whose natural scenerio is internal. I suppose that is why it is printed in red and in normal lettering, which separates it from the rest. However that may be, the discrepancy between the subjective, almost confessional commentary and the ostensibly deprivatized form of the poster poem is a factor of irritation, and interesting for that reason.

When is 'post-everything'? The little story that the poem recounts offers a reply, whose inadequacy, or adequacy, given point by the clarity of its formula, actively excites controversy, which is a kind of quality in its own right. It is as if the meaning were in the medium rather than in the message, or as if the poem's internal organization undid its intent, and led to conflicting ways of interpreting the poem.

Read as if it were prose, the poem exposes the paradox inherent in the desire to change everything. Everything is never everything, since beyond everything, there is always another, bigger everything. Doesn't this non-specific wisdom, of a rather antiquated sort, look somewhat insipid in a modern poet? Without denying other registers, which do exist, it's easy to feel the proximity of Conselheiro Acácio* or Vicente de Carvalho,** who was also right when he said that happiness 'Does exist: but we cannot reach it/because it's always where we put it/and we never put it where we are'. In the most advanced outpost of the avant-garde, what do we find but ancestral resignation?

However, it is not prose. Arranged on the page, the argument acquires other dimensions, which counterbalance its air of generality. Look, for

---

corresponding single words. Thus, the implicit subject 'I' mentioned by the author cannot be left implicit in English. 'All' might be a better translation than 'everything', because it is short, like *tudo*, but since it is not so commonly used as a pronoun, 'everything' seemed the better choice.

*A pompous, platitudinous character in the Portuguese writer Eça de Queirós's novel *O primo Basílio* |*Cousin Basílio*| (1878).

**One of the leading Brazilian Parnassian poets (1866–1924).

example, at the variations in the sense of the word '*tudo*' [everything], given prominence by the way the word is repeatedly lined up, in a column. When one looks carefully, between the first and the second of them we move from the absolute meaning, linked to a radical desire for change, to a relative meaning, linked to what is individually possible. Even so, '*mudei tudo*' (I changed everything) is one of those phrases in which pretentious-ness borders on folly. One cannot, therefore, exclude the other hypothesis, however outlandish it may seem to be, according to which the persona of the poem really might think that he has changed everything, in which case the second 'everything' would lose nothing in breadth of meaning *vis-à-vis* the first, but this latter, in exchange, would seem to have quite modest demands, unless one makes an absurd evaluation of the reality we live in. The third 'everything' takes in the previous two moments, the wanting and the doing, takes them in to the extent that they are now over ('*pós-tudo*'): for that reason it is no longer everything, and is, now according to the fourth meaning, 'ex-everything' ('*extudo*'). The poem ends with '*mudo*': that is, either the poet has concluded what he has to say, and is studying ('*extudo*') and staying silent ('*mudo*'), a possibility which the very existence of the poem gives the lie to, or after changing everything, he has resolved to change in his turn ['*mudo*' — 'I change']. This step indicates, moreover, that the general transformation planned did not include the transformation of the subject, another restriction on the sense of 'everything', which perhaps explains the monotony that accompanies a purpose which is apparently so mobile and radical.

Reading the right-hand column from top to bottom, we have the absolute, or fixed desire that the movement of the poem relativizes. In the left-hand column, on the contrary, we have variations on the verb 'mudar' ['to change']: 'to change', 'I have (now) changed', 'I am changing', or, from bottom to top, 'I am changing', 'I have changed', 'to change'. In the absence of further qualifications, they match the general, philosophizing character of the central argument, that I spoke of earlier. In fact, the preference for elementary relations between words, or between their external forms, to the detriment of syntactical ones, does thrust in that same direction. In spite of his technical stance, the poet puts his trust in such pious, empty hopes as the word 'to change', or, in other poems, in combinations like old/new ['*novo/velho*'] death/motor ['*morte/motor*'], etc. There is an important distinction to be made between non-specificness and lack of intellectual precision, but the distance between them is nonetheless small. Look, for example, at the poem 'Luxo' ('Luxury'), which also has the shape of a poster: printed in aggressively kitsch lettering, the title-word forms a module which, repeated and set out in the appropriate ways, allows one to form the word 'LIXO' ('rubbish') in rounded lettering. It was published in 1965, and it may be a response to the dictatorship and the meaning of wealth in the new regime. This does not prevent the link between luxury and rubbish being a commonplace of small-time morality, which the arrangement and the similarity of the words fails to redeem. But let's return to 'Póstudo'.

Unless I'm mistaken, the design of the letters quotes op-art and art deco. In this context, one can note the blinking, flickering effect, caused by the concentric circles, and the slightly passé air, which surrounds the modernist desire to change everything with distance and nostalgia. The present age defines itself in the same manner, with display-lettering and by arbitrarily quoting other styles, since it has no proper rationality of its own. Another effect of the large, fat lettering is a certain affirmative thickening of the lyrical voice, which becomes less evanescent. It is as if it were speaking in public: the first person functions like a third person, and acquires exemplary status as well as volume – which brings us to the central question, the one responsible for the aggressive impact of the poem, and which is merely underlined by the quietly factual tone of its narrative. Who is its subject?

Thinking about literature teaches us not to confuse the persona of the poet and the empirical author. On the other hand, since there is a signature, that impersonalization is not complete, and the link between author and work remains open to interpretation. This uncertainty can be used as an irritant: the objectiveness of the form implies the objectiveness of the lyrical self, a fictional being, and the question which perhaps takes shape around him is also objective; while on the other hand the signature, the self-explanatory tone and the claim on a prominent place in history all contribute to an empirical singularization of the subject: they make one feel the presence of personal pretensions and give the poem, so to speak, a tone of blowing one's own trumpet. We will see that this doubt about the appropriate register for reading creates instability, a wide-ranging oscillation, which is 'stimulating' in its way.

Let's suppose, then, to begin, that the subject of the poem is the poet himself, boasting of his own past deeds and explaining his present conduct. In this case what we had in front of us would be a short intellectual autobiography, and the 'I changed everything' looks very weird, unless the dash of irony in the title spreads to the pretensions and relativizes them.

The fact Is that the poem is set up on the basis of the confrontation between 'I' and 'everything', *tout court*, with no mediation: it is a formula of which illusions and *folie de grandeur* form an integral part.

However, the subject may also be rooted in a collective movement, and I imagine that is the way that most Brazilian readers will see the poem. For them, the poem will be about the Concretist experiment, in which, as everybody knows, the poet was a central figure. Even here, the 'I changed everything' will produce varied reactions, since it involves a judgement about the real state of affairs. There will be people who disagree, thinking that concentrating all change on one person and one group can only be a case of poetic licence. Others, and that includes me, will see the poem as the *n*th example of a key trick played by the concretists, always concerned to organize Brazilian and world literature so that it culminates in them, a tendency which sets up a confusion between theory and self-advertisement, as well as being provincial nonsense.

Finally, the lyrical subject could be broader, and a member of the international modern art movement, of which the poem, in this case, would be a summary and an evaluation. On this hypothesis, in which the field of operation and the criterion involved would be the entire modern world, the 'I changed everything' can be read without embarrassment, since it no longer represents the claim of an individual person. But it is read with a certain melancholy, since the 'everything' is saturated with the historical experience of our time, and if the result of the change has been what we see around us ... In this context, the 'I change' of the conclusion takes on something of futility and inconsequence, very interesting in fact, which registers (if the yardstick is the real necessities of humanity) the failure and the irrelevance of the cultural movements of the avant-garde in our century – which was, however, such an extraordinary development. There's no harm in reminding ourselves that change for change's sake is essential to the functioning of the market.

Moving beyond literature, the self of the poem could be the revolutionary after the revolution, leaving it on record that the world has not ended and that after one history another begins. It could also be the whole of humanity in our time, perhaps desirous of change, perhaps condemned to it. Separated from the title and the signature, which tie it down to the individual perspective, one could imagine the poem being realized in the open air, on a gigantic scale, in some socialist country: it would remind the passer-by of the transformation that has taken place, the condition of the collective subject and the continuity of life, and doubtless would look really good (in a more or less hypocritical way, depending on the host country).

When all this has been said, which of these is the correct reading? Rather than deciding the undecidable, it is better to see that the poem gives no clue that allows one to choose, and that that *is* significant. It asks for an interpretation in an external key – what is 'everything'? – at the same time as it leaves the question open, functioning like an empty allusion. The context for the interpretation is left to the individual choice of the reader: the biography of the poet, the history of the concretist movement, the destiny of modern art, the revolutionary cycle, they all fit, though none has any real, identifiable support inside the composition. So, since they are external, they will be cut to the measure of current opinion and the prior knowledge of the reader: opinion and knowledge which, given that this is the case, do not have to pass the critical test of whether they are pertinent or not. In other words, this is a form which is committed to the reiteration of commonplaces.

This non-determination of meaning is however not complete. Whichever reading one gives, it will necessarily bring with it the external features of the radical spirit, reduced, as it so happens, to a caricature: a reference to 'everything' and to changing everything. Thus, the urge of the poem is to proclaim that the poet is in the advance guard of History, though it doesn't matter on which particular frontier, and at the same time to suppress references which might allow one to see the reality behind these pretensions. It's what could be called abstract avant-gardism, chemically pure, or absolute (imaginary) authoritarianism, for all the variety of options open to the reader. And, by the way, there is a word hidden in the poem whose presence is stronger than all the others', even than the 'everything', repeated four times over. It is an 'I' in a state of acute paroxysm, which owes nothing to anybody: I wanted to change, I changed, I change.

As far as the poem is concerned, removing the author from the scene for the moment – which is an artificial move – the choice of interpretative context is fairly free. Once rid of the artifice, however, the reader finds himself between the devil and the deep blue sea. The concretist group themselves provide an extensive body of literature, essays, erudite and militant, which in the revolutionary meaning of their work is explained, and Brazilian and foreign precursors are identified. These are extremely debatable questions, in spite of the swarm of authorities that are quoted. They are relevant here because of their ultimate aim, which is to define modernity and, within it, their own position of leadership, in that adamantine spirit of which 'Póstudo' partakes, and which it realizes in its quintessence, with no need for the incidentals of proof. It proceeds by the strictly affirmative path, eliminating empirical reality in words, situations and arguments, suppressing – purging! – to the last drop the actual matter in relation to which the change being talked about might have a meaning, or in relation to which its meaning might leave room for doubt. As the object of transformation is 'everything', we know nothing about it. On the other hand, and this is the point I wanted to reach, the poem fuses together, for its own benefit, the authorities of the poet and the critic, of poetic and theoretical discourse. You either believe or you don't in the words and in the herculean task they proclaim has been undertaken; but how can one doubt the authority of the critic-historian, the other side of the poet, who assures us, within the poem and in his very own words, that what's important is what is said. Depending on the way it's done, the fusion of theory and practice and the breakdown of the frontiers between genres – both of them aspirations which are at the heart of modern art – can have a strongly regressive dimension.

Understanding and explaining oneself historically is a part of the modern condition. But it is also true that, right or wrong, historical explanations take part in reality too, and are elements of power. Subordinating them to propaganda, to the point where contradictions, which are the sinews of dialectics, disappear, is one chapter – on another level, distant but related – in the degeneration of Marxism. Seen from this point of view, the concretist claim to a forward position at any price has got something to do with bolshevik style in its dogmatic variant, something which naturally has nothing to do with the political position of the concretist poets themselves. What this parallel does indicate is the depth of their roots in the contemporary scene, and shows that their sectarian energy, which might seem aberrant to a dispassionate observer, corresponds to a real dimension of our age. Anyone familiar with political documents of that section of the extreme left for whom ignorance of the real world is essential ('this is serious, comrade, you're being empirical') may perhaps recognize in the Proletariat and the Revolution of this kind of writing, repeated *ad infinitum* but empty of real workers and of real social movement, the same attachment to abstractions as in the everything everything everything of the poem.

In an elementary sense the poem reveals a distinct shortage of empirical reality. The reader 'now after everything', may ask himself: 'But what has really happened?' In a complementary sense, this lack of definition has an expressive dimension, like a gesture, where one senses the authority of the

'I' who owes no explanations. I insist on these things because they do not belong to the surface intention of the poet: they are its unwanted byproducts, but they are real and eloquent, the price that has to be paid, the supposedly hidden but in fact obvious truth. Individual expression was certainly not in this project, which goes back to Mallarmé and comes by way of João Cabral:* in that tradition, the subject is cleansed of any individual contingencies in order to get at the pure creative act. Outdoing the masters, who trod the negative path and kept the traces of the empirical reality they negated, the poet here takes the 'positive' path: he wanted to transform, and, according to him, he did transform the real world. This latter, however, so that the transformation might not be partial and marked by contingencies, and would not fall short of the standards demanded by radicalism, in its turn found that it had been transformed into 'everything', which as far as reality is concerned is the same as nothing – the absence of obstacles. Where the negative way gave the measure of the resistence of reality, positivity makes it evaporate.

'Everything', while it means the suppression of the empirical, is the central empirical fact of the poem. What is 'changing everything'? The object is not specified, and neither is the subject. The same goes for the idea of change, which remains neutralized, neither good nor bad. In terms of climate, this effect captures something of the present day, and seems to be guaranteed by the irony of the title, which alludes to the contemporary debate about the post-modern. Briefly, what happens is this: 'changing everything' had a worthy opponent in bourgeois culture and property, which are seen as incapable of evolving. The threshhold was crossed by the Russian revolution, but also by the anti-traditionalist evolution of capitalism itself. Given that, as a consequence of this, large-scale change has become the norm, and has brought us to a situation of stability in terror, with no way out in sight, the term in its generality has become empty, or, better, has become ideologically conservative, and needs to be brought to the level of the particular in order to have meaning. In this context, one interesting reading of the poem would say that, between the body of the composition and the final 'mudo', now taken as cynical and resigned, lies the

---

*João Cabral de Melo Neto (1920–), poet from the Northeastern state of Pernambuco, and the leading figure of his generation: he has practised a deliberately impersonal, objective (and to that extent concrete) poetry, mixing social commitment with speculation about the nature of poetry and creation. The symbolist tradition, in particular Valéry, was a strong formative influence on him.

distance between those two moments, the modern and the post-modern: for the latter, change is so to speak a law of adaptation (to the market?) and has no connections with hope for revolution (expressed in the 'everything').

Something of this is in the air, and was recently formulated by Haroldo de Campos,* in a study of the present situation of poetry (*Folhetim*, 14 October 1984). In an extremely daring and unjustified leap, in which he transforms calamity into liberty, Haroldo explains that, given the impasse between imperialism and bureaucratic dictatorships, both of them equally dreadful, poetry is now entering into a 'post-utopian' world, one of the 'pluralization of possible poetics'. The situation has got better because it has got worse, so to speak. Paradoxically, if we want to risk an up-to-date understanding of our 'everything', a word so stubbornly resistant to anything relative, it is in this atmosphere of generalized softening that we must plunge it. Behind the globalized form of the real, from which contradictions, differences, and other marks of concrete reality are missing, maybe there is an element of indifference. In a more obvious key, it is realistic to say that the empty and all-embracing word used to define the world to be changed has within it something of a bureaucrat's mode of operation. Bringing together total ambition and total lack of definition, the 'everything' blends the inadequacies of messianic utopianism and the self-sufficiency of a bureaucracy, which promises nothing. However that may be, as far as the poet is concerned, poetry no longer lives in a situation of impasse, but in a world which it has transformed, and will go on transforming (what for?).

Thus, though the terms of the poem belong to a rarefied realm of absolute desires, I do not think that its meaning belongs to this same order. To illustrate this, note that the poem begins at the end of a line, with the 'I want', indicating right from the start that the accomplishment of desires demands a break: and that it ends at the beginning of a line, indicating that the change will be continued. There's no doubt that it is neat, and banal. As we have no parameters to judge by, what is left is the abstract gesticulations of the desire to transform, wrapped up in attractive lettering. This same alteration holds for the other thematic contexts we have pointed to: revolution, the literary struggle, the aims of modernism, the importance of

---

*With his brother Augusto, one of the founders of the concretist movement in Brazil. Haroldo is a poet, but is also well known for his critical essays (including revaluations of such figures as Oswald de Andrade) and for his wide-ranging activity as a translator.

the poet's past, all of them are present in this schematic form of trans-
formative action in general – the project, the transformation, the transformation of the transformer – which in the absence of an object is reduced
to being its own image, context, and ideology. Its cost, its advantages, and its
meaning disappear, and what is left is its profile, one more reputation from
the past among others, almost a kind of nostalgia, ready to be pop material
for the cultural market. The transformation of modern art's agenda into the
ideology of consumption and conduct is not peculiar to Brazil, but I think
that that is the historical moment marked by Augusto de Campos's poem.

Having said that, after the splendid 'dias dias dias' ['days days days']
(1953) this 'Póstudo' is perhaps the poet's most suggestive work. I have
already read it in enough ways, both against its grain and in its paradoxes.
To end in the same vein, we could note that read discursively, and taking
'ex-tudo' as intercalated, the poem is extraordinarily natural and would be
indistinguishable from the poetry which was born in determined opposition to the concretists, so-called marginal poetry, execrated by concretism,
in which the contingency and the self-exposure of the subject, endowed
with fluency and nothing else, serves to reveal the nature of the times.* In
this perspective, the 'all' would be read unpretentiously, as if in the context
of everyday speech. It wouldn't be a bad version of the poem.

---

*A poetic movement which grew in the wake of the atmosphere of gradual relaxation of
censorship in the mid-1970s, and produced some of the most important poets of the 1970s
and 1980s, such as Ana Cristina César and Francisco Alvim. Aesthetically, as Schwarz
implies, it was opposed to concretism and indeed to some extent it was a reaction against its
deliberate impersonality.

SIXTEEN

Chico Buarque's New Novel

Estorvo is a brilliant novel, written with skill and a light touch.[*] Within the space of a few lines, the reader knows he is in the presence of a form with its own texture and coherence. The narrative runs along with a fair speed, in the first person, and in the present: the action we witness consists of what the narrator/protagonist does, sees and imagines. The language reconciles aspirations that are difficult to keep together: it tries to be unpretentious – as if spoken by an ordinary person – but to be open, at the same time, to the more secret, unexpected side of things. The combination works very well, and produces a special kind of poetry, which is Chico Buarque's own discovery. The expression, for all its simplicity, is a vehicle for situations which are more subtle and complex than itself.

The novel begins with the narrator, half-asleep in front of the spy-glass in the front door of a bedsitter. The face on the other side of the door, neither

---

[*]It was decided to include this brief review in August 1991, when the novel was published (and this piece appeared in the Brazilian weekly *Veja*), since it gives an insight (admittedly a pessimistic one) into Schwarz's view of the present direction of his country. Chico Buarque de Holanda (1944–), as many will know, is one of Brazil's most famous popular singers and composers, who during the years of military rule on numerous occasions defied censorship in an attempt to recount the dramas of exile, repression, of the exploitation of the working class (in the famous 'Construção', for instance), and so on. The son of the important historian Sérgio Buarque de Holanda, Chico Buarque's fame has taken him far beyond the realms of literature – his novel was, of course, an immediate bestseller, and is translated into English by Bloomsbury Press (London 1992).

familiar nor unfamiliar, is what makes him decide to flee, and so sets the plot in motion. Was he right or wasn't he? Hallucinations and reality get the same literary treatment, and have the same importance in the text, even though the motivating force behind the former is greater: this explains the dream-like atmosphere of the story, in which everything seems foreordained. The interpenetration of reality and imagination, which requires considerable expertise, means that facts become permeable: this face is made up of others, I've seen this beard on another face, the present is made up of other moments. The dry, factual account of what is there, as well as what is not, or of absence within presence, is what sustains this transmutation of popular fiction into a more demanding type of literature, one which attempts to be up to life's complexity.

The necessities of the flight, with its moments of speed and slow motion, are what filter the sense we get of the city. Rio de Janeiro has a strong presence in the book, but in an intimate fashion, as if by chance, something far removed from any postcard view of the place. In the opening scenes there is what we could call the excitement of topography and of contrasts: the narrator rushes down the service stairway of a high-rise, goes round the corner which a moment ago he had been watching from the sixth floor, goes through a tunnel in the wrong direction, against the traffic, emerges, with some relief, in another area of the city, where he breathes another atmosphere, and begins to climb the hillside towards the greenery and the large houses with plate-glass windows, where he can see the ocean. The reader, in his own imagination, can follow the poetry of this sequence.

Depending on the point of view, the narrator is a nobody, or the alienated offspring of a wealthy family. The former lives in a bedsitter, goes around in jeans, a white tee-shirt and sneakers, drinks water from taps in stinking public toilets, and drags his suitcase round the streets. But we also know that his late father was the sort of man who was used to shouting at his employees, and that his mother is silent when she answers the telephone, because she thinks it improper for a lady to say 'hello'; we know that his sister, married to a millionaire, lives in a plate-glass mansion; that the family's beautiful country estate has turned into a marijuana plantation and a refuge for bandits.

We could also say that what we have here is the son of a rich family living like a bum, on the road to complete marginalization. What kinds of conflict are implicit in this kind of situation? It should be said that the dominant tone of the novel is not one of conflict, but on the contrary of fluidity and of a merging of the frontiers between social categories – are we in the process of becoming a classless society, under the sign of delinquency? – which might well be a way of defining the state of our country at this moment in its history. Even so, it is impossible to understand this levelling without first considering the opposing forces that it destroys.

The foreground voice, friendly and engaging, is that of the man in the street, whose ethics is an aesthetics, and whose disgust at social pretensions is represented, on the level of the style, by the exclusion of any kind of literary vanity or affectation. From this point of view, sophisticated enough in its way, and which belongs to the student radicalism of the sixties, the luxury of the rich is utterly improper. The concrete and glass house is wrong, as are the men with their country-club faces, and the sister with her manufactured look: 'Here's my sister in her peignoir, taking her breakfast at an oval table.' But times have changed, and his dislike of money doesn't stop the narrator taking advantage of a visit to steal the jewels which will pay for his passage into the world of marginality. For their part, the rich don't criticize his 'artistic' temperament, and in fact have no real antipathy for the world of crime. What excites his brother-in-law is the rape undergone by his wife, who, however, flirts with the detective engaged on the case, who in his turn gets on with the bandits, who may have committed the crime or may not, as the case may be: an apocalyptic promiscuity, then, which everybody seems quite used to, and which may belong to the imagination of the narrator, but then again, may not. Just like the geography of the city, History is also present only indirectly, but it is what gives the book its strength.

In a marvellous street scene, with a chase, police cars and TV, a short woman with an Indian face tries to stop her son being arrested, screaming, and with good arguments. The narrator feels he is going to be on her side, but then finds he has made a mistake, for the woman stops shouting when she sees she is not being filmed. This episode, which the narrator wishes hadn't happened, explains a good deal – perhaps indeed defines the horizon of an epoch. The desire to take the side of the poor, and to see them defending their rights in public rushes to the surface, only to be extinguished at the next moment. It's like an old, antediluvian reflex movement, which today is only a reaction in a vacuum, since all the poor want to do is appear on television. The desire for a different, better society seems to have lost its foundation. Am I taking things too far when I imagine that the suspension of moral judgement, the almost total apathy with which the narrator moves between situations and classes is an expression of the perplexity of the generation of 1968?

The other important setting in the book is the family's old house in the country. As the site of childhood, of simple people and of nature, it might seem to be a refuge, the remedy for the narrator's failures to adjust. When he gets there, however, he discovers a population – children included – organized and enslaved for the purpose of contravening the law, blitzed by videogames, motor-cycles, leather jackets and hair-dye, as well as quite prepared to negotiate with the authorities. In other words, closing the circle, we have the same thing as in the plate-glass mansion: in the place where the old virtues were supposed to be preserved, the water no longer runs so pure. So, after the times in which the ignorant poor were to be educated by the elite, and other times when the iniquities of the rich were to be removed by the virtues of the poor, we have now reached a mire which nobody wants to get out of and where nobody is happy.

By a profoundly modern paradox, the lack of internal definition of the characters has its analogue in an intensified visibility. Gestures and movements have the kind of clarity which cartoons, cinema gags and soap-opera acting, as well as dreams and nightmares, have accustomed us to. This precision, a notable thing in itself, comes in the first place from the literary brilliance and the sure observation of the writer, and also from detective novels. But there is another aspect, a much more disturbing one. It is as if now, at this moment, this clarity were not merely an artistic quality, but a real aspiration of things and people to the status of a model, a stereotype, as if they wanted to be their own logotype. The irresistible attraction of the media reveals to us, and puts into action, the figure who can be put over, communicated, and whose behaviour can be encapsulated in a simple formula: in whom word and thing coincide. Chico Buarque sees his characters, and defines them, in this way, as if they were clones, simple advertisements for themselves. The elegant sister goes up the stairs and moves her body, according to the precepts of a professional model; her husband looses his tennis serve with a grunt, just like the champions; rebellious kids rev up their red motor-cycles, in a scene they have seen in a film, and have huge rings, that blind you like their headlights. Crooks, millionaires, employees, bandits and of course the police, all participate in the world of images, where they shine, above and beyond the conflicts between them – which conflicts are relegated to a strange kind of suspended animation. It seems that the price of an entrance ticket to this spectacle of modern objects and relations is well worth the horrendous terms in which it is played out.

Seen as a whole, the line of the action has the strength of simplicity. The flight leads nowhere, or, better, the narrator keeps on coming back to the same places. These repetitions have no end in sight, though they cannot be infinite, since the situation is getting worse and worse. In the final scenes monstrosity takes over. With his sights fixed with a faint hatred on other people's grotesqueness – which in fact is extreme – the narrator fails to see the crust of filth, blood, wounds and bits of glass (not to mention the moral confusion) which he has gathered around himself and which must be disfiguring him. The reader has to put all this information together, and visualize this character who is talking to him, himself no less anomalous and acclimatized to this intolerable world than the fauna that inhabit the scenarios of luxury or of the underworld. At one moment, unconscious of what he looks like, the narrator tries to embrace in the street a man he thinks he recognizes. The latter doesn't hesitate to defend himself with a kitchen knife. With his guts ripped open, the narrator gets the bus and goes on his way, thinking that maybe his mother, a friend, his sister or ex-wife might give him 'a place for a few days'. This absurd readiness to carry on in just the same way in impossible circumstances is the potent metaphor which Chico Buarque has invented for contemporary Brazil: it may be that he has written its book.

Index

Adorno, Theodor 49, 124 n7, 158 n9, 182
Albee, Edward 138
Alencar, José de 19, 45, 50, 63, 65, 67, 71, 72, 74-6 n20, 76 n24, 76 n29
Cinco minutos 63
Diva 42, 61, 62, 64
O Guarani (The Guarani Indian) 42, 75 n20, 100
Iracema 42, 43, 74 n20, 100
O Jesuita 44
A pata da gazela (The Gazelle's Foot) 42, 61-2, 64
Senhora (A Lady) 42, 46-9, 51-61, 66, 69, 70
Sonhos d'Ouro 50
Til 42, 44, 76 n20
O tronco do ipê (The Ipê Trunk) 42, 75 n20, 76 n20
Alencastro, Luiz Felipe de 31 n8, 35
Allende, Salvador 172
Almeida, Manuel Antônio de, Memórias de um Sargento de Milícias 48
Althusser, Louis 49, 165 n2
Alvarenga, Silva 10
Alvim, Francisco 196
Amaral, Tarsila do 118, 121, 125 n22
Andrade, Carlos Drummond de 97, 124 n15
A rosa do povo (The People's Rose) 99
Sentimento do mundo (The Feeling of the World) 99
Andrade, Joaquim Pedro de 17 n6
Andrade, Mário de 1, 2, 3, 8, 17 n1, 27, 75 n20, 95, 110, 124 n8, 175
Macunaíma: The Hero Without Any Character 17 n1, 40, 43, 90, 119, 158 n6
Andrade, Oswald de 3, 7, 8, 9, 34, 40, 63, 90, 95, 110, 111, 112-23 passim, 195
Manifesto Antropófago 17 n8, 108, 116
Manifesto da Poesia Pau-Brasil (Brazil-Wood Poetry) 17 n8, 108
Araripe Junior, Tristão de Alencar 34

Arraes, Miguel 133, 134
Arrigucci, Davi 125 n20
Azevedo, Aluisio 94
O cortiço (The Slum) 94
O mulato 94
Azevedo, Manuel Antônio Alvares de 50

Balzac, Honoré de 42, 47, 49, 51, 52, 62, 73 n13, 75 n20
Comédie Humaine 48, 54
Bandeira, Manuel 125 n20
Barbosa, Rui 7, 122
Barren Lives (Vidas Secas) (Dos Santos) 159 n11, 161
Barreto, Afonso Henriques de Lima, Triste fim de Policarpo Quaresma (The Patriot) 4
Barreto, Pereira 32 n22
Baudelaire, Charles 94, 99 n1
Beiguelman, Paula 32 n22
Benjamin, Walter 121, 169, 182, 185
Charles Baudelaire: A Lyric Poet in the Era of High Capitalism 73 n14
Illuminations 74 n20
The Origin of German Tragic Drama 158 n5
Berriel, Carlos Eduardo 119
Black God, White Devil (Deus e o diabo na terra do sol) (Rocha) 40, 142, 159 n11, 161
Boal, Augusto 146, 149, 158 n7
and Gianfrancesco Guarnieri, Tiradentes 149, 150
Zumbi 148, 149, 185
Bopp, Raúl 8, 17, n9, 95
Bourget, Paul 77 n30
Branco, General Humberto de Alencar Castelo 36, 127
Brancusi, Constantin 124 n3
Brecht, Bertolt 40, 109, 124 n1, 138, 147, 148, 149, 163, 178, 185
Byron, George Gordon, Lord 42, 50

Cabra marcado para morrer (A Man Marked Out to Die) (Coutinho) 166, 167, 172
Cabral, Pedr'Alvares 123

INDEX

Os Cadernos do Povo (*The People's Notebooks*) 129

Callado, Antonio, *Quarup* 4, 133, 157

Câmara, Dom Helder 156

Campos, Augusto de 110
'Póstudo' 187–96

Campos, Haroldo de 108, 110, 124 n1, 195

Candido, Antonio 2, 3, 12, 32 n23, 34, 45, 48, 70, 71, 72, 75 n20, 95, 107 n7

Cardoso, Fernando Henrique 21, 158 n2

Carpeaux, Otto Maria, *History of Western Literature* 176

Carvalho, Vicente de 188

Castro, Fidel 173

César, Ana Cristina 196

Chateaubriand, François-René 42

Chekhov, Anton 29

Constant, Benjamin 10

Cony, Carlos Heitor, *Pessach: a travessia* 159 n11

Cooper, James Fenimore 42

Coutinho, Afrânio 44

Coutinho, Eduardo 171
Cabra marcado para morrer 166, 167, 172

Da Costa, Cláudio Manuel 10

La Dame aux Camélias (Dumas fils) 72

Dean, Warren 73

Derrida, Jacques 6

Diegues, Carlos, *Os herdeiros* (*The Heirs*) 158 n6

Dos Anjos, Augusto 63

Dos Santos, Nelson Pereira, *Vidas secas* (*Barren Lives*) 159 n11, 161

Dostoyevsky, Fyodor 29, 91

Dumas, Alexandre (Dumas fils) 42, 69, 77 n30
La Dame aux Camélias 72

Durão, Santa Rita 9

Eça de Queirós 94, 136
O crime do padre Amaro 136
O primo Basílio 136

Enzensberger, Hans Magnus 185

Estado de São Paulo 185

Eulálio, Alexandre 76 n24, 124 n15

Feuillet, Octave 70
Roman d'un jeune homme pauvre 69

Finnegans Wake (Joyce) 140

Folha de São Paulo 187

Foucault, Michel 6, 49

Franco, Maria Sylvia de Carvalho 33, 34, 36

Freire, Paulo 134, 142

Freud, Sigmund 181, 182, 184

Freyre, Gilberto 76 n29, 110, 120

Furtado, Celso 124 n12

Gama, Basilio da 10

Gasparian, Fernando 33

Gil, Gilberto 110, 158 n6

Gogol, Nikolai 29

Gomes, Paulo Emilio Salles 16

Gonçalves Dias, Antônio 50

Goncharov, Ivan 29

Gonzaga, Tomás Antônio 10

Goulart, João 4, 126, 133, 136, 139, 150, 155, 168

Guarnieri, Gianfrancesco 158 n8
and Augusto Boal, *Tiradentes* 149, 150
Zumbí 148, 149, 185

Guerra, Rui, *Os fuzis* (*The Guns*) 159 n11, 161, 162, 165

Guevara, Ernesto 'Che' 133

Guimarães Rosa, João, *Grande sertão: veredas* (*The Devil to Pay in the Backlands*) 44

Gullar, Ferreira 17 n6

The Guns (*Os fuzis*) 159 n11, 161, 162, 165

Gutenberg, Johannes 25

Hair 138

Hartmann, Eduard von, *The Philosophy of the Unconscious* 102

Hartmann, Nicolai 184

Hegel, G.W.F. 183

Holanda, Chico Buarque de 200, 201
Estorvo 197

Holanda, Sérgio Buarque de 13, 20, 32 n14, 110, 197

Hugo, Victor 42

Jacob, Max 124 n3

James, Henry 41, 72 n2

Joyce, James 165
Finnegans Wake 140

Kafka, Franz 40, 116, 124 n7

King, John 161

Klee, Paul 116, 124 n7

Kraus, Karl 182, 185

Lamartine, Alphonse 42

Lenin, Vladimir 133

Liberdade, liberdade 146

Lukács, Georg 60, 73 n13, 73 n16, 158 n10, 184

Macedo, Joaquim Manuel de 45
A Moreninha 42, 63

Machado de Assis, Joaquim Maria 2, 9, 13, 17 n4, 19, 25, 27, 28, 29, 30, 31 n12, 40, 41, 44, 46, 50, 52, 62, 67, 68, 73 n7, 78–83, 87, 88, 92, 94, 102, 103, 105, 106, 110, 123
Dom Casmurro 17 n4
Epitaph of a Small Winner, see Memórias

póstumas de Brás Cubas
Esau and Jacob 17 n4
Helena 80
Iaiá Garcia 80
A mão e a luva (*The Hand and the Glove*)
　80
Memórias póstumas de Brás Cubas 44, 63,
　84-5, 89-90, 95, 96-9
'The Present Generation' ('A nova
　geração') 37
Quincas Borba 26, 104
Resurreição (*Resurrection*) 80
Machiavelli, Niccolò 56
Macunaíma: The Hero Without Any Character
　(Andrade) 17 n1, 40, 43, 90, 119, 158 n6
Mallarmé, Stéphane 194
Mann, Thomas 40, 181, 183, 184, 185
Marat-Sade (Weiss) 138
The Marmot at Court 26
Martinez Correia, José Celso 150, 151, 158 n6
　O rei da vela 158 n6
　Roda viva 158 n6
Martius, Philip von 35
Marx, Karl 7, 73 n17, 97, 133, 181, 182, 184
　Critique of the Gotha Programme 99 n2
Massa, Jean-Michel 83 n2
Maudsley, Henry, *Crime and Madness* 102
Medeiros e Albuquerque 26
Médici, Emilio Garrastazu 155
Mello e Souza, Gilda de 125 n22
Melo Neto, João Cabral de 194
Memórias de um Sargento de Milicias (Almeida)
　48
Meyer, Marlyse 42
Miguel-Pereira, Lúcia 83 n4, 107 n7
Molière, Jean-Baptiste 54
Movimento 33

Nabuco, Joaquim 19, 44, 45
　Abolitionism 91
Nasser, Gamal Abdel 173
Nehru, Jawaharlal 173
Neruda, Pablo 172
Neves, Tancredo 172
Nietzsche, Friedrich 183
Norma (Bellini) 64

Opiniao 146, 147, 148, 149

Pasquim 155, 159 n12
Pedro, João 166
Peixoto, Afrânio 114
Peixoto, Alvarenga 10
Picasso, Pablo 124 n3
Ponte-Preta, Stanislaw *see* Porto, Sérgio
Porto, Sérgio 137
Posthumous memoirs of Bras Cubas (*Memórias*

póstumas de Brás Cubas) (Machado de
　Assis) 44, 65, 84-5, 89-90, 95, 96-9
Prado Júnior, Caio 110
Prado, Paulo 110, 119
Proust, Marcel 40
　Pastiches et mélanges 73 n14

Quadros, Jânio 133
Quarup (Callado) 4, 133, 157, 159 n11
Quincas Borba (Machado de Assis) 26, 104

Rego, José Lins do, *Menino de engenho*
　(*Plantation Boy*) 120
Ribot, Théodule, *Les Maladies de la mémoire*
　102
Rocha, Glauber 8, 17 n6, 142, 158 n6
　Antônio das mortes 40, 158 n6
　Brasil ano 2000 158 n6
　Deus e o diabo na terra do sol (*Black God,*
　　White Devil) 40, 142, 159 n11, 161
　Terra em transe (*Land in Anguish*) 40, 158
　　n6, 159 n11
Rodrigues, Nelson 63, 156
Rodrigues Pereira, Lafayette 107 n5
Romero, Silvio 3, 9, 10-15 *passim*, 17 n5, 27,
　107 n5
Rosenfeld, Anatol 175-85 *passim*
Rousseau, Henri 117

Sarraceni, Paulo César, *O desafio* 159 n11
Sartre, Jean-Paul 52, 92, 178
Schiller, J.C.F. 181
Schopenhauer, Arthur 183
Schwarz, Roberto, *Ao vencedor as batatas* (*The*
　Winner Gets the Potatoes) 44
Scott, Walter 42
Smith, Adam 21
Stanislavski, Konstantin 149
Sue, Eugène 42

Tiradentes (Boal and Guarnieri) 149, 150
Trevisan, Dalton 63
Tzara, Tristan 124 n3

Valéry, Paul 194
Vargas, Getúlio 47
Veja 197
Veloso, Caetano 40, 73 n11, 110, 158 n6
Ao vencedor as batatas (*The Winner Gets the*
　Potatoes) (Schwarz) 44
Verissimo, José 107 n7
Vigny, Alfred 42

Weber, Max 57
Weffort, Francisco 158 n2

Zasulich, Vera 7
Zola, Emile 94
Zumbi (Boal and Guarnieri) 148, 149, 185